D1267612

IN PRAISE OF
THE STRONG GRAY LINE

"In citing West Point's contributions to this great country, General Douglas MacArthur told the Corps of Cadets in the spring of 1962 'The Long Gray Line has never failed us!' It never has, and thanks to the heroism and sacrifices of West Point's young graduates, it never will. The moving tributes offered by members of West Point's class of 2004 to their deceased classmates who fought and died in Iraq and Afghanistan remind Americans again of this timeless truth." —**Daniel W. Christman**, Lieutenant General (retired), USA; 55th Superintendent, West Point

"The West Point class of 2004 has a story to tell that is unique in the twenty-first-century history of the United States Military Academy. For the first time in many generations, a class entered the Academy when the nation was at peace but was destined to spend the entirety of their time there in training and preparation for wartime leadership. *The Strong Gray Line* tells this story extraordinarily well, in a way that only those who experienced it first-hand can. From inauspicious beginnings during a rain-soaked first summer of initial training and through the myriad challenges that cadet life entails, that story has now become one of battle-hardened, experienced professionals who are doing the nation's work in a way that brings distinction to a class that has earned an honored place in West Point's illustrious history." —**Eric T. Olson**, US Army retired; Commandant of Cadets, United States Military Academy, West Point 2000–2002

"Remembrance has always been one of the duties of the soldier, and *The Strong Gray Line* is in keeping with that vital tradition. With this book the West Point class of 2004 honors their fourteen members who have fallen in service to their country, and they provide us a window into the diverse experiences of one class during the past decade of war. In that regard, this books stands as a further act of service to their country." —**Phil Klay**, author, *Redeployment*

"While you will likely never walk a mile in their dusty boots, reading *The Strong Gray Line* will help you understand, and certainly respect, the courage, sacrifice, and leadership of the West Point class of 2004." —**Craig Mullaney,** *New York Times* bestselling author of *The Unforgiving Minute: A Soldier's Education*

THE STRONG
GRAY LINE

THE STRONG GRAY LINE

WAR-TIME REFLECTIONS FROM THE WEST POINT CLASS OF 2004

Edited by Cory Wallace

ROWMAN & LITTLEFIELD
Lanham • Boulder • New York • London

All photos in this book are by Roger Pettengill, Academy Photo.

The authors will donate all proceeds from this book to charities chosen by the family members of our fallen classmates. For more information, please visit our website at www.thestronggrayline.com/.

Published by Rowman & Littlefield
A wholly owned subsidiary of
The Rowman & Littlefield Publishing Group, Inc.
4501 Forbes Boulevard, Suite 200, Lanham, Maryland 20706
www.rowman.com

Unit A, Whitacre Mews, 26-34 Stannary Street, London SE11 4AB

Distributed by NATIONAL BOOK NETWORK

British Library Cataloguing in Publication Information Available

Library of Congress Cataloging-in-Publication Data

The strong gray line : War-time Reflections from the West Point Class of 2004 / edited by Cory Wallace.
   pages cm
  Includes bibliographical references and index.
  ISBN 978-1-4422-4975-2 (cloth : alk. paper) — ISBN 978-1-4422-4976-9 (electronic)
1. United States Military Academy. Class of 2004—Biography. 2. United States Military Academy—Biography. 3. United States. Army—Officers—Biography. 4. Military cadets—United States—Biography. 5. Iraq War, 2003–2011—Personal narratives, American. 6. Afghan War, 2001—Personal narratives, American. I. Wallace, Cory, 1981- II. Title: The Strong Gray Line
  U410.M1A46 2015
  956.7044'342092273—dc23

2015011489

CONTENTS

Foreword   xi

Acknowledgments   xiii

Introduction   1

PART I: THE FALLEN: LISTED IN CHRONOLOGICAL ORDER OF THEIR ULTIMATE SACRIFICE   7

First Lieutenant Dennis W. Zilinski II, KIA in Bayji, Iraq, on November 19, 2005   9

First Lieutenant Benjamin T. Britt, KIA in Baghdad, Iraq, on December 22, 2005   21

First Lieutenant Garrison C. Avery, KIA in Baghdad, Iraq, on February 1, 2006   27

First Lieutenant Robert A. Seidel III, KIA in Abu Ghraib, Iraq, on May 18, 2006   35

First Lieutenant Amos "Camden" Bock, KIA in Baghdad, Iraq, on October 23, 2006   43

Captain Michael A. Cerrone, KIA in Samarra, Iraq,
on November 12, 2006   53

Captain John R. Dennison, KIA in Balad, Iraq,
on November 15, 2006   61

Captain David M. Fraser, KIA in Baghdad, Iraq,
on November 26, 2006   69

First Lieutenant Jacob N. Fritz, KIA in Karbala, Iraq,
on January 20, 2007   75

Captain Adam P. Snyder, KIA in Bayji, Iraq,
on December 5, 2007   85

Captain Paul W. Peña, KIA in Arghandab, Afghanistan,
on January 19, 2010   93

Captain Daniel P. Whitten, KIA in Zabul Province, Afghanistan,
on February 2, 2010   101

Captain Jason E. Holbrook, KIA in Tsagay, Afghanistan,
on July 29, 2010   121

Captain Dave Hortman, Killed in a Training Accident
on August 8, 2011   125

PART II: INTERLUDE   131

Classmates   133

"A Place in the Fight"   139

PART III: THE WAR   141

Hope   143

Have you Passed through the Night?   145

"Walking the Last Mile Home"   153

In God I Trust   161

Anger   173

Hier kannst du nur Krieg fuhren
(Here You Can Only Wage War)   175

"Economy of Force": My View of Hell from Deep within
the "Triangle of Death," Kargouli Village, Iraq, 2007   187

Love   199

Clearing Barrels: Iraq's Amusement Parks   201

All the Things I Didn't Know   211

Choosing   221

Dismay   233

All the Pieces Matter   235

The Men I Went to War With   247

It's a Small World: Southern Baghdad 2005   255

The Day the Elephant Came to Town   265

PART IV: THE STRONG GRAY LINE CONTINUES   277

The Fire Inside of Us   279

Glossary and Terms   287

Notes   293

Bibliography   309

Index   311

About the Editor   317

FOREWORD

From the distance of our television screens and Internet video clips, the advanced technologies wielded by America's armed forces have had the effect of often portraying war as an antiseptic affair. But on the ground where combat is waged, nothing could be further from reality. War in the contemporary age is much as it always has been: arduous, grueling, and costly. For most who experience war, their lives are irrevocably changed. For the men and women charged to lead our nation's soldiers in combat—and for their loved ones—the experience takes on even greater weight.

To preserve the memory of their service during the tumultuous decade since their commissioning as Army officers, members of the West Point Class of 2004 have written *The Strong Gray Line*. This is foremost a story of remembrance. Each chapter honors one of the fourteen members of the class who has died in the service of our country. It is fitting that the lives of such exceptional young officers be remembered, not only as examples of selfless and intrepid officership but also as monuments to the thousands of fellow Americans who served alongside them.

Their stories offer an unvarnished glimpse into the now-famous "Iraq Surge" and other defining moments of the Global War on Terror in both Afghanistan and Iraq. These vignettes often are uncompromising in their accounts of the unrelenting demands of warfare in the modern world. For those who have not felt the heartrending grind of months and years in a war zone, these dispatches provide insight to better understand today's veteran.

As the Class of 2004's combat record demonstrates, soldiers are not relieved of the emotional burden of war when they return home. Rather, they bear a burden in body and mind that affects their well-being and the well-being of their friends and family, and often transforms into an enduring struggle to restore normalcy to their lives. Yet this is also a story of triumph and noble service. The Class of 2004 represents what is best about the United States. Their willingness to serve in uniform and to dedicate their lives to leading their fellow citizens in both peace and war is a testament to the greatness of our army and our nation.

I hope you find this work to be a meaningful glimpse into the journey of one class of West Point graduates, and that through it you find a measure of understanding about the nature of combat, the resiliency of our junior leaders, and the titanic courage that so many soldiers and their families display on behalf of the United States of America every day.

General Raymond T. Odierno
38th Chief of Staff of the Army

> The Strength of our Nation is our Army,
> The Strength of our Army is our Soldiers,
> The Strength of our Soldiers is our Families,
> This is what makes us Army Strong.

ACKNOWLEDGMENTS

First and foremost, the contributors of this book want to acknowledge all Gold Star families of the Global War on Terror as well as every other armed conflict fought to protect this country. Yours is a debt that we as a nation can never fully repay. While we can never understand what it is like to be in your shoes, please understand that you will always have our respect and admiration.

Next, we want to express our gratitude for the assistance provided by Lloyd Remick and the employees at Zane Management, Inc., of Philadelphia, Pennsylvania. The generous guidance and mentorship you provided us was extremely helpful and absolutely crucial to bringing this project to fruition.

We would also like to thank Academy Photo, Marianne Carr, and photographer Roger Pettengill who so graciously provided the photos of our classmates at no additional cost.

We'd also like to thank classmates Kevin Powell for assistance on the project's website (www.thestronggrayline.com) and Tim Hsia for contributions to editing, obtaining endorsements, and project inspiration. Finally, we would like to recognize Jim Wilson who somehow found the time to bring the Amazon Fire to market and handle all of this project's promotion for both social media and vendors.

Finally, we would like to thank all of the soldiers and noncommissioned officers with whom we served over the past years. Though the times may change, the bravery and selflessness of the American soldier has remained the same from Valley Forge to the sun-scorched sands of Iraq and desolate mountains of Afghanistan.

INTRODUCTION

Jim Wilson and Cory Wallace

And when our work is done,
Our course on earth is run,
May it be said, "Well done;
Be thou at peace."

—P. S. Reinecke, USMA Class of 1911,
"West Point Alma Mater"

Originally composed as a furlough song by Cadet Paul Reinecke as he marched disciplinary tours, the "West Point Alma Mater" today is sung at nearly every West Point gathering from football games, to reunions, to funeral services.[1] The third verse hits a powerful crescendo on "May it be said, 'Well done,'" before reverting to a quiet, solemn "Be thou at peace" as graduates pay their respects to those members who have passed on. The tune is powerful, but it is abstract for cadet candidates when they arrive full of excitement and anxiety for "Beast Barracks" their first summer. With time, however, the meaning of the "Alma Mater" grows for graduates as we come to appreciate the institution's values and the bonds we hold with our fellow comrades past and present.

We, the members of the United States Military Academy's Class of 2004, arrived at West Point for Reception Day (R-Day) on June 29, 2000. Our class was composed of 1,187 "new cadets" beginning the journey to become members of the Long Gray Line.[2] We hailed from across America, representing one of the truest cross sections of the country, but we were bound together by the goal of becoming officers in the United States Army. While the day began bright and sunny, by midafternoon storm clouds threatened the evening parade and Oath Ceremony. As we stood in formation awaiting marching practice, it began to rain. Our cadre asked us, "New cadets, it's raining on your R-Day, do you know what that means?"

"No, Sir! No, Ma'am!" many of us responded, unsure what to say in the situation as we only had four responses we were allowed to use.

"It means your class is going to war!"

While the details of the folklore are unclear (some believe it's rain on R-Day, others believe it's Acceptance Day, while others say rain on Graduation Day foreshadows war), the notion of war at the time was a bit ridiculous. Most of us had watched the Berlin Wall fall and the U.S. military lead a coalition that wiped out Saddam's Iraq army; it was difficult to envision another war breaking out anytime soon.

Due to the rain, the cadre canceled our R-Day parade and moved the Oath Ceremony to Eisenhower Hall. Storms continued throughout most of the summer, hitting us on most of our road marches and almost our entire week of training at Lake Frederick. Rain became such an integral part of our experience that it seemed fitting to include a storm cloud in our class crest. At the time the cloud symbolized the trials and tribulations we overcame as a class in our pursuit of becoming officers in the army, but like the "Alma Mater," it has come to symbolize much more as time passes.

Our world forever changed on a beautiful September morning when Osama bin Laden's al-Qaeda network hijacked four airplanes and crashed two into the World Trade Center and one into the Pentagon, killing nearly three thousand people. What seemed so unimaginable the summer prior, our country was now at war. The enemy was not a nation-state, but a dispersed network of organizations and individuals. We were in shock, angry, and eager to help in any way we could. We wanted to get in the fight, but it was not our time. Our time would come. We became more focused as cadets knowing the stakes were higher, but it was still not clear what role we would play.

Academy cadets do not incur a service commitment until a formal ceremony the night prior to academic classes starting their junior year. Our Affirmation Ceremony in August 2002 was the first to occur following the attacks of September 2001. Our class had some members leave, deciding that the military was not right for them, but we did not experience a large exodus. West Point's Class of 1969, which graduated at the height of the Vietnam War, had an inscription in the front of their Howitzer (cadet yearbook) that reads "This is the Sign of the True Professional, To March to the Sound of the Guns." Like the class of 1969, our nation called and we marched to the sound of the guns.

In spring of 2003, while most of us were on spring break, President Bush announced the start of combat operations in Iraq to remove Saddam Hussein's regime from power. The "Global War on Terror" (GWOT) now had two fronts, and the likelihood that many of us would deploy soon after graduation increased significantly. We continued our march to the sound of the guns.

We graduated on a warm spring day in May 2004. It was apparent that operations in Afghanistan and Iraq would not be quick and simple like the conflicts of our youth, and a mixture of excitement and anxiousness filled us as we prepared to head out to the "real Army." Noon meals were increasingly interrupted with announcements of graduates killed in combat; we had a purpose and a job to do. The sounds of the guns grew louder, but they were still distant.

In November 2005, our class received word that an improvised explosive device had killed Dennis Zilinski while he was on patrol in northern Iraq with his platoon from the 101st Airborne Division. Dennis was the first member of our class killed in combat. The shit immediately got real—no longer was the GWOT an abstract concept or a theoretical discussion. Our time had come—the sounds of the guns were all around us.

From 2005 to 2012, our class lost thirteen members in combat and a fourteenth to an aviation accident, by far the most of any class for Afghanistan/Iraq. As foreshadowed on our R-Day, our class very much went to war. The pieces that follow are a collection of personal experiences from deployment and tributes to our fallen comrades. They recount our passions, strengths, and triumphs, but also our fears, our vulnerabilities, and at times our stupidity.

We hope that these stories help the reader understand how a decade plus of war has changed us and provide some insights into the amazing classmates who left us too soon. This book is divided into four parts: "The Fallen," "The Interlude," "The War," and "The Strong Gray Line Continues." The first part, "The Fallen," covers the life and death of each of our fourteen classmates that were killed during the Global War on Terror. Each piece connects the reader to a close friend of the deceased, but more importantly, a West Point classmate. While each chapter tells the story of one of our classmates who never made it home, it also provides the reader with an understanding of the bond forged at West Point and how it can survive even the most brutal combat conditions and continue to unite classmates even after the end of their lives. This emotional union serves as a mechanism for the authors to both reconcile their combat experiences and alter the tragic loss of a classmate into a cathartic moment. These memorials might make the reader laugh or perhaps cry; however, they all combine in a narrative arc that ultimately defines a bond that was founded at West Point, preserved through combat, and maintained after our classmates left this world.

Part II, "The Interlude" section only consists of two entries that create a pregnant pause in the book's tempo. Joe Myers uses a photo that he and his cadet company mates attached to a wall of the Firstie Club, one of the few bars on West Point that serves libations to cadets, and realized that for the rest of his life, he will be unsuccessfully searching for a bond akin to the one he feels with his fellow classmates. We chose this story as a transition between the two main parts of the book because it helps the reader understand the vital connection between each author and West Point that will manifest in each personal experience monograph, albeit in a slightly different permutation. We also included a poem by our classmate Nick Horton, who wrote the poem after reflecting upon his connection to West Point several years after he left the army. He wanted to express his disbelief of how it would take the death of fourteen of our classmates to open his eyes to a greater reverence for something that he once considered a sort of hyperbole. Both Nick's poem and Joe's vignette are crucial for the reader to understand the subtle undertones of a connection that takes each vignette author back to either West Point itself or the people with whom he or she met while there.

Part III, "The War," consists of personal experience monographs that are organized into four emotive categories that everyone, whether they be a combat veteran or a civilian, can understand: Hope, Anger, Love, and Dismay. Initially, we struggled with organizing these seemingly disparate combat vignettes into some semblance of a narrative arc. The last thing we want wanted to present the reader was a "shotgun blast" of war stories that fails to transcend the barriers of a troupe of combat snapshots. After much reflection, we realized that the aforementioned cohort of emotions linked certain vignettes to others and presented four distinct taxonomies that enable the reader to glean a deeper understanding of each experience.

A recent West Point graduate wrote the final portion of the book during his final year at the academy. In this part, the author captures the bond he feels that he shares with previous graduates despite the fact that he never met them during his life. The names of fallen graduates spoken over a loudspeaker during lunch are not the names of strangers; rather, they belong to people to whom he feels connected in a supernatural manner.

While many of us have left active duty for other pursuits, others continue to wear a uniform. We all carry a burden of living a life worthy of the sacrifices of our classmates and so many others. To those who bore the ultimate cost and who now grip our hands from the shadows, we dedicate this book.

May it be said, "Well done; Be thou at peace."

I

THE FALLEN

Listed in Chronological Order
of Their Ultimate Sacrifice

Dennis W. Zilinski II

FIRST LIEUTENANT DENNIS W. ZILINSKI II, KIA IN BAYJI, IRAQ, ON NOVEMBER 19, 2005

A Legacy of Love: The Story of Dennis Zilinski II

BJ Kraemer and Charlie Lewis

Greater love hath no man than this: that a man lay down his life for his friends.

—John 15:13[1]

So there they were—Ron Garberson, BJ Kraemer, Charlie Lewis, and Dennis Zilinski—proud, no, cocky, second lieutenants, who just graduated from West Point and were surrounded by family and friends.

Forty-seven months earlier, the four arrived at the historic institution as high school kids and met for the first time in swim coach Ray Bosse's backyard in a bucolic West Point neighborhood the day before reporting to West Point. They bantered with each other, distracted by what the summer ahead held for them. They were just boys, full of questions and fear of the unknown summer of Beast Barracks that lay before them. Despite limited conversations over America Online in the months leading up and the precious few hours at Ray's, each one left the picnic that day with a little bit of comfort knowing they were all going through the summer together.

Now here they were, more mature, aged, and standing together as men, filled with nothing but pride of accomplishing this milestone and excitement for the future. However, in their hearts they knew their smiles were hiding something—something no one was talking about. Again, each feared the unknown and knew there was the unknown. They were joining an army at war, and although the excitement of the day was beaming from them, they chose a special place for their commissioning as a reminder of what would be asked of them. Their commissioning took place at the West Point Cemetery.

One by one, Ron, BJ, Charlie, and Dennis stood at the grave of their former teammate, First Lieutenant David Bernstein, where their family members pinned on their second lieutenant bars. A Firstie (senior) when the four were plebes, Dave was the ideal of what a cadet should be—smart, fit, driven. Dave graduated fifth in his class, and although he was not the fastest swimmer on the team, he was the fittest. It was earlier that year that the four learned that Dave was killed trying to save his driver in northern Iraq on October 18, 2003, earning a Silver Star. They chose this place to honor Dave's sacrifice and as a reminder that, while they were celebrating an accomplishment, they would soon lead soldiers in war. Dave was a reminder of the reality of war and a reality of the responsibility bestowed upon each man.

They left the cemetery that day in May, excited but wary of what the future might hold. The four did not know that the same spot would soon hold one of their own for eternity. While the reality of the war was in their hearts that graduation day, no one knew how badly it would come crashing down on the group seventeen months later when, before the brass on their second lieutenant bars could tarnish, Dennis was killed in Bayji, Iraq.

This is a story of lessons learned from one man's life, a life that impacted many and continues to impact others through his memory. This isn't a story of loss. This isn't a story of war. This is a story of Dennis's legacy. This is a story of love.

LOVE OF COUNTRY

So there they were, no longer the bottom of the barrel. Plebe year was officially over. Camp Buckner was in the rearview mirror, and the fall was off to a fresh start.[2] The yuks, or yearlings as the sophomore class is referred to, moved to new companies. The group became closer; plebe year left few opportunities to socialize much outside of the Academy other than swim meets, but summer training gave them a glimpse of the friendships they were building. BJ and Dennis enjoyed the "full cadet experience" while they were stuck in STAP, missing out on summer vacation.[3] They met back up with Charlie later in the summer out at Camp Buckner, and while they did not get to hang out as much because of different schedules, they still found some time to have fun in between training.

No longer plebes, there was not much more they could ask for. BJ and Dennis started what would become their daily routine of walking to swim practice together for most morning and afternoon workouts. They had a new coach, who brought in a brand new staff and a sense of excitement. As sophomores, classes seemed more manageable, and social freedom picked up; life was good.

But a few weeks into September, their lives and the world were sent on a new path. September 11, 2001, shook the entire campus. In the weeks that followed, the mission of the Army and the lives of all cadets were changing faster than they could realize. The Class of 2004 had a big decision ahead of them. At the end of their sophomore year, each member of the class would commit to their path of graduating and serving by staying at the Academy after the first two years of commitment-free education.[4]

In the days that followed 9/11, Dennis often shared his desire to deploy immediately. There was talk of the days when cadets graduated early to go serve. Dennis even considered enlisting to go "over there." It was in those moments that Dennis's love for his city of New York and commitment to service came through. He felt personally attacked, and this sentiment did not fade. He knew his country needed him, and he wanted to answer that call. That was the day he taught them about love of country.

LOVE OF FAITH

So there they were, senior year. They were Firsties! Nothing is better at West Point than being a senior. Your privileges are virtually unlimited—you can have a car, leave on weekends, go to the Firstie Club.[5] Firstie life was the first real taste of freedom and was almost like being a normal student at any other college.

Some of the seniors held leadership positions within the Corps. Dennis was the obvious choice for team captain. Everyone, including his peers and coaches, looked up to him. He had a maturity and balance that came naturally. Dennis knew how to work hard, but that didn't get in the way of making sure practices were focused on having fun as a group, then on just swimming laps. Dennis was competitive . . . the team constantly played soccer, football, ultimate Frisbee, and basketball, often with a lot of trash talking. Dennis set the teams by class—creating additional bonds outside of those built during typical class experiences. The games were heated, but they brought the team closer and closer.

BJ and Dennis continued their routine of walking to and from practice together most days. One afternoon, BJ was early and Dennis was in his room, reading his Bible. BJ waited as he wrapped up reading a section, and the two headed to practice. BJ knew Dennis had gone to Christian Brothers Academy, attended a couple of Christian events while at USMA, and participated with him in Fellowship of Christian Athletes events, but BJ never really dove deep in his faith. In spring of their senior year, Dennis invited teammates to come to the reenactment of the Last Supper. He was not showy about it, but he made it seem more social. A few teammates attended and found out Dennis was playing the part of one of the apostles. Tan makeup and all, he played the role. That was Dennis—he was comfortable in who he was, not worried about being judged, and just did what he felt like he wanted to. He never proselytized and was not forceful with his faith, but Dennis's devotion to his afternoon Bible readings intrigued BJ. Then one October night, the team was meeting up at Grant Hall for dinner. BJ was rushing to meet up with Dennis to walk over when he received an email and a call from his dad, who had just read that David Bernstein, a senior swimmer from when they were plebes, was killed in Iraq. BJ ran over to Dennis's room to let him know before they would make an announcement to the rest of the team. When BJ got there, the two cried, hugged each other, and without skipping a beat, Dennis said, "Let's pray for Alex and Dave's family." And that was the day he taught them about love of faith.

LOVE OF THE GAME

So there they were, coaching a Little League team. Dennis always loved baseball. The Yankees were his team, and he proudly adorned his Derek Jeter jersey and fitted hat whenever attending a game. He played the game—

or at least home run derby—well. Despite this love of the game, there was no reason for Dennis to volunteer as a Little League coach. Swimming was over. For the first time in three and a half years, Dennis's time was his. And unlike Charlie, who sought relief from disciplinary lockdown, Dennis was not facing a brigade board and the associated punishment.[6] Yet when Charlie asked him to help coach Little League, Dennis jumped at the opportunity. Dennis saw coaching as a way to give back to the community that helped him through his four years at USMA.

What Dennis, Charlie, and their graduate assistant and friend Ryan did not know, however, was the league's toughness. This was not T-ball. Winning was the goal, and the other teams entered ready to win. To top it off, most of the coaches were senior faculty at West Point with kids and neighborhood friends on their teams. Most teams wore their jerseys and hats, along with purchased white pants, cleats, and high socks. Leftovers filled Dennis, Ryan, and Charlie's team, the Orioles, however, and tested their knowledge of baseball, teaching, and patience. The team was lucky to have enough kids to play, and most wore jeans with crumpled jerseys and flat-brimmed caps. Despite the ragtag team, Dennis's love of the game shined through in his infectious smile at practice. The kids flocked to him as if he were the fun uncle—someone who brought candy, laughs, and fun. To Dennis, compassion and love of others was part of service. His love of everything appeared in a variety of ways. This one-victory-and-nine-loss baseball team showed how Dennis's care and love of service infiltrated everything he did, large or small.

After a dismal start to the season, the team finally came together. For Dennis, serving as a coach was an honor; the best way to repay those parents sitting uncomfortably in beach chairs on humid Tuesday and Thursday evenings in May was with a victory. With the best pitcher on the mound and an aggressive shortstop, Austin, covering the left side of the infield, the Orioles were poised to shut down the opposing team's offense and earn that win. Then the coaches' focus changed.

With a runner on first, a ground ball was hit toward third base and (miraculously) was scooped by the third baseman. With Charlie yelling, "Throw to second," the third baseman spun and threw with all his might toward second, or so we thought. In all his excitement, the player whipped the ball right at Austin, who was watching the play unfold, unprepared to catch a ball flying at his face. With a dull thud, the ball fell to the hard-packed dirt of the small field at West Point. Shocked, Ryan and Charlie looked at each other and for ice. Before he could do anything, though, Dennis was with Austin, kneeling to inspect his eye. Austin was frightened but unhurt; Dennis whispered a few words in his ear, ending the tears and causing a smile to form. When asked what he said to Austin, Dennis just smiled, clapped his hands, and yelled, "Let's get 'em, Orioles!" And that was the day Dennis taught them about the love of the game.

LOVE OF THE BULLDOGS

So there they were, Dennis and Charlie, standing as teammates again as members of 3rd Brigade, 101st Airborne Division—the "Rakkasans." The Rakkasans are more than the typical infantryman. They have a different kind of pride that appears through one symbol, the most prominent of which is a bright red *torii*. Representing the regiment's time in Japan following World War II, the torii is a gateway consisting of two large poles supporting two crosspieces. With the symbol adorning their helmets, trucks, and buildings, Rakkasan soldiers rally around the torii.

Dennis's pride in the Rakkasans and its iconic symbol was no different. Arriving after Ranger School, many classmates assigned to 1st Battalion, 187th Infantry, "Leader Rakkasans," recommended Dennis to their leadership. Dennis immediately took over the third platoon of Bravo Company, aka the "Bulldogs." Combat proven during a suicide bombing in Tal Afar, Iraq, during their first tour, the platoon was respected as one of the battalion's best. To add fuel to their pride, one team leader, who lost an eye in the suicide bombing, graced the cover of *Men's Health* magazine as the first Ranger School graduate with that kind of injury. Dennis was not intimidated. In fact, he accepted the challenge to prepare these men for another tour and served with a focus unseen before in Dennis by those who knew him. Dennis's men soon fell in love with him for his leadership, personality, and care. His love of service and of others was soon obvious to all who witnessed him lead.

Tests for Dennis as platoon leader sometimes appeared when they were least expected. A hard worker, Dennis earned the battalion leadership's respect by planning a large range—the last major one prior to deployment.

His focus on training demonstrated Dennis's devotion to not just his unit but also to those with whom he served. But the first big test as a platoon leader came not while at a range or briefing his unit, but on a platoon run. Rakkasans do not work out in the normal gray Army t-shirt. Rakkasans instead work out in navy blue shirts with the company logo on the back. The Bulldog T-shirt was like the rest in the front but with a large bulldog defending a torii in the back. The T-shirts caused Rakkasans to stand out while conducting physical training, leading to the inevitable smack talking and shoving. On one humid summer morning, Dennis led his platoon on a run toward the Air Assault School. As his platoon crested a hill, another group of soldiers ran in the opposite direction. When those other soldiers saw the eye patch, one snickered and made a remark. Unlike most platoon leaders who might continue on, Dennis stopped and chased the snickering soldier. Defending his team leader, Dennis discussed the incident with the offending runner. He ensured that soldier would never snicker again at the soldier while simultaneously earning the respect of his men. What Dennis saw as a basic defense of his soldier was something else to his platoon. They knew then that their platoon leader would do what it took to defend them. It did not matter; they were his and he was theirs. And for the rest of us—there was no platoon leader better. And that was the day that Dennis taught them about the love of brothers and his Bulldogs.

LOVE OF MARIE

So there they were, two young men discussing relationships while Dennis conducted guard duty at FOB Summerall. Dennis was engaged to Marie, a West Point classmate. They were a young couple who spent their last days together before Marie boarded a plane to head to Kuwait and then Mosul, Iraq, in August. When they said their goodbyes and gave their final hugs, they both knew they would be worlds apart despite Dennis leaving for Bayji, one hour south of Mosul, one month later.

Dennis and Marie were going on four years together. After requesting a new partner for group assignments, her instructor placed Marie into a three-person group with two classmates—Courtney Carey and Dennis. Marie was a hard worker at school. She was famous for attention to detail and is still a whiz with numbers. Dennis, on the other hand, was not known for his book smarts but knew how to organize groups to get work done. The charm and smile Dennis used to organize any group in which he was a member started to win Marie over. She liked his confidence and the way he treated her. Slowly, the two became more than just math partners.

Their relationship continued to grow. The swimmer from Jersey and Rabble Rouser from Florida spent more time together.[7] As their sophomore year finished, the two found ways to meet back together during summer training. Their love grew during the fall of their junior year. The strength of the relationship showed itself in a variety of ways, but it was most evident during football games. The swim team stood in the back of the Corps of Cadets at Michie Stadium. Dennis focused less on the game and more on the cheerleader on the field, with whom he exchanged waves and smiles. The team caught on quickly and started to rib Dennis, whose smile gave it all away.

Firstie year had its ups and its downs. They received their class rings together, and both celebrated earning their top branch choices—Dennis to the Infantry and Marie to the Adjutant Generals Corps. Reality hit, however, when Marie posted to Fort Campbell but Dennis received Fort Lewis, Washington, after infantry slots to Campbell ran out. The prospect of living across the country was daunting, especially knowing the struggles they faced living only a quarter mile apart at the Academy. Still, their love grew, and the two graduated and joined the Army as second lieutenants.

Their officer basic training put them about five hours apart. Marie was in South Carolina at Fort Jackson and Dennis was in southwest Georgia at Fort Benning. The time apart was tough, but Marie made the drive often as Dennis's training went late into Friday nights. Marie was there when Dennis put on his cherished infantry cord for the first time and waved goodbye as he left to start Ranger School. While at Ranger School, the sleepless and lonely nights led Dennis to realize something—he would never find a woman like Marie again, and it was time to ensure she knew that. On Christmas leave from the school, Dennis called his friends and let them know he would propose over New Year's weekend.

On December 29, Dennis took Marie through Central Park where he proposed while crossing a picturesque bridge. Thrilled, Marie said yes and put the beautiful three-stone diamond ring on her ring finger. Signifying their intention to spend their lives together, that ring changed much as Dennis traded Fort Lewis with another lieutenant and moved to Fort Campbell. The two purchased a house together and settled down to enjoy their final summer before deployment. While Marie left first, the two remained in touch. When Dennis got to FOB Summerall, however, the communication slowed to emails due to limited phone connectivity. It was tough, but they persevered.

The week before Dennis's final patrol, his platoon provided base security. This required Dennis to sit in a room in a maintenance bay for eight hours and conduct regular checks on his men. Charlie swung by to talk one day and asked about Marie. Dennis opened up during this conversation, describing the sadness experienced when she left before he did and how he could not wait to get home and spend the rest of his life with Marie. Charlie left the shack that day, amazed at the depth of Dennis's love. The raw emotion contrasted with the bleakness of Iraq. Dennis's love was true. And that was the day Dennis taught them about his love of Marie.

LOVE OF MISSION

So there they were, thousands of miles away from home and living on an airfield in the Sunni Triangle. FOB Summerall once served as a helicopter base for Saddam's army. The base bordered a small town, As Siniyah, to its east, with an open desert to the west. A major route, Hershey, ran by the base, and connected it to a major highway, Tampa, that ran through the main city in their area—Bayji. Divided by Tampa up the center and blocked to the east by the Tigris River, Bayji had the elements of a once bustling city, with a large market and beautiful main mosque. Beneath the beauty and the dust, Bayji was a messy city. Primarily Sunni, it was a bastion of Saddam supporters and was a natural crossroads for insurgents coming into Iraq through Mosul and heading south.

The Bulldogs were tasked with the northeastern portion of Bayji, along with towns that bordered the Tigris. This area was one tribe's stronghold and required a lot of patrolling to meet the community. Dennis was up to the challenge. Constantly outside the wire, Dennis forged relationships with the Iraqis he met, creating a level of trust with the Iraqi sheikhs that others could only dream of building. Sheikhs sought Dennis's attention, and Dennis gave them his time; he knew their importance in securing Bayji.

Dennis's importance to the security of Bayji was most apparent on November 19, 2005. Just off a week of guard duty, Dennis patrolled with his platoon that morning. Despite having finished a morning patrol, Dennis went out again with his company's headquarters for a meeting. Riding as the third truck in a five-vehicle convoy, Dennis headed out to continue his efforts with a sheikh.

On the way to the meeting, the patrol drove down a dirt road along the Tigris called Smugglers' Road. Just off the edge of one side of the road were reeds; the other side was tall grass and shrubs. The patrol found the road crowded and turned around to take an alternate route. Dennis, along with the men in his truck, knew this, and in spite of the long day, followed. As the convoy headed south, there was a large explosion and a lot of dust. Dennis was gone. And that was the day Dennis taught them about love of mission.

LOVE OF FAMILY

So there they were, attending "A Toast with Dennis" in the fall of 2012 for the First Lieutenant Dennis Zilinski Foundation. The event occurred in a charming neighborhood along the Jersey Shore and was filled with people honoring Dennis's memory. BJ and Charlie were honoring Dennis's memory together for the first time when they met his parents at the event. Dennis's family was a huge part of his life. Dennis was a cherished son, brother, uncle, grandchild, and nephew, so it was no surprise that much of Dennis's family became an extended family to classmates and teammates at West Point. With Dennis's childhood home only two hours from school, the Zilinskis attended most football games or invited cadets to their home. Roommate, classmate, teammate, or just someone who did not have somewhere to go, everyone was a guest of the Zilinski family.

It was obvious family was a priority in his life. He was proud of his father, "Mr. Z," a leader in the New Jersey State Police and a Vietnam veteran, who taught Dennis service and sacrifice. He adored his mother, "Mama Z," who was his shining example of faith and love and always his biggest cheerleader in whatever he was doing. Dennis would often share Mama Z's letters that she wrote every day with BJ—always encouraging, motivating, and loving the son, of whom she was so proud. Dennis made you think his older siblings, Dougie,

Shelly, and Tiffany, were yours with the way he spoke of them. The youngest Zilinski was Dennis's best friend and brother, Matt. You could tell from the first time you met them the love, respect, and pride the two had for each other.

BJ and Charlie mingled that night. While everyone who knew Dennis knew his family's closeness, it was not easy to quantify that love. Everyone there shined with pride at the chance to talk about him. The energy and love that poured into celebrating Dennis's life through a cause so great was a mirror image of Dennis's love for his own family. Mama Z said a few words of thanks and told the attendees a bit about her son before reading Dennis's final letter. Like so many others, the letter began with "Mom and Dad, Well if you are reading this letter then I have paid the ultimate sacrifice for our country." The letter continues in a way that was the quintessential Dennis: "I want to thank you for this wonderful life that I have lived. . . . Take care. I love and miss you, Dennis."

And that was the day Dennis taught them about love of family.

CONCLUSION

So there they were, reminiscing about Dennis. BJ and Charlie thought that to summarize a life—especially a life that was filled with as much love as Dennis Zilinski's—in a few pages was impossible. The stories are as endless as the laps they swam. While Dennis may be gone, his memory lives on through his family and his friends. It lives on in the "Run with Dennis," the First Lieutenant Dennis Zilinski Foundation, and the causes they support. His memory lives on in the donations he shared through his will—to his church and to his team. Dennis was an extraordinary young man with a life full of potential in front of him. While his death is tragic and stories that are told give a glimpse into the life of this big-smiled, big-hearted, all-American guy, the true legacy Dennis leaves are the lessons of love, service, and sacrifice. Dennis Zilinski's legacy is not in the number of years he lived but in the number of lives he touched. Dennis wouldn't want us to weep for him; Dennis would want us to love for him. Love each other, love our lives, and love our families and our friends. Have faith in God and faith in people and do your best to serve others in whatever way you know how.

Take a lesson from Dennis Zilinski—make people better.

Benjamin T. Britt

FIRST LIEUTENANT BENJAMIN T. BRITT, KIA IN BAGHDAD, IRAQ, ON DECEMBER 22, 2005

" . . . And the Party Never Ends."

Brett Walker

I wish I could be a man like Benjamin Thomas Britt. He was certainly the kind of man I hope my son, Benjamin Thomas Walker, will someday become. I could never identify why he chose to tolerate my presence, much less befriend me. Ben was a rising star in the cadet ranks—a disciplined, inspiring, physically fit, and academically gifted Texan. I was something of an anomaly within the corps of cadets—a San Francisco liberal whose principal talents lent themselves more to contesting conformity than any of West Point's preferred skills.

Given the constrained nature of social life at West Point, our relationship relied heavily upon on our nightly shared dinners. Of course, on the limited occasions we were allowed to leave the West Point campus, we would usually do so together—play an away rugby game, visit my house in Massachusetts, play poker at a Connecticut casino, or spend the night in New York. While all these escapes were indeed a luxury, the dinners were the most important aspect of our relationship. According to a set routine, we would attend our classes during the day, proceed directly from our last class to rugby practice, then from rugby practice back to our dorms for a shower and then convene in the Mess Hall. Three of us partook in this tradition every night without fail. There was Benjamin Britt, Brent Pafford, and me; that is to say, Britt, Brett, and Brent. The phonetic similarities in our names coupled with our constant proximity to one another served as the source of endless confusion for our rugby teammates and coaches.

Typically, the dinner conversation would focus on politics. Ben was, borrowing the term used by then presidential candidate Hillary Clinton as I proudly did, a member of the "vast right-wing conspiracy." I was, and remain, a bleeding-heart liberal. Our debates on current events were an event to behold. Often we would put as much effort into preparing for each evening's political debate as we did in preparing for the next day's classes. On occasion, no agreement could be achieved, so we would take it to the boxing gym for final resolution. Ben was bigger and stronger than I was, but I was a bit wilier, making our boxing matches nearly as exciting as our verbal debates.

Brent Pafford, the third member of our trio, was not as adamant about politics as Ben and me. In sensitivity to Paff, we would occasionally discuss nonpartisan subjects. One day Ben began waxing on the miniseries *Lonesome Dove*. The subject resonated with Paff, a product of New Mexico, and dominated that evening's conversation.

"My favorite part of *Lonesome Dove*," said Ben, "is where the guys bring their dead buddy all the way across the country for a proper burial in his beloved Texas hometown."

Ben paused. "If I get killed, I want you guys to bring me back to Wheeler, Texas—God's country—for a proper burial."

It was 2002. The war in Afghanistan had just begun, and the war in Iraq, the one that would claim Ben's life, would soon follow.

Ben loved football. In fact, his friends eventually came to understand that we could never be so brazen as to ask him to socialize on the Saturday of the annual Red River Shootout, when University of Oklahoma would play the University of Texas. He had been a standout player in high school and took it quite hard when his tiny alma mater was relegated to a seven-man football program as opposed to the traditional eleven-man program. He had played college football at Trinity College in Texas before transferring to West Point.

The prospect of playing football at West Point did not seem to interest Ben. Instead, he opted for football's athletic ancestor—rugby. Though capable of playing nearly any position on the pitch, Ben became a hooker mostly in recognition of his humility and toughness. For those unfortunate souls unfamiliar with rugby, the hooker is a tirelessly worked yet rarely appreciated position akin to the offensive guard in football. One of the hooker's duties, the one from which the position derives its name, is to be suspended above the ground in the middle of the scrum and try to hook the ball backward toward his own team with his dangling legs. To do so, the hooker must pin his own arms behind the back of the two biggest members of the team—the props—leaving himself unprotected during the initial collision of the two teams in the scrum and unable to escape in the common instances of scrum collapse. It is a dangerous, difficult, and thankless position, but at the same time a crucial position. It fit Ben's ethos perfectly. Ben never sought recognition for his accomplishments. In fact, he would rarely discuss them with anyone. It took much of the rugby program by surprise when Ben received an award for highest academically ranked rugby player. Very few people knew that Ben was selected to receive a Marshall Scholarship for graduate study but refused to accept, preferring instead to hasten his deployment to the Middle East. Nearly nobody knew that Ben was engaged to be married.

Ben's humility was often misleading. His refusal to acknowledge accomplishment, his insistence on Spartan living standards, and his rigorous work ethic all gave the impression that Ben failed to revel in traditional sources of enjoyments. While it is true he often denied himself pleasures while in his role as cadet or soldier, Ben became an entirely new person outside of a professional setting. For instance, each year immediately following spring finals and just before our class was scattered across the world for summer assignments, I would host a party at my family's home on Cape Cod. Many of those contributing to and memorialized in this collection attended those parties, including Jerry Eidson, John "Dave" Hortman, Jay Ireland, and Nick Ziemba. During those three-day stretches each year, Ben became a totally different man—a joyous and excitable man. There, on Cape Cod, Ben was able to detach himself from any duty and simply enjoy himself.

Back at West Point each fall, Ben returned to his business-minded, development-focused self. During those periods, he derived his greatest pleasures from assisting others with intellectual, ethical, or doctrinal problems. That quirk offered some indication of the basis of our relationship—I was constantly in need of such mentorship. The movie *Fight Club* had recently been released, and Ben likened himself to the narrator. He was a regular guy with good judgment and values. In juxtaposition, Ben likened me to Tyler

Durden—a far more impetuous and excitable character. But ultimately, in the movie as between Ben and me, we were of a united spirit.

Ben was always sensitive to structure his advice indirectly, never giving his advice in an authoritative manner and rather prefacing it with some softening phrase. It was a disclaimer. He did not consider himself to have the definitive answer, merely thoughts. Oftentimes it came in the form of "Dad always told me." Though he was not one to articulate it specifically, Ben considered his father's perspective to be that of old cowboy wisdom born of many days on the metaphorical trail—the sagest of all wisdoms to a Texan.

"You know, my dad always told me, it is not a real problem if simply writing a check can make it go away," counseled Ben when I was hysterically angry about the rugby team not reimbursing me for a clinic I attended.

"I guess I am determined not to let anything in this early part of my life define me," sympathized Ben when I received discouraging news about a position for which I believed myself best qualified but was ultimately denied.

"Some of the guys seem to think you are too controlling," explained Ben between missions at Ranger School. "You might want to trust some of the subordinate leaders to do their thing."

"The way I see it, those who have trouble sleeping at night either have a guilty conscience or don't work hard enough during the day," said Ben, when I expressed concern about a mutual acquaintance's claim that he had to drink to get a restful night's sleep.

A long-standing tradition calls for West Point cadets to pen the yearbook entry for their closest cadet friend. Ben, Paff, and I struggled to decide who should write each entry. Eventually we settled upon a triangular model: Ben would write for me, I would write for Paff, and Paff would write for Ben. Paff wrote, in part, "Ben's conservative past guided him to study economics and spend his free time playing the market." Ben indulged my fancy for American literature by paraphrasing Mark Twain, when he wrote of me, "It's good he didn't let schooling interfere with his education because he sure didn't learn anything studying psychology." All three entries concluded with the chorus lyrics from a Robert Earl Keen song, "The road goes on forever and the party never ends."

I was never a big fan of Robert Earl Keen. I am more of a Lynyrd Skynyrd fan. Sitting in my dorm room one day with Ben, the Skynyrd song "Simple Man" came on the radio. After listening for a bit, I lightheatedly quipped,

"Hey, Ben. This is you. You are a Simple Kinda Man." Ben fixed me with a serious stare and with steady conviction responded, "You're right. I am a simple kinda man and I like it that way."

Later that year it came time to select assignments for our postgraduation service. Ben was at the top of our class and thus eligible for any assignment he desired. He could have selected helicopter pilot, military intelligence, or engineer stationed in Hawaii, Italy, Japan, or Germany, but Ben naturally chose a simple assignment. Infantry in Fort Campbell, Kentucky.

It was in keeping with Ben's simple tastes, but it was also a calculated decision to bring him to the front lines of the war in Iraq. He was among the first members of the Class of 2004 to deploy to Iraq. A finer ambassador of the class could never be known. He wrote me regularly to describe his experiences, both good and bad. He frequently complained of his company commander. In his final email to me, he expressed his frustration that his company commander ordered him to clear a dirt road every morning, fully knowing that the insurgents would recapture it each evening.

It was on that dirt road that Ben was killed just shy of Christmas Day 2005. He was struck by one of the infamous improvised explosive devices that claimed so many American, and civilian, lives in Iraq. I received the phone call from Paff on Christmas Eve. The Christmas Eve church service that evening was a constant reminder of Ben's death. Ben had introduced me to organized religion. I am now a leader in my home church, but it was Ben who first brought me to church.

In the dark days that followed, I spoke to Ben's parents often. In one conversation his mother, Mary, asked if I thought Ben would prefer to be buried at West Point, in Arlington, or in Texas. Reflecting on the *Lonesome Dove* conversation in West Point's dining hall two years earlier, I knew exactly how to respond.

Ben was buried in a fitting manner. He was interred in a beautiful, ornate coffin provided by the army, with his name spelled incorrectly. There was some talk as to whether to replace the coffin. Ben, an ardent advocate of responsible government spending, would almost certainly have asked to be buried in the deficient coffin to avoid imposing additional costs upon the taxpayer, and so he was.

Also, though Ben was straight, a group of demonstrators from the Westboro Baptist Church of Kansas lined the road to the cemetery protesting the perceived allowance of homosexuality in the Army (the "Don't Ask, Don't Tell" policy was still in effect). A motorcycle club called Rolling Thunder also appeared to cordon off the protestors and offer their respects for the fallen. I believe Ben would have enjoyed this. Conservative as he may have been, Ben was dedicated to the U.S. Constitution and our fundamental freedoms. He would have supported the free expression of the Westboro Church and enjoyed the interplay created by the appearance of Rolling Thunder.

Ben's body now rests in the town cemetery of Wheeler, Texas, but much of his blood was spilled on that dirt road in Baghdad and absorbed into the soil. To this day, that blood is now ever entangled with the terrain of Iraq—part of the earth, part of the legacy. The road goes on forever and the party never ends.

FIRST LIEUTENANT GARRISON C. AVERY, KIA IN BAGHDAD, IRAQ, ON FEBRUARY 1, 2006

Gripping Hands from the Shadows: Remembering Garrison Avery

Nicholas Ziemba

I was fortunate enough to have worked with Gary during our time at the academy. It may have been on a math project or something similar . . . no doubt he carried the group. I remember him as a team player we all expected to do amazing things for the people of the world. It was during a recent talk with civilians in Mahmudiyah, Iraq, that I realized the magnitude of his character and the impact it had on literally everyone he came in contact with.

The Brigade I'm assigned to, 2nd BCT 10th Mountain, assumed control of 2-101's sector last September. Since then, we have been fighting the South Baghdad fight with mixed and moderate successes. Recently we have started to enlist the help of Sunni volunteers for security in Al Qaeda infested areas. During a talk with leaders from one of these areas, a couple of the Sheikhs brought up, out of the blue, an "LT Afry." It took me a couple seconds to see through the pronunciation [sic], but it all clicked when they started to talk about how he had been their absolutely favorite American, had visited and worked with their local schools numerous times, had recognized the tribe's potential over a year before we stumbled upon them. As we exchanged our favorite stories about Gary, I could see that some of the sheikhs were shedding tears in his memory. I just wanted everyone to know that Gary's legacy as a kind, insightful, and amazing human being still lives

Garrison C. Avery

*strong even here, in what many of you know to be an utterly un-
forgiving and ruthless place.[1]*

—Written by the author on Garrison's eulogy webpage

While the writing of that eulogy seems like a lifetime ago, I remember
the described events as if they happened yesterday. Gary was talking to me, to us, supporting our effort from the shadows in communion
with the Long Gray Line; something like this one never forgets. I, like the
rest of our classmates, wish we could have had more time with Gary—with
his ever-upbeat outlook, undying care for others, and MacGyver-esque
ingenuity, he was a beacon for our class. He refused to accept Army mo-
notony as a given under which to suffer. Instead, Gary infused every day
with trademark originality and a fresh perspective, bringing us all along
with him on the journey. I count myself lucky to have had the opportunity
to communicate with him in this way, after he was so cruelly taken from
us. His legacy of love in that scary time and place spoke volumes through
the darkness—this legacy had far-reaching positive consequences in South
Baghdad, helping to set the conditions for security gains that contributed
to an amazing reversal of the war.[2]

Most importantly, this legacy will always speak to his genuine concern
for his fellow man.

Every new cadet undergoing the rigors of Cadet Basic Training is required to learn and recite verbatim the lyrics to the poetic hymn "The
Corps." Written in 1902 by USMA Chaplain Bishop H. S. Shipman to
commemorate the Academy's centennial, it serves as a testament to the
legacy of the Long Gray Line, the expectations of cadets and graduates, and
connections bonding us together. As a young plebe, I remember thinking
the hymn a bit morose when it spoke of ghostly assemblages, shadows, and
marrow. Now, as a graduate looking back on more than two centuries of
USMA sacrifice, especially that of the last decade of war that has claimed
so many of my classmates, "The Corps" holds a special meaning for me. I
think of those killed in action since the War of 1812, I think of their costly
contributions to our freedom, and I face gladly the expectations to uphold
that legacy. Most personally, though, I see Gary, along with our other fallen
classmates, firmly demanding us to carry the torch.

In the summer of 2006, my unit had replaced Gary's unit in the patch-
work of seemingly never-ending farmland south of Baghdad, known then by
the unfortunate nickname "the Triangle of Death" due to its well-publicized
violent reputation. At the apexes of the triangle were the small cities of
Mahmudiyah to the north, Yusufiyah to the west, and Lutfiyah to the south.
These cities, like most across the country, were at times vicious and at others
vibrant: overflowing markets full of brilliant spice displays and hanging, fly-
pestered goat carcasses were equally likely to attract shoppers and suicide
bombers. The buildings and streets reeked sourly of raw sewage and were
run down with both years of prewar neglect and more recent battle scars, but
the people who inhabited these places had, at some point, made the fatalistic
decision to keep on living amid the despair.

Out of the cities the noise died down, but the danger remained.
Sociopathic bands of terrorists, not to be confused with romanticized
freedom fighters, roamed the countryside, killing entire families, blowing
up mosques, and targeting well-intentioned coalition and Iraqi security
patrols with ever-increasing volumes of explosives. To the unacquainted,
however, the Triangle might seem perfectly pastoral. Geometrically
planted and mercifully shady date palm groves interrupted open fields
brimming with tomatoes, cauliflower, and some of the biggest green pep-
pers known to man. Isolated farm compounds dotted the lush landscape,
serving as tiny spots of civilization. These mini oases, dirt-floored, quiet,
and equally the domain of people and livestock, remain for me a near
perfect representation of an agrarian ideal. If only we could all live so
simply in harmony with nature, how much better off would we be? On a
few occasions, I let my imagination entertain the thought of taking up the
biblically blissful way of life, only to be jolted harshly back to reality by the
crack of a passing bullet or the unexpected "whump" of an enemy mortar.
As my comrades and I used to lament, "If it weren't for the [insert form of
violence here], this place would be beautiful."

What did the members of the Long Gray Line think when they left the
hills and valleys of southern New York and first saw America's fruited plains
while fighting the Indian Wars? How about Italy's Apennine Mountains
in World War II? What about the dense jungles of Vietnam? Issuing forth
from the Hudson Highlands, our Long Gray Line has been stitched into
the historical fabric of so many contested, beautiful places and traditions.

This last decade of war has seen our class and others add to the history of the cradle of civilization in Iraq and play the next round of the Great Game across Afghanistan. The beauty, whether considered in the context of war or not, reminds us of our small but lasting role in human history.

I am sure Gary appreciated both the natural beauty and the beauty ingrained in the spirit of the tough and determined people he met in Iraq. One such spirited and beautiful group, the al Saidi tribe, inhabited the northern part of the Triangle along the road between Mahmudiyah and Yusufiyah. For generations, they had been successful chicken farmers and still maintained a scattering of pungent and noisy coops with easy access to local markets. The thoroughfare their lands abutted was a rare paved two-lane road, pockmarked with small roadside bomb craters and hand-railed on the north by a major canal. Thick stands of ten-foot-tall elephant grass curtained the road on both sides, limiting sightlines and isolating travelers in a green tunnel. The typically peaceful route was not the most dangerous in our area, but insurgents still occasionally targeted wayward American or Iraqi military convoys. The al Saidi tribe was caught in a rough position—easily reached by friend and foe alike alongside a relatively safe roadway, and too close to roadside bomb detonations to escape suspicion. In hindsight, our best assessments deemed the al Saidis innocent of the bombings, hopelessly lodged between insurgents and their American and Iraqi targets. With each year bringing a new American unit to the area, the tribe had to start fresh the battle of perceptions. One can only imagine the frustrations of having to reprove one's innocence year after year; exuding great inner peace, these ancient people had accepted and grown accustomed to their lot. With so much understanding lost in the rapid turnover of American units year to year, the tribe had become a perennially targeted entity in the fight to eradicate roadside bombs. The first time I met the al Saidi tribe was around December of 2006 when we barreled an M1151 brashly through their heavy, steel front gate to kick off a raid in which we detained seven tribe members. Admittedly, not the best introduction.

The al Saidi tribal lands were quiet for much of the ensuing year until the momentous fever of the "Awakening" movement reached our corner of the country. The movement, a response to the particularly murderous tactics of al-Qaeda in Iraq and Abu Musab al-Zarqawi, empowered tribal leaders to stand up internal, ad-hoc security forces to protect their lands. They wore makeshift uniforms, built checkpoints, and most importantly, received a paycheck courtesy of Uncle Sam. Insurgents, flush with cash from foreign and domestic financiers, recruited unemployed, disaffected young men to their cause; our alternative of a reliable paycheck and the opportunity to honorably protect their families erased the insurgents' monetary edge and led to unprecedented security gains across the country. The wildly successful movement made its way to the Triangle in the summer of 2007, and the al Saidi tribe was at the front of the line, begging for the opportunity to secure their people. After a vetting process during which we determined the tribal leadership could control their area, we invested wholeheartedly in the tribe. Consider again how our unit had introduced ourselves to the tribe, and you can imagine how surreal such an arrangement seemed at first—sitting down to talk security cooperation with al Saidi leadership took a measure of mutual, near-blind trust at the onset, but their warm welcome and amazing ability to let bygones be bygones quickly overcame this awkwardness. As we approached the end of our deployment, we felt a small sense of triumph in being able to hand over an area to our replacements markedly safer than how we found it. Furthermore, the al Saidis, loyal members of the Awakening movement and central to these successes, felt they had secured for their tribe a place in their country's future.

But that was not the whole story of the al Saidi tribe's elevation.

Frequent and lengthy tribal dinners served equally as security meetings and social gatherings; we would put away mountains of fatty lamb on rice, vegetables, bread, and ever-present sweet chai and talk about the insurgency, about the family, about life. At one such dinner a month before our scheduled return to American soil, I was having a quiet side conversation with one of the tribe's English-speaking leaders, known familiarly as Abu Hadi, when he started to recount the tribe's recent war history and interactions with coalition soldiers. Sitting outside on cheap plastic lawn chairs, precariously pliable in the one-hundred-degree heat, he repeated the all-too-familiar frustrations of being stuck in the middle, targeted from both sides, and beholden to the passing whims of the American operations cycle. But he also spoke of rare connections with certain Americans that helped to showcase the tribe's goodwill since the invasion in 2003. Abu Hadi believed that these glimmering instances were what kept the tribe from aligning with the insurgency. In spite of repeated wretched treatment from the Iraqi government and capricious American reactions to local bombings, the al Saidi tribe maintained the faith that one day their fortunes would change.

Our side conversation had gathered a small group of listeners, expanding our circle of lawn chairs into an interested, white-garbed gaggle. One of the white-bearded tribal elders said in a reedy voice something almost imperceptible about a "Luu-tent Afry," to which the conversation ring all nodded in agreement, muttering in Arabic somber words of gratitude. Abu Hadi, a sensitive man by Iraqi standards, looked to me through misty eyes and asked me in broken English, "Luu-tent Afry, maybe you know him? He was very good man. He take good care of us." When he saw the look of confusion in my eyes, Abu Hadi talked about how this young American officer had gone out of his way to help the tribe but was killed by a roadside bomb more than a year before.

He was talking about Gary.

"Yes, yes, I knew Lieutenant Avery," I responded haltingly, belying my astonishment at the connection. "I went to school with him, and yes, he was a very good man."

More than eighteen months since his passing, Lieutenant Garrison Avery's radiant legacy with that ancient tribe was still burning bright; the conversation echoed around the circle, with each elder sharing an emotional tribute to "Luu-tent Afry" that Abu Hadi attempted to translate for me. I could see that Gary was, for them, a point of positive light in the otherwise troublesome darkness since 2003. We shared stories, reaffirming what we all knew of Gary and his capacity for caring, leadership, and inspiration. He gave the al Saidi tribe hope for a fair deal, for peace and prosperity, and for better days ahead. Our efforts were merely building on the solid foundation of goodwill Gary had shared with the tribe; he had identified their potential well before we had, and we were all safer because of it. This relationship and pact with the al Saidi tribe, started by Gary, focused on shared goals for a better Iraq, and for the opportunity to live freely and in peace. He had honored the Corps, the Long Gray Line, and, in doing so, our country by being a model human being in the midst of such violence and chaos. At that somber but thrilling moment, I was immensely proud to count myself among the ranks of the Line that had been strengthened, like so many times before, through the heroism of our fellow graduates.

Gary was reaching up from the shadows to help a classmate, soldiers, and a persecuted people, and that is something eternal indeed. The Long Gray

Line is built on thousands of such deeds, such gifts from one to the next. I will always remember what Gary gave to me and to all of us, out of the enduring goodness of his heart. I hope my sharing of this war memory helps you to remember Gary and all those who have gone before us, and to consider how you and your legacy will grip hands with those who follow.

FIRST LIEUTENANT ROBERT A. SEIDEL III, KIA IN ABU GHRAIB, IRAQ, ON MAY 18, 2006

Deeds Not Words: Remembering Rob Seidel

Dave Strickler with Colonel (R) Kevin Brown

Although I no longer recall the exact date, I can say with absolute certainty that I remember the day I met Rob Seidel. During the first summer at West Point, known as Beast Barracks, there is a brief respite for new cadets halfway through the three months of Cadet Basic Training. This eight-hour break, which one might mistakenly believe is a nice gesture to new cadets, actually exists because it is logistically easier for the upperclassmen who are moving into and out of the barracks.[1]

Nonetheless, it is a terrific, albeit brief, escape for new cadets. Rob and I met during this break at the house of Major Jeff Logan—our future sponsor for our remaining years at West Point.

When I first asked Rob what he thought of our experiences at Beast, I was somewhat surprised when he remarked, through his trademark wry smile, "It sucks, but whatever . . ." Though I did not realize it at the time, this was classic Rob: brief, honest, dry, and witty. Rob had a rare ability to keep things in perspective while maintaining an exceptional tolerance for bullshit. This pragmatic humility was surprising for a young man who was carrying the pride of his entire hometown on his journey and would ultimately hold the distinction of being the first West Point graduate from Emmitsburg, Maryland. But not so surprisingly, Rob's demeanor served him well both during his time at West Point and as an Infantry officer in combat. As we lounged around at Major

Robert A. Seidel III

Logan's house and talked about literally anything but West Point, I had the feeling that I was gaining a close friend, but I had no idea how close we would become in the six years that would follow.

I have no doubt that Rob always wanted to be a soldier. Growing up in rural Emmitsburg, Rob stood out as a young man who was passionate about service, God, and family. He was clearly interested in the Army at a young age, and many who knew him well would say that he was born as the perfect infantryman. Rob was mentally sharp, physically tough, and struck an exceptional balance between idealistic and pragmatic. From what I have come to know about Rob's childhood, his desire to serve something larger than himself took him to West Point, and ultimately to Iraq, where he died doing what he firmly believed was the right thing.

During our four years at the Academy, I came to value Rob's perspective on our experience as cadets. He had a broad view that was quite rare for a West Point cadet, and his sense of humor always put me in a better mood. As we entered our final year at school, I was not even remotely surprised when Rob chose Infantry as his branch. Any other job in the Army would be a letdown for Rob Seidel. Furthermore, Rob truly doubled down on his bet when he chose Fort Drum, New York, as his first duty assignment. The joke that "the sun never sets on the 10th Mountain Division" is actually not a joke at all.[2] The unit that Rob and I joined in early 2005 had recently deployed twice to Afghanistan, and as we joined the team, we already knew we would be going to Iraq in a few short months.

As we arrived to Fort Drum, Rob met with the Army's version of human resources that placed him in the first available position for a newly minted Infantry Second Lieutenant, which just so happened to be in the Special Troops Battalion to serve as an executive officer. Rob had a mission: to find an Infantry rifle platoon to lead as soon as possible! Rob was certainly not shy about carrying out this mission; he walked into the personnel office at 2nd Battalion, 22nd Infantry Regiment, the "Triple Deuce," and let the head personnel officer know that "a mistake had been made" in his assignment to anything other than a line Infantry unit. Our battalion commander, LTC Kevin Brown (USMA 87), had seen Rob hanging around our battalion and was impressed with his demeanor and his initiative in trying to become part of the team. After a number of leaders went to bat on Rob's behalf, he became a rifle platoon leader.

As we approached our deployment and conducted a number of high-intensity training events, it was clear to me that Rob's men were very happy to have him as their platoon leader. As we packed our bags and boarded a plane bound for the Middle East, Rob stood out as a young man who was resolute in his commitment to our mission, and would do absolutely everything in his power to bring each of his men home. During our deployment, Rob came to be a living example of our battalion motto: "Deeds not Words."

Rob and I adjusted to life as young lieutenants in the Abu Ghraib district of Iraq, and we developed a regular routine of keeping each other laughing through some tough times. I remember a particular mission in which Rob's platoon supported a Special Forces Team's raid that took place in a neighborhood we normally patrolled. Rob and a number of other folks from our unit talked with the team leader and team sergeant and helped them develop their plan to conduct the raid. As the cocky special forces captain explained the route he planned to take to the target compound, Rob informed them that the road was blocked. Moreover, after the team leader showed the alternate route, Rob smiled and said, "That will work, but I think you may get lost. I would be glad to lead you guys to the target." Of course, the team refused the offer for help, and later that night they conducted a textbook raid on a house *exactly one block east* of their planned target. Rob grinned from ear to ear, and radioed the team leader with one of the best "I told you so!" messages I have ever heard. Fortunately, the team moved to the correct target and completed its mission. Every few weeks, we got to hear Rob tell his story of how "those SF dudes couldn't land nav[3] their way out of a wet paper bag."

As our deployment wore on, Rob and his platoon saw a decent amount of action, and they were a natural choice for the decisive operation[4] on many company- and battalion-sized kinetic missions. Rob had the absolute trust of his subordinates, peers, and superiors, and we all knew he had a bright future in the Army. He considered applying to serve in the Ranger Regiment, and he seemed especially interested in assessing for Special Forces. During a counseling session in April of 2006, our battalion commander tried to convince Rob that, while his goal to become a special forces officer (ostensibly to replace guys who couldn't land navigate!) was achievable for a guy with his skills and abilities, that the best place for a guy like Rob was leading men in a conventional Airborne Infantry unit, where his leadership would have a broader reach, and his ability and personal example would impact the conventional force in a positive way.

In the nearer term, the battalion commander planned to move Rob from his platoon and make him the mortar platoon leader. This was not only recognition of Rob's abilities and potential for future growth but also a signal from the battalion commander that he had immense trust in Rob because the Mortar Platoon served as the Commander's Personal Security Detachment and was out of the wire nearly every day. A little over a month later, LTC Brown described Rob Seidel as "the type of second lieutenant I wish I could have been—confident, competent, and humble." Our company commander balked at the idea of losing him from the Company, and the battalion commander put the move on hold. It seemed that Rob's professional development as a lieutenant was at a crossroads.

Over the course of the next two weeks, Rob and his platoon doggedly conducted a search for caches in the farmland northwest of Baghdad. They recovered thousands of pounds of cached ammunitions and explosives; so much so that when the controlled demolition of the stockpile was detonated it was felt fifteen miles away on the large coalition base at Baghdad International Airport. Rob was bringing the war a little closer to those who never left Camp Liberty! Two weeks later, around May 7, 2006, the battalion commander pinned an Army Achievement Medal on Rob's chest for his leadership in the enormous cache effort, and then, over "near beer" and cigars, publically reiterated to Rob his belief that "Rob was the kind of guy who would stay Infantry and command a battalion one day in the 82nd Airborne Division." After our commander left, Rob laughed and said something to the effect of "Yeah, I don't see that happening. I can't say I like jumping out of a perfectly good airplane all that much." We all laughed, and all definitely admired the fact that our battalion commander would make such a public statement of how he viewed Rob's potential as a leader in the army. Without a doubt, no matter what path Rob Seidel could have chosen or what path was chosen for him, he would have made a positive impact on his men, and on his mission.

Much like the day I met Rob back in 2000, May 18, 2006, is a day I will never forget. Sadly, I will always remember this day because it is when I said good-bye to Rob. I wish I could recall our last conversation, but honestly, I don't remember. I was with our company commander patrolling in the eastern portion of our assigned area when we received a radio call stating that Rob's platoon was in trouble. I can't remember the exact details, but when I heard Staff Sergeant Brandon Gardner reporting on the radio instead of Rob, I already expected the worst.[5] Rob's platoon had been conducting assessments of local farms with an Army veterinarian and was called to track down some insurgents who had fired at the Marines assigned to our west. In doing so, they had moved to a rural area, and they were traveling along hard-packed dirt roads. Unfortunately, insurgents in the area were able to dig IEDs under some of these roads. At times, these buried IEDs are massive, and Rob and the other four men in his vehicle almost certainly never knew what hit them. Though it is somewhat morbid to discuss, I do take comfort in knowing that Rob and his men died quickly.

By the time I arrived to the area, Rob's platoon had done a good job of establishing security of the area. We were now concerned with making sure there were no secondary explosive devices in the area targeting other American forces who responded to the scene. In fact, there were two other bombs, and fortunately, the damage from these devices was relatively minor. We spent hours searching the area and recovering what was left of Rob's vehicle. Losing a friend or family member is never easy or pleasant, and doing so in combat is even more confusing and surreal. During the hours that followed, I made the conscious decision that I would deal with the task at hand and think about what happened once we were back at our base. After sunset, we finished our work at the site of the attack and prepared to drive back to our firebase.[6] The drive back was miserable; every one of us was on edge and nervous after seeing the events that took place that day. On a normal day, soldiers (myself included) start to get somewhat complacent and even laugh and joke as they get close to their base. On that night in May 2006, we did not say a word until we were safely within the walls of our firebase, and even once we arrived, no one was in the mood for jokes.

As I talked to my men that evening, I tried to craft a compelling story about how we should think about the good times we spent with the men who died, and not dwell on the horrible events of one specific day. I kept my own emotions guarded, and told the men that if anyone wanted to talk about their feelings, the chaplain was an excellent resource. Overall, I thought the message was well received, but one young NCO definitely called my bluff and asked who I was planning on talking to about the loss of Rob. The question floored me, and I realized that I had still not fully processed the events of that day or the fact that I had lost a close friend.

In the months that followed, we were able to come to terms with the loss of Rob Seidel. His premature death left a gaping hole in his platoon, and made me feel very grateful to be alive. My parents were able to attend Rob's memorial service. They said that the town of Emmitsburg must have completely shut down that day because it seemed as if every single resident was at the funeral. My dad told me about the ceremony and that he was able to meet Staff Sergeant Johnny Rowell, who served as Rob's platoon sergeant. "Johnny T," as we called him, was an exceptional platoon sergeant, and he and Rob definitely shared a special bond. My dad commented that in hearing what Johnny said about Rob, and more importantly how he said it, it was obvious that Rob was exactly what Infantry NCOs and soldiers want in a young officer. And in the years that passed following Rob's death, his legacy and impact have clearly lived on in many different ways. There is now an annual Rob Seidel Memorial golf tournament, and each year his former NCOs organize a trip to attend the event and honor Rob's memory. And Rob's high school in Maryland honors him and his love of baseball with the annual First Lieutenant Rob Seidel Memorial baseball tournament.

Clearly, Rob was a great man whose departure left a significant impact on those who were fortunate enough to know him. One development that I did not ever expect was the discovery that Rob was an impressive author. As we collected the things in Rob's living area in Iraq, we found a number of well-written poems and short stories. I feel that it is appropriate to share his work, which describes his feelings leading a platoon of Infantrymen in combat.

> Cloaked under the darkness of the soft desert sky, I feel a strange
> likeness between my father and I
> For now I am the father of 30 young men, related only by the blood that
> we shed
> And they look up to me, to lead them through the fight
> For we know not what awaits us this cold desert night
> But I vowed to protect them and bring them all home, so may I find
> strength in the courage they have shown
> And now like my father, I ask the Lord as I pray—Watch over my boys
> if today is my day.

In reading this poem, I am struck by the clarity with which Rob described his role as a lieutenant, and the wisdom he showed in being able to keep things in perspective. Sometimes I think about what an awesome father Rob would have been, and I am sad to think that he never got to experience the awesome responsibility of raising a son or daughter. However, it is clear that the men of 1st Platoon, B Company had an exceptional father in Rob Seidel, and that they are living Rob's legacy to this very day, and honoring his memory.

On a far lighter note, one of my favorite memories of Rob interacting with the men in his platoon was captured in a video that showed some of the highlights of our deployment to Iraq. It was filmed by Rob's team on patrol in their HMMWV.[7] The video starts with one of Rob's sergeants, Brian Kilheffer, egging Rob on, saying "C'mon sir, do it!," after which Rob breaks out in a hilarious impression of the chorus from Bone Thugs N Harmony's rap song "The Crossroads." The vehicle absolutely erupts in laughter as Rob begins rapping in a near perfect rendition of the song.

Right now, I picture Rob kicking back and enjoying a glass of mead in Valhalla, telling war stories with his fellow fallen warriors, writing poetry, and maybe even doing his best Bone Thugs impression to generate some laughter. We miss you buddy, and we are fortunate to have known you. And as the next line of the song Rob sang for the camera that day says, we'll see you at the crossroads.

FIRST LIEUTENANT AMOS "CAMDEN" BOCK, KIA IN BAGHDAD, IRAQ, ON OCTOBER 23, 2006

Amos Camden Bock: Missourian, Friend, Warrior

Travis Marks with contributions from Michael Anderson, Ryan Harbick, and Simon Welte

It is better to remain silent and thought a fool than to open one's mouth and remove all doubt.

—Mark Twain

I imagine Amos would have liked a story about himself to start with a very sarcastic comment from an influential figure like Mark Twain, especially since they both hailed from Missouri. He may have been sarcastic, but he was the most loyal person we knew. His loyalty was probably a product of growing up in "small town" America—New Madrid, Missouri, to be precise—that helped form his character. Born on January 30, 1982, to Jill and Riley Bock, this red-headed, 5'10", 145-pound man was easy to underestimate. However, Amos was one tough cookie. He not only completed some of the most strenuous training that our Army can offer, he was also an outstanding friend, peer, and combat-proven leader.

One trip to New Madrid will really make someone understand Amos. The people of New Madrid make it a special place. It is one of those towns where everybody knows one another. It was customary for Amos to introduce his friends to many of the local spots in New Madrid, such as Rosie's, and you could see how much people admired Amos and his West Point ties. But the true essence of the town went beyond just being friendly and

Amos "Camden" Bock

polite. Some of his friends experienced this during Amos's funeral as we saw another side of the town that really made us understand his love for it. It all appeared that every tree in New Madrid had a flag on it; people came outside to line the streets as the funeral procession drove by, every pew in the church was full, and neighbors offered their homes to Amos's friends who came to the funeral so they wouldn't have to pay for hotel rooms. It is easy to see why Amos loved his town so much. They loved him back just the same.

Coming out of high school, the natural progression would have been for Amos to attend the University of Missouri as the majority of his family had done. However, from a very early age Amos showed an interest in the military. As a young boy, he particularly enjoyed reading military history or dressing up as a soldier. He joined the Missouri National Guard just before he turned eighteen, with the intention of using the extra money to attend the University of Missouri. Amos's West Point ambitions quickly blossomed when a friend of the family, Colonel Broughton, convinced him at a Missouri football game to apply. Considering it was already the fall of his senior year, Amos was not confident there was enough time to pull off the lengthy West Point application process. This process not only involves the normal application process for most American universities, but it also requires candidates to have a nomination from an official government source (congressman, chain of command, etc.), conduct a physical fitness exam, and pass a medical evaluation. So of course, Amos and Colonel Broughton made a gentlemen's bet on Amos meeting all of the West Point application milestones on time to be eligible for the upcoming class. Amos's hard work and dedication paid off as he was accepted to the United States Military Academy's Class of 2004. The caption under Amos's photo in the West Point yearbook his Firstie year reads, "Best bet I ever lost."

Amos started off in Cadet Company G-1 as a Plebe, spent his Yearling and Cow years in H-2, and his Firstie year in F-3. Many of Amos's friends at West Point were made during his time in company H-2, and he continued those relationships after graduation. In between Cow and Firstie year, one of Amos's friends, Ryan Harbick, did his cadet summer training period at Fort Leonard Wood, Missouri, which is about an hour away from Amos's hometown. Amos came to pick Ryan up and drive him out to his family's cabin on the Lake of the Ozarks for a weekend. They fished during the day and would go around the lake at night to see what "good times" they could find. They talked about everything that twenty-one-year-old cadets would talk about: girls, fishing, and their futures in the Army.

In 2003, at the beginning of Firstie year, West Point had their ring ceremony for the upcoming graduating class. Ryan's family came out from California to attend the ceremony. Amos, Ryan, and Ryan's mom decided to head to the Firstie Club for a few beers while waiting for Ryan's dad to return from the airport with Ryan's sister and her friends. Ryan went to go talk with some classmates he knew and, after a few moments, he turned to look at the booth where his mom was sitting. There was Amos, getting his mom up to dance. They danced to several fast songs, his mother having a blast and Amos laughing along with her. Through the years, Ryan's mom would always talk about the fun she had that night at the Firstie Club and how Amos helped make it such a great time.

During his West Point days, Amos was remembered as a staunchly loyal friend, fiercely stubborn, and a small town country boy through and through. He loved to have a good time, but when it came to something that he was passionate about, there was no getting in his way. He loved being outdoors, either hiking, hunting, or fishing, and he took great pride in being on the Skeet and Trap Team at West Point. Few, if any, knew this little-known fact about Amos—he loved blacksmithing! He had his own forge, hammer, and anvil all set up. On the outside, Amos hated institutionalization, particularly because he believed institutions lacked common sense or independent thought. But on the inside, he loved structure and was honored to be a cadet at West Point and a soldier serving his country. He took pride in the fact that he was from the South. He acted like it, looked like it, and talked like it. He loved inviting friends home, taking them to the local store for a sandwich, riding down all the back roads, and grabbing a six pack to drink while sitting on the old bridge, tossing the empties in the water below and shooting them with his rifle as the bottles floated away. His easygoing demeanor and country ways were endearing and the true core of his person.

After graduation from West Point, Amos was commissioned as a Field Artillery officer. He started training at "the best post in the Army" (it says so on the front gate), Fort Sill, Oklahoma. While at Fort Sill, Amos met a couple of former classmates, Travis Marks and Sean Quinn, who would be joining Amos at Fort Campbell, Kentucky, so they decided to be roommates. Travis, Sean, and Amos had many adventures in their rental house on Andrews Drive. Between an Amos-designed horseshoe pit, frequent trips to Nashville in Travis's SUV, and many freshly made weekend breakfasts by Amos, it was a real bachelor's paradise. A favorite ploy of Amos and Travis, both redheads, was to try to see how many girls they could fool into thinking that they were brothers. Even though they did not look much alike, they were usually able to pull off the prank as everybody thinks redheads are the same.

Amos was always Mr. Reliable—whether it meant taking relatives to the airport in Nashville on his day off, backing his friends up if things got a little "squirrely" in Nashville, doing needed maintenance on the rental house, taking buddies to his house in New Madrid for a weekend, or packing up all of Travis's stuff and putting it in a storage unit while he suffered through Ranger School for the third time (Amos passed Ranger School on his first attempt). Frankly, Amos was not only a great friend but also a very good roommate, as he rarely complained, unless it was about Travis's PlayStation skills. This easygoing attitude was probably attributed to the fact that he loved his job. In a profession where complaining is ubiquitous, Amos would rarely, if ever, be caught speaking negatively. In fact, he usually had a smile on his face when he came home from work each day. It was no secret why he was such an effective officer. He really had a passion for it.

Michael Anderson, another fellow classmate of Amos's, witnessed this passion firsthand as they served as platoon leaders in 4th Battalion, 320th Field Artillery Regiment, aka "The Tomahawk Battalion." It is common for teams to name themselves in the Army, and Amos's platoon was known as the "Dark Side." During OIF 05-06, in the greater Karadah area of eastern Baghdad, they had a reputation among their enemies, but an even stronger reputation among their friends. Amos was a typical redhead. He never settled well with leadership, as he cared little for the political "give and take" required to stay in the good graces of his bosses. Instead, he was driven by two things: the desire to be an effective combat leader and the need to take care of his men.

One April evening, after returning from a patrol, Mike found Amos at his door with a couple of cigars and a big smile on his face. Repeating the frequent ritual, Amos and Mike grabbed the cigars, climbed to the roof of their three-story Baghdad home, and smoked in the camping chairs that Mike's mom had sent them from Virginia. While sitting on their lawn chairs, watching the hustle and bustle of Baghdad traffic as people rushed home to avoid violating curfew, Amos and Mike smoked and bullshitted for the next hour. It was the typical conversation: Mike complained about Iraqis, and Amos made a series of sarcastic remarks that weren't the least bit comforting. It was a part of his charm; he was a smart ass, but a good one. Like many of their smoking excursions, they were accompanied by many of their soldiers briefly grabbing a cigarette break. It was one of the things Amos enjoyed the most about Iraq—he relished the moments when he would get to talk with his men.

As they neared the end of their smoke, Gunny Reel joined them, sitting on his personal folding chair.[1] He said something to the effect of, "What are you two assholes doing up here?" Gunny Reel and Amos were attached at the hip, a real combat leadership team. Gunny was a tough man in his late thirties, he was on his sixth deployment, and although he displayed the rough exterior of a weathered line soldier, he was the "mother hen" that was always looking out for Amos.

As he sat down with us he calmly said, "Hey LT, the Hajjis are celebrating something, we best get inside soon, celebratory fire is starting." Amos smiled at his worrisome platoon sergeant and calmly said, "Eh." Soon Gunny forgot about his previous warnings, and the three of them sat on the roof, gabbing the night away as they always did. They started to observe the random celebratory gunfire when all of a sudden they jumped out of their chairs as they heard, "POP, POP, POP." A volley of celebratory gunfire ricocheted off the roof's top floor. The three of them quickly jumped inside and considered each other lucky not to have been shot. Mike shot a quick glance over to Gunny, and he looked at him with an expression of relief that only a survivor of multiple wars could display. Gunny and Mike then turned toward Amos and observed the scratchy bellowing of their feisty friend.

"Hah, ha . . . HAHAHAHA," laughed Amos.

"LT, you are god damn crazy, are you in shock? I told you it was stupid to be out there, we almost got shot," said Gunny.

Amos, in his typical manner, replied with premeditated sarcasm, "Bet your butt hole is puckered old man, you should see the look on your face!"

After catching their breaths they moved downstairs and resumed their normal nighttime activities. Amos continued to chuckle a bit, and walked back to his room to start another one-hour stint of spider solitaire on his laptop. This wasn't a crazy man. This wasn't a man who laughed at death. This was just a man who simply wasn't scared of it.

It was a cool October night, and fighting had picked up in eastern Baghdad. As the Tomahawk Battalion continued its aggressive patrol presence in Karadah, all of its soldiers couldn't help but have one foot out the door. They all had about two weeks until they started "right-seat rides" (handovers) with the 1st Infantry Division. It seemed the end was near, and that they would all be back with their loved ones soon. At that time in the deployment, tensions were high. Soldiers and officers were tired, as the brutal conditions of a tough Baghdad deployment took their toll on the war-weary men.

On the night of October 22, Mike laid down for some much needed rest. He blissfully thought about how he couldn't wait to get home and go to the pub with Amos in Nashville. His sarcasm was bound to be poorly received by all the women they would hit on, and he couldn't wait to see that little redhead stir up the hen house.

"LT, LT! Wake up! Dark Side got hit, we gotta go!" Mike remembers SSG Walters waking him up as if it were yesterday. He ran down the hall to get Smoke Marquez, and they both ran down to the trucks to meet their boys.

They didn't know much about what had happened, but one of the Battle NCOs came down from Battalion HQ to give them a quick update before running out of the gate. "LT Bock's platoon got hit off Route Wild, LT (Andy) Jesser's patrol just got out the gate and are on their way. We have broken comms with the platoon. One KIA, multiple wounded. Looks like an EFP." The Explosively Formed Penetrator was an IED that was relatively new to eastern Baghdad, yet had begun being employed with devastating effect to Coalition Forces.[2]

Smoke briefed the boys; they hopped in their trucks, and moved quickly down the main roads to get to Dark Side platoon. Mike had a sinking feeling in his stomach. They had little information except that one of their brothers had passed. As they moved through the traffic circle that provided access to the local Iraqi police station, they saw a truck on fire and Lieutenant Jesser's trucks cordoned around the contact site. They rushed toward the quick-response platoon and set up a security perimeter so they could safely exit their trucks. Mike jumped out of the lead vehicle and ran toward Lieutenant Jesser.

"Mike, it's Amos, he's gone," Andy said.

Mike stood in front of Andy, and asked him where Amos's boys were. It was a natural response, as pain had become a standard part of their lives. But there was a physical and emotional duality in receiving the news. Mike's body was ready to react, to help Amos's men, but his heart had stopped. The greatest man he ever knew was gone. None of them would ever be the same; none of them would ever love fully again, and a part of their heart had been violently cut out.

Smoke Marquez stood behind Mike and put his hand on his shoulder as he heard the news. He turned around. Smoke gave him a quick hug, looked at him, and said, "I'm sorry LT. Now let's go to work." Mike reflected on Smoke's brief statement years later and thought that this was a befitting reaction to the death of a great, young leader. His sorrow for the loss of Amos could be encapsulated by a simple "I'm sorry." His show of love and respect for the man who had passed could be encompassed by "Now let's go to work."

We were escorted by one of Andy's squad leaders into a shop about thirty yards west of the contact site. Smoke and Mike walked inside to find almost all of Amos's men huddled in the shop, the less injured treating and guarding the more severely injured. The Dark Side had been hit by an EFP as initially thought. The EFP made contact with the first and second vehicle in the patrol. It killed Amos and his interpreter Ali instantaneously, while critically injuring four of his soldiers. In fact, the EFP's blast radius was so large that it had injured nearly half the soldiers in the platoon. After the EFP was detonated, the platoon received small arms fire and moved quickly for cover. The men who could still walk valiantly carried the injured to cover and began treating their wounds. The Dark Side had been through a fight like this many times before. They were well trained, and in that horrific moment, they represented their platoon leader like true warriors.

Mike and his fellow soldiers remembered very little between that night and the memorial service. The time in between was a waking nightmare; the grief was like poison in their veins. They wanted revenge, they wanted blood, and they wanted someone to die for the cowardly act that killed their brother, but before they could resume their duties and get back to the fight, they first had to memorialize their friend.

As Mike walked up to the podium of the FOB Loyalty auditorium, he thought about what he wanted to say. He had not written a speech, nor jotted down talking points. How could he capture the words that would adequately describe his best friend? It seemed impossible. Standing at the podium, he looked over to the front right corner of the auditorium and observed the Dark Side platoon huddled together in the front three rows. Now many might expect that such hard men would be sitting at attention in their seats, with looks of pain and anger on their faces. This was not the case. They sat crying, some inconsolably. The only feeling these tough men couldn't contain was the sense of loss they felt for their brother, their leader, and their friend.

Amos Camden Riley Bock was a great man. He was great because above all else, he loved his soldiers more than he cared for himself. As a platoon leader in 4th Battalion, 320th Field Artillery Regiment, Amos really found his niche in the Army. Amos's ability to lead is even more apparent through the thoughts and actions of his soldiers since his passing. "I attribute my growth and success to your outstanding leadership," said SSG Brad Crozier on Amos's West Point eulogy page. At least three of his former soldiers have named their children after him, so they "will grow up to know the origin of their name," said SSG Grant Lawrence. It is obvious that Amos touched many lives during his short time with us on this earth. As his gunner, John Hardesty, said about that tragic day in October 2006, "I still remember moments before the fatal explosion you had noticed I was in the gunner's turret instead of the driver's seat . . . the last thing I remember was you looking back at me with the half grin." Well, Amos Camden Riley Bock, we are looking right back at you with your signature half grin, keeping your memory close and with us forever.

Michael A. Cerrone

CAPTAIN MICHAEL A. CERRONE, KIA IN SAMARRA, IRAQ, ON NOVEMBER 12, 2006

Illegitimus non Carborundum

Jordan Garrett

When I was a child, I used to look at two pictures my father kept on display. They were both of the same man: one of him looking smart, dressed in those impressive navy whites, and the other of him climbing into a jet, fully kitted in his flight suit with a helmet tucked under his arm, looking like something out of a movie. I can't remember when I came to know who he was, because he was always there. I imagine I asked my father at some point, and he explained, "That's Mack. He was my best friend from college. We rushed the same fraternity at Baylor. After school, I went to the army, and he joined the Navy to be a fighter pilot." Sometime later—when a father is comfortable with sharing these things, I suppose—my dad finished the explanation: "Mack passed away in a flight training accident when he attempted to eject from his plane." I remember feeling some sadness, and I was also disappointed that I would never be able to meet my dad's buddy, who was a real fighter pilot. Until very recently, I had not thought about Mack and what he could possibly mean to me and my life; he had always existed only in the context of my father's.

Last Christmas, while visiting my parents, I was sitting talking with my father in his den. In the midst of our conversation, I looked over and saw that the pictures of Mack were still there, as impressive as I remembered, if not more so. This time, however, he looked a bit younger to me. Younger than I am now. He had that aspect that all young men seem to have when they are newly minted officers: confident, energetic, and a little fearless, perhaps. What struck me immediately, though, was that I have two similar photographs on my dresser at home. Not of a man in whites and a flight suit, but one of a man around the same age as Mack, in full dress gray, and the other in army combat uniform (ACU) and body armor, briefing his men before a patrol. Michael Cerrone was my roommate for two years at West Point and one of my best friends. I write this in hope that I can relay to those who did not know him how special a person he was. To those who did have the privilege of his love and friendship, forgive the inadequacy of my words.

Mike grew up as a military brat, which perhaps explained his nondescript accent. He was born in Clarksville, Tennessee, and spent his formative years following his father, who moved from one successful assignment to another at various posts at home and abroad. His father was a colonel and picked up his brigadier star while we were at the Academy. During his time at West Point and in the Army, soldiers would frequently approach Mike and ask, "Is your dad . . .?" With neither reluctance nor a sense of entitlement, he would respond with a "Yeah," or, where appropriate, "Yes, sir." Mike was proud of his father and his accomplishments, but in an environment like the Army's, where many think success is a function of "who you know," Mike was determined to let his actions and hard work speak for themselves.

The idea of "getting to the real Army" was something that always seemed to guide Mike and how he dealt with the challenges and stresses of cadet life. Being a platoon leader was his ultimate goal, and until he achieved it, he did not let much else get to him. I never saw him flustered or upset about much. He did not worry about the little things, and often, for him, schoolwork was a little thing. Having the cleanest room in the company wasn't high on either of our lists, but when a Saturday Morning Inspection (SAMI) was coming the next day, I could always rely on him to pick good movies to watch until midnight and to stay up until morning formation cleaning with me so we didn't get hours. His ability to not sweat the small stuff also influenced the way he treated others. Whenever one of us might be down, Mike was there to point out the positive and to provide encouragement—usually delivered with the quote, "You're so money and you don't even know it!" His attitude was infectious, and when you were with him, it was hard not to crack a smile or burst out in laughter after too long. It wasn't an attitude of indifference that he carried about him but a true realization of the things that were important, and during that time, before we were in the midst of the realities and dangers that awaited our profession, the most important thing was to have fun and not take ourselves too seriously. It makes sense, looking back on it now, that it was Mike who recommended to several of us that we inscribe the old E-1 motto inside our class rings: *Illegitimus non Carborundum*—"Don't Let the Bastards Get You Down."

Mike was never lacking in confidence or personality. So it was natural that a guy somewhat short in stature but with those outsized attributes was occasionally called "Big Mike." He lived in the weight room, frequently consulted Arnold Schwarzenegger's *Encyclopedia of Modern Body Building*, and took his daily doses of protein and muscle-building supplements. When Mike and I came to E-1, the company was known for having an awesome weight room (called the Cell Block) and our share of upperclass meatheads who, from their looks, would make good candidates for the next cast of *Jersey Shore*. Mike quickly gained their respect for his ability to throw weight around and for his penchant for smack talk and grapple with guys twice his size. It was not uncommon to walk around the company area and find Mike, in the uniform of the day, either delivering or receiving a chokehold to or from a guy who was quite a bit larger than Mike was, laughing all the while. From time to time, he took out his aggressions in an appropriate setting with the grappling team, but I personally think he liked to put on a show.

Mike's ease of character and appreciation for the truly important things also bled through to his treatment of others in a military setting. When walking the campus of West Point, one can sometimes find examples of bad leadership and individuals who torment plebes because they themselves had been tormented. Mike would never flex what little authority we had for its own sake. I remember walking to dinner with him one night when we crossed paths with a plebe that seemed to be having a particularly hard day. As the plebe bumbled through a greeting, Mike told him to stop, and we approached. Instead of piling more grief on this kid, Mike took a good ten minutes to engage in a considerate inquiry as to why the plebe was having such a hard time. With ease, Mike deconstructed the plebe's problems, provided him with a little advice, reassured him that this was all little stuff, things could be worse, and then sent the plebe on his way, a little better than he had found him. It's not like Mike was out to save the world or that he thought that he could solve everyone's problems, but he was very perceptive, possessed genuine concern for people, and knew the appropriate times to step in and help.

As already noted, Mike had a talent for procrastination. "If you wait to the last minute, it will only take a minute," he used to say. So as each semester neared its end, you could find Mike and me napping during the day and frantically hacking out papers at night and until the early morning. Second semester of our yearling year, Mike thought he could make our all-nighters a little easier by purchasing an espresso machine. While one cup of espresso might add a little focus and pick-me-up, the four, five, or six cups we would have over the course of a night well surpassed the point of productivity. Sidebar conversations or breaks to play computer games would go on for hours as our jittery, hyperfocus directed itself to things other than papers and projects. Neither of us would sleep right for days after consuming that much caffeine, but as I look back on it, I remember moments I would not trade for anything.

Mike also had an appreciation for the finer things in life. He liked scotch and cigars and was especially happy when he could find those two things in a dimly lit bar with a little Sinatra or Deano playing in the background. He liked old movies and the cars that guys like Newman and McQueen drove. When we got our Cow Loans,[1] Mike hunted down this amazing 1966 Pontiac GTO and took care of it like it was his own blood. I remember riding around post with him in that car and watching him light up as he received compliments shouted at him above the throaty idle of the engine. We both, separately, spent time in Germany over our summers and would later discuss the various beers we had tried and made plans to find them the next time we caught the train to New York City. What Mike really wanted to do was to wrap up all of these things and the feelings they induced into a nice, laid-back bar that he would own and operate. His GTO would be parked outside, and dark wood, leather, some cigar smoke, and pool tables would fill the inside.

Mike stayed close to his family and was quick to bring his friends into the fold when they needed a place to go for a long weekend. I accompanied him to D.C. one long weekend, and his Italian background was evident in how both he and his family showed their hospitality. We were amply fed, met with good conversation, and had time to go out on our own when we visited the Cerrone household. I remember stories about Mike as a kid and an amazing rum cake from his mom, and his dad giving us some good scotch and wisdom about the Army while we were there. I also got to see the interaction between Mike and his younger brother, Tony. They had the typical younger-older brother relationship characterized by close friendship and the occasional teasing and challenges for strength. Mike, like any good big brother, watched out for Tony and had the occasional worries and hopes for his little brother's best interests. He was immensely proud to see Tony pursue a commission in ROTC and become a father. He would be prouder still to see how Tony picked up the torch where Mike left off and became an accomplished infantry officer as well.

Once we graduated from West Point, I had the good fortune of going to the Infantry Officer Basic Course (IOBC) at Fort Benning with Mike. We weren't in the same platoon but had ample time to hang out, play pool in Columbus, take weekend trips to the University of Georgia, and do the stupid things lieutenants like to do before they have any real responsibility. Mike was more in his element at IOBC than he was in the cadet environment. He had a passion for shooting, thinking about tactics, and traipsing around the woods in the middle of the night. He often spent his free time at indoor and outdoor ranges working on both his pistol and long gun marksmanship. As relayed to me by both Mike and others, he was often the compass man for his platoon at nights because he had a knack for finding his way that others—especially his platoon instructor—didn't seem to have.

Mike and I eventually left Fort Benning, and while my knowledge of him as a young lieutenant is mostly secondhand, it appears he made the same impressions on others that he made on me. We would talk on the phone every couple of months about the excitement and challenges of being platoon leaders. I could tell from the sound of his voice that he was finally where he belonged. It would be easy for me to tell you that Mike was a physical stud, a great shot, and a natural at tactics, but I don't really think it was the adventure or romanticism that drew him to the profession. All Mike wanted to do was take care of soldiers at a personal level—nothing else. It is true that all those physical and military traits are necessary in a good leader, but it's the interpersonal attributes that make people like Mike great. For instance, the afternoon after he graduated from Airborne School, Mike was driving around post and happened to see a junior NCO from his class sitting on a curb with his duffel bags. Mike pulled over and learned that the E-5 had another forty-eight hours till his flight home and was trying to figure out what to do before his bus to the airport left the next day. Refusing to take "no" for an answer, Mike had the NCO throw his bags in the back of Mike's truck and drove him to the Atlanta airport—a four-to-five-hour round trip—so the NCO could make an early flight home to see his family. Sometime after Mike passed, the NCO wrote Brigadier General and Mrs. Cerrone commending them on raising "a pretty squared-away LT." Mike carried that same sense of care to his platoon. Any time one of his soldiers' wives went into labor, Mike would go and sit with the family in the waiting room until the child was born. Knowing that these are only a fraction of such stories, I am not surprised to hear that when Mike's men spoke of him, they said they would "unquestionably follow him into battle."

When Mike left us, I was a company executive officer in Mosul getting my unit ready for relocation to Baghdad. Word of his passing hit me very hard. I was able to take a detour on my flight down and attend his memorial at FOB Brassfield-Mora. Many of our classmates made the trip, and we were able to trade stories of him and find consolation. I managed to find his platoon sergeant and men and could tell, firsthand, by the looks on their faces what he meant to them. I don't know that it is necessary to recount the specifics of Mike's passing here, but needless to say, he went out front. People call it being a warrior—which he most certainly was—but Mike was just taking care of his guys. I don't feel the need to expound on why, but being at that memorial with the men who fought alongside him was one of the most important moments of my life.

It would be easy for me to tell you that Mike was a West Pointer, infantry officer, and soldier who epitomized Duty, Honor, Country, the Honor Code, and the Warrior Ethos, but Mike was so much more than that. He was a real person with hopes and dreams who made us laugh and feel better about ourselves. He wasn't complicated; he just cared about and looked out for his family, friends, and soldiers. On days when you questioned why you took such a hard path, you could look at Mike and say to yourself, "Because I never would have met guys like him." Before I went to West Point I asked my dad and several other veterans this question: "How often do you think about your time in service and the war?" Every time, I received the same, simple response with so much meaning: "Every day." Now I understand all too well. Those who have served think not so much about the war or the things we saw, but about the people and how they affected us. We think about guys like Mike and Mack. They had such an impact on our lives over a relatively short period of time that we cannot allow ourselves to forget them. We have to carry their memory with us forever because we know life would be a little less meaningful without theirs touching us in some way. So we wear their names on bracelets and display pictures in our homes like the ones of Mack in my father's and Mike in mine. I take solace in the fact that Mike, Mack, and all the others who paid the ultimate sacrifice adorn the walls of many homes.

Like so many others, I will always keep Mike in my thoughts and in my home, his picture sitting on a dresser or hanging on a wall somewhere to be seen. I'll think of him often and await the day that my son or daughter asks me, "Dad, who is the man in those pictures?"

To Brigadier General, Mrs., and Captain Tony Cerrone, thank you for sharing your wonderful son with us and continuing to care about the comrades he left behind.

John R. Dennison

CAPTAIN JOHN R. DENNISON, KIA IN BALAD, IRAQ, ON NOVEMBER 15, 2006

Singleness of Heart

Jack Morrow

While there are a number of ways to evaluate a person's life, I can't help but think of John Ryan Dennison's life in terms of its magnitude relative to its duration. By any objective measure, his life was short. Ryan gave his life in service of his country at the age of twenty-four. Taken on its own, this fact would seem tragic. If you examined his life more closely, though, you would think differently. If you learned of the impact Ryan had on the lives of others, before you knew anything else about him, you would be surprised later when you discovered his age. If you examined his words and actions, you would see a disciplined and principled life that could withstand the scrutiny of philosophers, theologians, and all thinkers in between. Ryan's life on its own had impressive amplitude. What is more substantial and important, though, was the way in which his life fit in with those around him. He was a source of strength and inspiration for more people than one would expect from someone so young, and he altered the trajectory of those who knew him in a substantially positive way.

My primary hope in writing this is that I may somehow illustrate certain qualities of his character and personality so that those who knew Ryan can be spared in part from the cruel effects that time has on their memories of him. In making this attempt, however, I understand that Ryan had an enormous identity. He meant so many things to so many people. He was John, he was Ryan, he was Denny, he was JR, and although all of these aliases belonged to the same man, the depth of Ryan's character and personality was such that it often revealed substantively different things to different people. It follows, then, that any single account of whom Ryan was and what his life meant will be incomplete and will lack consensus.

While we had English 102 together as freshmen, I didn't really start to know Ryan until we roomed together the following autumn. Looking back, it seems as if we spent most of our second year struggling through homework and cleaning for inspections, grinding through those late evenings with the help of Iron Maiden and The Clash. Like most cadets, we were always tired, and by the time I finished my homework each evening I went to bed as soon as I could. Ryan always stayed up later. This was his time for reflection; this was how he would grow and develop the sophistication and discretion that characterizes the best leaders. On most evenings of that semester, I would wake up in the middle of the night and find Ryan sitting at his desk, reading *War and Peace* and thinking. I don't know how he managed to stay awake each night, though I do know that through this habit he contracted mononucleosis. Even then, however, he probably wouldn't have noticed but for his spleen having swollen to the size of a grapefruit, protruding obnoxiously from his abdomen.

Mental exhaustion was just one of many things that Ryan endured with dignity and class. Physical fatigue was another. Ryan could push through anything: running ten miles through knee-deep snow as a plebe while pushed by a bullying upperclassman, casually running ultramarathons on B-weekends, consistently scoring off the charts on his physical fitness tests, graduating from Sapper School and Ranger School with a yawn—you name the physical challenge, he could take it. Yet Ryan was not being stubborn, egotistical, or competitive by pushing himself as hard as he did. He competed only against himself. Toughness was something Ryan knew you could never have too much of in life, and he constantly tested—and thereby expanded—the limits of his endurance.

Ryan took a similar approach to his social and spiritual life as well. Although busier than most cadets, he always made time for others. If someone was having a hard time with school, girls, or life in general, Ryan was there for them. He could listen as long as necessary, providing affirmation and reassurance. Ryan did this regardless of whether that person was a close friend, a mere acquaintance, or even someone far senior to him. I understand that most of the problems we faced as cadets weren't that big of a deal. They were usually little things, troubles of young adulthood. But there were countless little things that competed for your time and consumed your energy at West Point, and their collective weight is what made them so difficult to deal with. They tested one's patience, discipline, and resolve to a great degree. Yet I can never think of an instance when Ryan became impatient or antisocial, and he certainly never exhibited selfishness of spirit. He listened and he helped, all the while unconcerned that his sleep for that night was slipping from five hours to four or to three.

One of the things I always liked about Ryan was the exceptional wild streak he had. Ryan knew how to party, and most of the time Ryan was the party. If you hung out with him on a Friday night, you were going to have a good time, and you were going to tread the fine line between mischief and trouble. Having said that, it is important to note that Ryan somehow managed to always stay on the right side of that line. He certainly lived for the moment and enjoyed the ephemeral, but there was never any doubt that he lived life with eternity in mind. Ryan was unabashedly open minded and willing to entertain all of life's possibilities, but anything that would impinge upon his honor was out of the question. But it isn't enough to say that Ryan was honest and had a strong sense of integrity; a lot of our classmates at West Point possessed those attributes. What set Ryan apart in this regard, what made his life honorable, and what made his soul noble was the fact that he lived his life for others.

When we became cadets, we did so with the expectation that we would dedicate ourselves to a lifetime of selfless service. For some this was probably a stretch; for Ryan it was really just a formalization of who he already was. I honestly can't recall Ryan ever talking about selflessness or serving others; he simply lived that way. Even before he went to West Point, Ryan sought to help others. He was an active member of the Big Brothers Big Sisters program in Fredrick, Maryland; a loving son; and a caring brother. And it wasn't just with organized activities either. It was the little things Ryan did that made you realize how much he cared for those around him. Ask Erik Wright about his knee surgery during plebe year and how Ryan went with him to dinner every night after that surgery so Erik wouldn't have to carry his dinner tray while hobbling around on crutches. You could also ask one of Ryan's classmates at the Infantry Officer Basic Course who got sick and shit his pants during a field exercise. While others made fun of the lieutenant, Ryan instead stepped forward to help him clean up with canteens of water. Ask anyone who knew Ryan, and they too will tell you similar stories, and if you collected all of those stories together, you would marvel at the sheer volume of them.

Yet as impressive as some of those stories may be, the most meaningful example of honor in Ryan's life was the way in which he loved Haley. I knew Ryan only briefly before he started dating Haley, yet that was enough time for me to see clearly how transformative were the feelings he had for her. Ask anyone who was close to Ryan at West Point, and I think they would echo my sentiments. Don't get me wrong; it's not as if Ryan went from bad to good or heathen to ascetic. Ryan's feelings for Haley simply magnified the qualities he already possessed, the overwhelming majority of which were incredibly positive. The more Ryan got to know Haley, the more he sought to better himself. The more her reputation was linked with his, the more he would dignify her through his words and actions. And while Ryan was always a Christian, it was through his relationship with Haley where he would really grow in his faith. As their relationship progressed, you could see that through Haley, Ryan would come as close as he could to living out God's desire to give up ourselves to love and serve others. In his love for Haley and the unequivocal way in which he committed himself to serving her he would honor God to the greatest extent he knew how.

Looking back on the time that I knew Ryan, I can think of any number of instances in which a different person would have worked less feverously and would have been a little more selfish. This lesser performance, of course, would have been perfectly acceptable. That person's behavior still would have been worthy of respect. In so many instances, Ryan could have given in to exhaustion, he could have lost his patience, and he could have thought of himself, but he chose not to. I know that being around Ryan compelled me to put forth more effort, to laugh more enthusiastically, to do more for others, and to accomplish more than I would have otherwise. Even today, when I'm at my best, I'm trying harder and I'm shouldering more responsibility in large part because of the example that Ryan set for me. I am a markedly better person and a better officer because of how I changed and evolved while I was friends with Ryan.

If the story stopped right here, it would be easy to think Ryan's accomplishments and character were preordained and inevitable, but this simply isn't the case. Were it not for the efforts of his parents, his life might have taken a completely different course. While Ryan was still very young, Jack and Shannon Dennison took the courageous step of adopting Ryan and providing him the stability and love that he most likely would not have otherwise had. Having been adopted myself, I am somewhat familiar with what Ryan experienced growing up. Ryan raised some hell as a teenager, but his parents disciplined him when necessary and loved him always, throughout all of his ups and downs. In a sense, they planted in him the seeds of virtue that would come to fruition during Ryan's time at West Point and continue flourishing later as an infantry officer. They helped guide Ryan down a path that would keep certain opportunities open to him, and at the end of the day, he was still a good kid.

Like most popular teenagers, Ryan lived an all-star high school life and pushed the limits and boundaries set by his parents. He worked at a pharmacy after school to earn a little cash, played football in the fall, wrestled in the winter, and chased girls in the spring and summer. On Friday nights, Ryan would usually go with his friends to eat at some fast food joint, like Long John Silver's, and order three platters of fried everything. Before stepping on the gridiron for the Urbana football team, he and his friends would stop by Checkers so Ryan could slam three bacon cheeseburgers. On weekends Ryan and his buddies would pile into a pickup truck and cruise the county roads, drinking beers, four-wheeling, shooting guns, knocking over small trees and mailboxes, doing all of the things any self-respecting, rebellious teenager should do. Ryan was a guy who could tell you what it felt like to wake up face down in a pizza box in the middle of a cemetery on a Saturday morning, not really sure about how he got there. He could tell you about the disappointment of a girlfriend who planned a nice, quiet twenty-first birthday evening for him but was still kind enough to let him go out for a "couple" beers with the boys only to have him stagger back sloppy drunk and pass out, still smiling, in her presence (sorry about that, Haley). But there's something important about all of those stories that make a mother mad and a father secretly proud. These stories let your soldiers know that although you are their leader, you are still one of them. They can relate to you and trust you, in part, because you traveled a similar path to adulthood marked with mistakes, wild experiences, and strange waypoints.

And Ryan's soldiers did trust him, not only for the aforementioned reasons, but for far more substantive things as well. Like most lieutenants, Ryan's first chance to make an impression with his troops was during PT, and he blew them away. Of course, all lieutenants have times when they make mistakes, but even in his mistakes Ryan earned the respect of his men. In one instance, Ryan disregarded the better judgment of his platoon sergeant, SFC Robert Cobb, and grappled against all eighteen soldiers in his platoon. Ryan held his own against the first few, but after a while he began to tire, and he ultimately got beat up pretty bad—in front of his on-looking squadron commander. But his soldiers admired his physical courage, the fact that he wasn't afraid to take a beating and demonstrate what he was made of. Ryan trained his soldiers hard, and they respected that because they knew it would keep them alive in combat. But they also respected Ryan because he cared, because he would stand watch next to a tired soldier and share his food with another who was hungry. They discovered the depth of his character while patrolling New Orleans in the wake of Hurricane Katrina, and they saw his selflessness while evacuating residents of the 9th Ward. They learned that Ryan was a man of values they could believe in and a man of unquestionable integrity who they could count on to make the right decisions once they got to Iraq and the stakes were higher.

Ryan deployed to the Diyala Province of Iraq with the 5-73 Reconnaissance, Surveillance, and Target Acquisition (RSTA) Squadron in August 2006. On his very first patrol in theater, he and his men made contact on the Iranian border while working in a combined formation with an Iraqi Border Patrol unit. That patrol, like many after them, involved a lot of close calls and Ryan making a number of difficult decisions. On November 12, 2006, Ryan was conducting an aerial reconnaissance with his squadron commander and other key leaders when the rotor wash from one of the helicopters uncovered a major weapons cache. His squadron commander dropped off a team, including Ryan, to keep watch over the cache, while the rest of the squadron made preparations to move in and occupy the area. On November 15, gunfire erupted, marking the beginning of a fierce four-day fight that would later be remembered as the Battle of Turki. Before the day was over, Ryan would be dead—gunned down at point-blank range by an insurgent concealed in the dense foliage.

Early on in Ryan's time as a platoon leader, he told his men the story of Roman soldiers who would sound off with "Integris!" while striking the breastplate of their armor. This single word was a verbal assurance to the inspecting officer of the physical integrity of the armor and the moral integrity of the men who would wear it into battle. Ryan's men soon began sounding off with the same, striking their front ballistic plate when he conducted precombat inspections of their weapons and equipment. In a macabre twist of fate, Ryan was killed because four bullets missed his front plate entirely and struck him in the thigh, forearm, armpit, and neck. His platoon sergeant found him lying face down in the dirt and knew he was killed instantly. Ryan was too strong to be lying that way; if he had been alive for even a minute he would have turned himself over and continued fighting for life. But Ryan never had that chance; his life ended before he knew it was leaving him. Finished. Complete.

Ryan's was a great life, one that still resonates strongly with me today. His is a beautiful memory, and that memory is something we should always honor. We all die someday, and we have no choice in that. What matters is what we do before that happens. Ryan chose to live with humility and charity, in service of others. In doing so, he developed a nobility of soul that blessed everyone who knew him. It's tempting to look at Ryan's life and declare it tragic because it ended so soon. But applying that word to Ryan would be shameful; it simply doesn't do justice to who he was. It would be tragic to pass from this earth having mattered little to anyone. It would be tragic if Ryan had lived selfishly, maliciously, better off forgotten, a passing vision of a stranger that disintegrates inconsequentially, like ash in the breeze. Ryan was none of these things. His life bounded with such arcing amplitude that if you witnessed even a minute of it, you could not mistake how important it was. He possessed a richness of character and virtue that rivets his memory fast in the hearts of those who knew and loved him. For those people who did know Ryan, you are lucky. Not everyone had that chance. Hold on to his memory always; it is a gift whose value you are only beginning to realize.

With special thanks to Jack and Shannon Dennison, Haley Uthlaut, Robert Cobb, Chris Kline Jr., Erik Wright, and Jeremy Benvenuti.

David M. Fraser

CAPTAIN DAVID M. FRASER, KIA IN BAGHDAD, IRAQ, ON NOVEMBER 26, 2006

A Friend's Lasting Tribute: Running a Well-Lived Life

Seth Chappell

While I have known Dave longer as a memory than as a presence on this Earth, in the brief time that I was fortunate to share his company, he made a profound impact on my life. It is an impact that is much larger than what corresponds to our short time together. I know that I am not alone in this sentiment. Though I feel inadequate to capture the full effect and essence of Dave's existence in this short memorial, I hope that my effort provides some insight into the gift of his life.

For me, giving testimony of Dave's life serves to do more than sustain his memory, since he remains very much alive in the hearts of everyone he touched. This tribute serves as a gesture to a friend for whom I will always have a tremendous debt of gratitude for his presence in my life.

To fully describe Dave is tough. He stood about 5′8″ and had a big Texas grin and a swagger that anyone could spot from a mile away. He may not have been the most physically imposing person, but his winning charm, easy confidence, and sense of honor always made him the biggest person in the room.

The best way I can describe Dave's personality was as a special type of redneck Renaissance man. He was widely knowledgeable in a great multitude of ways and activities. He tied his own flies and was an amazing fly fisherman. He raced mountain bikes (fixing his own bike) and worked on

his old, but beloved, Chevy truck: Big Blue. He knew how to make a potato gun from PVC pipe and was a fantastic woodworker. He could cook a
fish over an open fire. He played a mean acoustic guitar. He knew how to
pack a can of Copenhagen (even though he didn't dip). When I wanted to
upgrade the sound system in my old Jeep, Dave helped me install the new
player and the speakers. I remember when our team's van blew a tire at Bear
Mountain Park, Dave had it changed in about fifteen minutes. A passerby
briefly stopped and commented, "I bet you're glad *he's* here." And we were.

Everyone was always happy when Dave was around. Not only due to the
fact that he was the guy who could replace a fan belt, but he simply was a lot
of fun. Dave was always looking for a good time, squeezing it out of every
day (oftentimes, a hard task to accomplish at West Point). He was the guy
who took the plunge off the seventy-six-foot cliff into Lake Champlain during our team's camp (the forty footer was good enough for me, thank you).

Dave was also the guy who came up with the brilliant plan of rafting the
Winooski River during that same camp. He and I bought a twenty-dollar
kiddie raft at a sporting store, found some 2x4s to use as "paddles," and
spent the day playing Huck Finn. We floated the river, pushed through rap-
ids, and waded through shallows, making very slow progress but laughing
all the while. When the sun went down, we were well short of our planned
debarkation point, and so we put ashore in some farmer's field and high-
tailed it through a cornfield back to camp.

After graduation, Dave visited me in London (where my father was working at the time). It was his first trip to Europe, and the agenda was his for the
planning. Therefore, Dave, our friend and classmate Garrett Cathcart, and
I found ourselves being chased by half of a ton of angry, snorting beef down
the streets of Pamplona. It was easily one of the best and most memorable
trips I have ever taken. We slept in a parking garage at night and lived with
nothing but the clothes on our backs.

Yes, Dave played hard, but he also worked hard too. In the classroom
and on the trails and track, his commitment to excellence and self-improve-
ment was for him a way to honor God. Dave understood better than most of
us that to whom much is given, much is required.

The way that Dave lived day-to-day life at West Point—how hard he
trained on the track, invested his time to his academic studies, dedicated
himself to worship services, or completely engaged himself in just having

a good time with friends—made it clear that life was a gift that should not be squandered. For Dave, anything worth doing was worth doing well. He pushed himself to become a contributing varsity member of the cross-country and track teams, posting mile times in the low four-minute range. He excelled in his civil engineering classes, where he and I worked on countless problem sets[1] and projects together. I would be hard-pressed to find a problem set in which I did not seek his assistance, and I remember feeling strangely proud on the few occasions when I could help him work through a concept.

In the beginning of our Firstie year at West Point, Dave and I selected a civil engineering project that we hoped would leave a defining mark. We chose to design and build a footbridge over the creek passing by the West Point Youth Activities Center. Dave drafted a beautiful arched bridge de-sign, and we spent what felt like the majority of our nights and weekends working to bring this dream to fruition. We conducted site surveys. We shaped laminated wood, bent rebar, and constructed concrete footer forms in the F-level basement of Mahan Hall.[2] While sometimes I would have been happy to take a shortcut and pack it in so as to wrap up work for the night, Dave was unflagging. He was driven by his vision of what this bridge could be, unwilling to put his name on anything less than quality. When we stood on that bridge on May 29, 2004, for our commissioning ceremony, I knew that all the late nights were worth it. The bridge represents but a small frac-tion of the impact Dave made on the world around him. His larger influence was on the hearts of others.

As a young cadet at West Point, Dave possessed a self-knowledge that many older men still work to find. He never swore, and he rose above petty conversations. Though Dave wasn't one of the fastest guys on the cross-country and track teams, as an upperclassman, he was a voice of steady lead-ership and inspiration for younger athletes. His maturity, self-awareness, and dedication to others derived from his very devotion to God. While other cadets slept in on Sundays, Dave served as the Cadet-in-Charge of Protes-tant Sunday School and shared God's love with the children of West Point.

Dave commissioned into the Engineers with orders for Fort Hood as an officer in 4th Infantry Division. I was fortunate to be in the same Engineer Officer Basic Course (EOBC) and Ranger School class. At EOBC Dave maintained that same "don't waste a day" attitude, buying a compound bow to take advantage of the hunting opportunities in the Ozarks (he had never bow hunted in his life, but he felt Fort Leonard Wood was a great place to learn). While most young lieutenants were buried in their blankets in the wee hours of the morning, Dave was stalking the woods for his prize buck. When he finally brought down his quarry, rather than pay someone else to field dress the deer, he paid them to teach him how to perform the task himself.

As one of nine engineer lieutenants selected for Ranger School out of our EOBC class, Dave committed himself to finishing the course despite the hardships. For instance, when an error on the Darby Land Navigation course forced him to redo the Benning Phase, Dave took his lumps and saddled up for another round. While he was waiting to reenter the course, he worked on behalf of the 4th Ranger Training Battalion to build a new wooden deck on the headquarters building. As always, Dave took the challenges in stride and worked to make the most of a difficult situation.

After graduating from Ranger School, Dave reported to 3/67 Armor Battalion, 4th ID in Fort Hood. As one of a handful of Ranger-qualified lieutenants in the battalion, he was selected to lead the battalion's personal security/quick reaction platoon for the upcoming deployment to Baghdad. I was deployed in Afghanistan concurrently, and we sent a couple emails back and forth. Dave sent a number of photos with one of his distro emails, showing him climbing a wall in some abandoned palace; driving some busted Iraqi tractor that he apparently found and repaired on his Forward Operating Base; and sitting with one of his wounded soldiers in the hospital. Dave carried the same enthusiasm for life, ability to turn the mundane into a source of joy, and dedication to others that rested on a firm belief in God to war's many challenges.

Dave transitioned from the QRF platoon to lead a Route Clearance Package during his tour, and spent months hunting for roadside bombs on the streets of Baghdad. In late November, just prior to his redeployment to Fort Hood, he helped the incoming unit prepare to take over his unit's battlespace. On Dave's last patrol, an explosively formed penetrator destroyed his vehicle, killing him instantaneously. In two weeks, Dave would have been home.

I received the news of my friend's death while deployed in Ghazni, Afghanistan, from my father. He titled the email, "Horrible News from Iraq." But like so many of us who have had friends in harm's way while deployed ourselves, I had no time to grieve. I had a patrol to lead that morning. It was only after I returned home that I could begin to process—going to meet with his parents, visiting his room, looking through some of his old journals. It felt like a last conversation with a friend.

Today, I believe that we still "grip hands" with our fallen classmates, and I know that they grip back. A couple of months ago, while navigating some difficult personal trials, I received a message on Facebook from a cross-country teammate who I hadn't spoken with in years. He related to me a dream that he just had. He was at the starting line for the Army Ten Miler (a congregating place for Army Distance alums) where he saw me standing with Dave. He asked me, "Seth, what is Dave doing here? He's dead." In the dream, I replied, "I know, but he runs with me still." For my teammate to unexpectedly contact with such a story was incredible and timely. For me, it was Dave's reminder of his constant presence to help me through my tough times. To all who knew him, Dave continues to be a friend. His memory guides all of us to choose the harder road and to make the most of our precious lives. Well done, my friend.

Jacob N. Fritz

FIRST LIEUTENANT JACOB N. FRITZ, KIA IN KARBALA, IRAQ, ON JANUARY 20, 2007

From Farm Fields to the Battlefield: Remembering Jacob Fritz

Tom Nelson

January 20, 2007. Karbala, Iraq. Late afternoon. A swarm of nine to twelve insurgents disguised themselves as American soldiers, donning U.S. military uniforms, carrying weapons that appeared to be American, and speaking English. They drove a convoy up to the U.S. military base of Provincial Joint Coordination Center, authentically resembling a U.S. diplomatic convoy. First Lieutenant Jacob Fritz was captured along with three other soldiers, taken from the base, and later killed by the abductors.

But this is far from the full story of Jacob's life. Jacob was a brother, a son, an athlete, high school sports team captain, president of the Honor Society, a dedicated volunteer at his church, a proud farmer, a soldier, a leader, and an officer in the U.S. Army. He was born and raised in the small, rural community of Verdon, Nebraska. The son of a farmer and a high school teacher, Jacob grew up on his parents' four-hundred-acre farm. He was the eldest of three boys, spread out over eleven years. It was a large, working farm. They grew corn and soybeans, and raised cattle, hogs, and occasionally chickens. Jacob and his two younger brothers were an active part of the farm life. They had daily chores such as dispersing the hay, corn, and silage to the cattle and calves. Jacob learned early in life what being a member of a team and putting the needs of the many above his own needs really meant.

Jacob followed in his father's distinguished footsteps of military service. His father, Lyle, served in Vietnam in 1969 to 1970 during his three years of service in the U.S. Marine Corps. He served another seventeen years in the U.S. National Guard.

I met Jake during what West Point cadets derisively refer to as the "best summer of their lives" after our freshman but before our sophomore year at Cadet Field Training. The training took place primarily in the mountainous wilderness of Camp Buckner, eight miles from the West Point main campus. As second-year cadets, or "yearlings," we muddled through various exercises designed to introduce us to the close ground fight and the associated challenges of leading soldiers at the team and squad levels in a tactical environment. For ten weeks, we lived in long, crowded, metal buildings lined with bunk beds and wall lockers from end to end. However, the limited personal space was not an issue because we spent nearly every waking moment in some kind of training event.

Jake and I were both assigned to 8th Company during that summer of 2001, and that's where I first met this barrel-chested young soldier from rural Nebraska. He immediately identified himself as a proud Cornhusker. Being from rural Wisconsin, I thought I understood what he meant. However, I did not fully appreciate the almost religious overtones of being a "Husker." Apparently, corn is to Nebraska what cheese is to Wisconsin. He joked with me that my hometown of 2,100 people must have been a "big city" compared to his hometown of Verdon, population 215. It's possible that the population of livestock outnumbered its citizens by as much as ten to one.

During this summer experience, West Point introduced us to all the branches of the Army. These included demonstrations by active Army units, helicopter flights, firing of artillery, and many in-depth operations during the field training exercises. For many West Point cadets, this is the time when they choose in which branch of the Army they will ultimately serve. Both Jacob and I were drawn to the combat arms branches. He was particularly impressed by both the mental and physical requirements of accurately firing artillery. Jacob would eventually select the Field Artillery branch and I would select Infantry. Eventually, both Jake and I would be assigned to and deploy with one of the army's elite airborne units.

For the next nine months, we shifted our primary focus from military tactics back to the rigors of academic life. During that fall, Jake converted us all into Cornhusker fans as the University of Nebraska football team went on a tear, winning its first eleven games of the season and rising to become the number-two-ranked team in the nation. Although Nebraska eventually lost the Rose Bowl to the number-one-ranked Miami Hurricanes, we couldn't help but cheer for the Cornhuskers. Of almost equal importance to Jake was the fact that University of Nebraska's quarterback, Eric Crouch, won the Heisman Trophy that year, a bit of trivia he rarely let us forget. Based on how much he bragged about the accomplishment, it seemed that Jake must be related to the guy. But in truth, for those who knew him, it was just one of many great examples of how proud Jake was of his home, family, and the great state of Nebraska.

As a cadet, Jake was a member of the West Point Glee Club. He was extremely proud of his membership in this prestigious organization. The Glee Club not only provided him with another source of camaraderie with his fellow cadets but it also gave him the opportunity to travel across the country and perform. During Jake's tenure, the Glee Club performed at Carnegie Hall, Lincoln Center, the Kennedy Center for the Performing Arts, and Ground Zero on the first anniversary of the World Trade Center tragedy. He sang in the beautiful recording of "Mansions of the Lord," which played in the closing credits of the 2002 film *We Were Soldiers*, starring Mel Gibson.

One of my favorite memories of Jake is from one of the many infamous weekends in New York City. A favorite destination of cadets, the city is just fifty-five miles south of West Point and accessible via a one-hour train ride. Through a friend's mutual acquaintance, we found ourselves in a dorm room at Columbia University. We were playing a card game in which one player selected a category and then the other players were required to state an item within the category without repeating prior responses. Typical examples were flavors of ice cream, NFL teams, or colors of the rainbow. So we were not only surprised but also utterly baffled when Jake selected the category Breeds of Cattle. Apparently, there are over eight hundred recognized different breeds. Before we knew it, Jake was on a roll, naming cattle breeds. Needless to say, he won that round of the game.

A fellow West Point classmate and roommate of Jacob, James Gibson, wrote:

> The characteristics I remember most about Jake were his gentle and "good" nature: I never remember him being hostile or confrontational with anyone. He was one of those "good-ol-boys" from the country who, at my best guess, was never accused of demonstrating any ill treatment or bad feelings towards anybody. And, like "good-ol-boys" from the country usually do, Jake always embodied what I believed to be a sincere love of both his family and his Country to which he dedicated himself to serve.

Jake's most striking trait was his positive attitude and outlook toward life. I don't remember him ever being "down in the dumps" or needing to be cheered up in any way. In fact, he was usually the one who was always in high spirits and could be counted on for a kind smile or a shared laugh. Jake seemed to make the conscious decision to always see only the greatest qualities in every person he met and to believe in the best possible outcome of any situation he found himself in. There never seemed to be any room for negativity in Jake's life, and I have a lot of respect for that personal quality.

Following graduation from West Point, Jake attended the Field Artillery Officer Basic Course at Fort Sill, Oklahoma. The mission of the course is to prepare newly commissioned lieutenants to be proficient in the core skills necessary for a Field Artillery officer. At the course completion, they can then serve as platoon leaders, fire support officers, and forward direction officers in combat units throughout the Army. The Field Artillery branch is known as the "King of Battle," and most Artillerymen are not shy in proclaiming this.

After successfully completing all requirements of this course, Jake was assigned to an elite Airborne unit in Fort Richardson, Alaska. There, he was assigned to be a platoon leader in Alpha Company, 2nd Battalion, 377th Parachute Field Artillery Regiment (PFAR). Traditionally, a fires battalion supports ground troops with indirect fire and provides immediate counterfire attack to confirmed enemy targets. However, the nontraditional war fought in Iraq and Afghanistan has often resulted in artillery units needing to perform important nondoctrinal missions and tasks such as armed reconnaissance missions, convoy and logistical security, joint security patrols, cordon and searches, raids, security force training, and various other civil-military operations.

This was the case for First Lieutenant Jacob Fritz and his platoon of thirty-eight soldiers in Iraq. They were given the mission of embedding with an Iraqi police unit in Karbala in order to secure, train, and coordinate logistical support for the Provincial Joint Coordination Center (PJCC).[1] The PJCC served as a place for Iraqi officials, Iraqi security forces, and coalition forces to coordinate security actions within the province. It was in the PJCC that Jacob spent most of his deployment, working directly with his Iraqi police partners. Lacking many of the amenities of the bigger bases in Iraq, Jacob served in austere conditions as the senior liaison officer between the Iraqi police and U.S. forces in Karbala province.

In addition to the work of Lieutenant Fritz's security element, there was a U.S. Army Reserve Civil Affairs (CA) team that frequently worked at the PJCC. The civil affairs team, led by Captain Brian Freeman, was developing plans and actions to provide security for pilgrims participating in that year's Ashura.

In the early evening hours of January 20, 2007, Captain Freeman and Lieutenant Fritz were meeting with their Iraqi counterparts at the PJCC. Approximately nine to twelve gunmen conducted a precise raid on the PJCC. Disguising themselves as an American Diplomatic convoy, they entered the compound dressed as U.S. soldiers, speaking English. There were reports that they carried American-looking weapons. Such convoys were not uncommon during operations in Iraq.

Once within the compound, the raid was initiated by a grenade and quickly followed with a barrage of small arms fire. In the initial attack, one U.S. soldier was killed and three others were wounded. The assailants then split into two groups. The first group captured two U.S. soldiers operating a HMMWV at the entrance of the compound and provided cover fire for the other maneuvering element. Those soldiers were pushed into the insurgents' vehicles, while the insurgents destroyed or disabled the U.S. vehicles with explosives to prevent an immediate pursuit after the raid.

Meanwhile, the second team moved directly to the room where Freeman and Fritz were meeting and captured them both. Reports indicated that the raid was conducted so quickly that some U.S. military members in the compound only saw the vehicles racing out of the compound before they could react. The U.S. soldiers remaining in the PJCC alerted the army unit's quick reaction force, which responded to the attack.

The insurgents' vehicles sped out of the compound, blew through an Iraqi police checkpoint, and crossed the Euphrates River. Their ultimate destination was unknown, but their vehicles were eventually found, thirty miles east of Karbala, abandoned near the town of al-Mahawil. The kidnappers successfully fled the area, but not before they murdered the four U.S. soldiers. Two soldiers were in the back of one of the vehicles, bound together and dead from gunshot wounds. Another soldier was shot dead and lay nearby on the ground. The fourth kidnapped soldier died of a gunshot wound to the head while Iraqi police rushed him to a nearby hospital. This raid was described as one of the boldest and most sophisticated attacks by insurgents during Operation Iraqi Freedom. A total of five American soldiers were killed in the incident, and another three were wounded.

In 2010, I deployed to southern Iraq as a Company Commander. One of my primary tasks was the maintenance of a PJCC located at a local Iraqi police station in the capital city of Maysan Province. For twelve months, I was responsible for the maintenance, security, and logistical operations of this combat outpost. Although I was in a different province during a different time, many of my duties and responsibilities were virtually identical to those of Jake's in Karbala Province three years earlier.

The reality of the embedded security station concept was that we literally lived, ate, and slept with our Iraqi police counterparts. It was a symbiotic relationship where we depended on each other for security, intelligence, and safety. Our lives were placed in each other's hands. Understanding the circumstances of the Karbala kidnapping incident from both a personal and professional perspective shaped my command philosophy and emphasis on force protection. The incident surrounding this kidnapping event was made into a case study for the Army's Training and Doctrine Command's Intelligence Handbook for future leaders to improve situational awareness and understanding, identify significant force protection issues, and learn from operational observations and after-action critiques. It also offered suggestions on how a kidnapping can be integrated in unit training readiness.

Knowing that a kidnapping incident or similar attack could happen at my security station at any time, I made sure that every soldier in my command understood what happened in Karbala, and we took many proactive steps to prevent such an incident. I attribute our hypervigilance and increased awareness to the lessons we were able to draw from the Karbala incident. Although the base was attacked once during our twelve months, no one was killed or seriously wounded. I attribute that fact to the legacy of Jake Fritz and the other four soldiers who died that day in Karbala.

Although our overlap in life was brief, it was more than enough time for Jacob to make a lasting impression on me. His story reminds me of the importance in connecting with people, with family, with community, and in the immeasurable value in making a difference in people's lives, regardless of the form that may take. Jake's legacy was illustrated quite simply by the more than 1,500 people who showed up to his funeral in the small rural Nebraska community of two hundred to show that he had touched their lives through his presence. He was and is an American hero, and his life, his actions, his brave deeds, his big heart, and his room-lighting smile will always be remembered by all who had the honor of knowing him.

In January 2007, days before he would give the ultimate sacrifice, Jake wrote to his local Nebraska newspaper in appreciation for all the support the community had shown him during the holidays. In one of his last correspondences home, Jake's words are a reminder of the proud soldier he was, bravely defending his family, his community, and his country that he so fiercely loved.

To Friends and Family—

I deployed to Iraq back in October of 2006. I made the trip from Alaska to Kuwait where I waited and trained in 110-degree weather for two weeks before finally flying into Baghdad International Airport. It has been quite the experience so far, as I'm definitely not doing the job that I thought I would be doing.

I was trained to be a Field Artillery officer, but I have found myself acting as a liaison officer between the Iraqi Police in Karbala to the US Forces on my Forward Operating Base. It has been quite the rewarding experience so far, as I am getting to experience first hand the inner workings of the Iraqi Security Forces.

I am in charge of 38 soldiers over here, and I must say that we have become quite the close-knit group over here thus far. Not all of us get to do the same missions together, but there is a corps that I get to work with fairly often. Of that group, I have my Gunnery Sergeant (Gunny), approximately 15 soldiers that vary each trip, and myself each time out on a mission. We have gotten to know a lot more about each other than I think that we ever would have hoped to learn or ever thought that we would learn. Everyone wants to say that they have the best group of soldiers or work with the best, so I guess that I'll follow the pack and say the same thing. I just want to put a little more emphasis on mine though!

My guys have gotten to know a lot of the Iraqi Police that we work side-by-side with here in Karbala. We have made some really good friends, and are getting to know more and more about each other every day. Even though we can't speak Arabic, and they can't speak English, we can sure communicate through body language, hand and arm signals, as well as facial expressions. Even if you don't know what they're saying, you can figure it out by how they're saying it. Then you start to pick-up on words or phrases. Then you're able to start having conversations. It's just amazing how much we've been able to accomplish in the past months.

As for the weather, you wouldn't believe how cold it gets over here. It is starting to warm up a little bit now, but back in mid-December it was getting down right cold over here. We would get a high temperature of maybe 45 and then a low of 27 some nights.

That's right, freezing temperatures in Iraq. Almost made me wish I was back home a few times after calling and finding out that Nebraska was having some nonstandard Nebraska weather back in Falls City. But, give it a couple months, and I'll be wishing that I was as cold as I was in December.

Speaking of December, one always thinks of Christmas. I know that this was my first one away from home, as it also was for most of my guys. A few of us were even "lucky" enough to be able to spend it away from our FOB, and got to spend Christmas together in Karbala. We had a great Christmas MRE and just had a great time spending it together as best we could. It was an experience that we won't soon forget.

What I meant to write in this letter was a thank you. I know that my address was published in the *FC Journal* in one of the issues. I have received so many packages and letters of support that I can't possibly find the time to thank each and every one of you that have sent me something.

I asked my mom how to best do this, and she was the one that suggested writing to the *Journal* and asking them to publish this letter. Words just can't begin to describe how much the letters and packages mean to me. I spend anywhere from five to nine days at a time out on a mission, and don't receive any mail. When I return, I get all my mail at once, and it just does so much to raise my spirits when I finally find time to sit down and open them all. What was really touching were the Christmas letters that people would normally send out to their families. I felt very special and in a small way a part of their family at least for that Christmas. I just don't know what else to say, other than I can't begin to write how much your words of support mean for me. I also share them with my soldiers, and you can take comfort in knowing that they also appreciate the support. Regardless of when we come home, my soldiers and I want you all to know that we couldn't have made it this far through the deployment without your support from back home.

We all thank you very much, and wish that you all have a safe rest of the year.

Very Respectfully,

1LT Jacob Fritz[2]
2/A/2-377th PFAR
Platoon Leader, FA

Adam P. Snyder

CAPTAIN ADAM P. SNYDER, KIA IN BAYJI, IRAQ, ON DECEMBER 5, 2007

The Faith of a Centurion

Michael Fish (USMA 2004) with contributions from Fran Frazer (Adam's mother), Patrick Brice (USMA 2004), and Adam Christenson (USMA 2004)

Admittedly, I only knew Adam Snyder through our USMA Glee Club experience and an encounter in Ranger School shortly after our graduation from West Point. In getting to know him better while writing this memorial, I have come to learn that the best word to describe Adam is humility. The following modest account provides a glimpse of who he was as he matured from a child into a man and a cadet into a seasoned combat leader who would ultimately lay down his life for those he loved.

Adam was raised by his mother, Fran, for the first nine years of his life in the coastal city of Fort Pierce, Florida. Growing up he always made time for extracurricular activities and sports, all the while excelling in academics. His interests were broad, including baseball, football, track, Cub Scouts, and theater. His pursuit of unfamiliar sports was not uncommon. In high school Adam took up pole vaulting on the track and field team despite lacking experience, knowledge, and even a coach. He also threw discus and ran the 400 and 800 meter races. Cadets and soldiers would later come to know him for his love of fitness.

Theater and the arts were a large part of Adam's life from early times. He would dedicate a significant amount of his spare time learning his lines for various roles as well as building and painting sets for plays and musicals. His passion for theater led him to audition for *The Music Man*, not at his high school, but at *another* school; his talent even won him the leading role. But because Adam downplayed his achievements, he declined to tell his mother about his role until just shortly before the performance.

Adam was also known as a man of humor and wit. In keeping with the spirit of homecoming week at his high school, Adam and his best friend participated in "twins' day" where they both dressed identically. Adam was very troubled and confused when he was written up at school for a uniform policy violation; after all, he and his friend had gone to great lengths to find the perfect matching dresses and high heels! Despite the infraction, the picture of them still made it into the yearbook.

This dry humor and wit Adam displayed started at an early age. When Fran began dating Larry Frazer, who would soon become Adam's stepfather, Adam would make concerted efforts to wedge himself between them, creating an awkward separation. Fran also recalled that when he was a young boy, Larry had asked him to help out with some yard work by sweeping the grass clippings off the sidewalk. Later on, Larry learned that Adam had done *exactly* what was asked and nothing more; he swept only the walkway, leaving all other paved surfaces scattered with blades of grass. His parents learned early on that Adam was detail oriented.

Even with his jovial prods and pranks, Adam exhibited a sincere humility throughout his life. Along with Adam's long list of achievements came meekness and a desire to stay out of the spotlight (except on stage, of course). Throughout his school years, Adam always qualified for gifted programs and curricula. He was recognized as the citizen of the month several times and student of the year in four of his six classes his senior year of high school. He generally kept to himself and maintained a small group of close friends. Still, his genuine character and admiration from his classmates elected him as the homecoming king. Adam downplayed it. At the end of school days, Adam would work humble and typical teenage part-time jobs at fast food restaurants or bussing tables. Adam carried himself as ordinary but lived extraordinarily.

Adam was very involved with his home church, Westside Baptist Church in Fort Pierce, and lived a life serving the Lord. He was a part of the youth group, took part in their Christmas pageant, and served in the community with projects such as Habitat for Humanity. He formed strong relationships with church leaders for friendship as well as mentorship in growing in his faith. While many teenagers were coming home late after a night of mischief, Fran would find Adam arriving home late at night after hanging out with his pastor all evening. After Adam's passing, Fran had learned how much he was loved by the entire church community, not just a small group. He had warmly affected so many with his genuine personality that it pleasantly surprised Fran at Adam's memorial service just how loved he was by everyone.

Adam formed a very deep bond with his stepfather, Larry, which extended into Larry's side of the family. Larry's father, Bob, who had served in the Army, mentored Adam and inspired him to apply to the United States Air Force Academy, where his only disqualification was his vision. Encouraged by his grandfather's love of military service, Adam later applied and was ultimately accepted to the United States Military Academy.

I knew Adam Snyder best from our time together in the USMA Glee Club. There were distinct differences between clubs centered on contact sports or tactical skills and those related to the arts, but Adam didn't exactly fit the stereotypical mold of a "Glubber" (an endearing term by which we called ourselves). He was easily the biggest guy in the Glee Club, and it was clear that he spent a lot of free time in the gym; very few of the other singers were built like a stack of bricks. I used to tease him that if he wanted some pointers, he could come by and spot me sometime. His response was always a sly smile that seemed to say, "Yeah, right," but he was still humble about being looked up to by the others. His love of singing and acting led him to a significant part in our 100th Night Show with the unforgettable and hilarious song "I'm a Toolbag."

Adam's connection with music to the West Point Glee Club took him to new venues that honored senior Army and government leaders as well as fallen heroes who gave their lives on September 11th. As part of the Glee Club, Adam's voice was heard at a number of prestigious venues, including performances for the Army Chief of Staff, President George H. W. Bush and Donald Trump, audiences at the historic Carnegie Hall, and for movie director Randall Wallace, who wept after listening to us record a song for the soundtrack of his movie *We Were Soldiers*.

Our first performance our Yearling year was with the Boston Pops just after September 11. At taking the stage, without even having sung one song, the audience gave us a roaring standing ovation—not for our performance, but for our chosen profession in light of the tragedy that struck our country. I like to think that perhaps the applause was in anticipation of the sacrifices we would make, and in Adam's case, the most precious gift of laying down his own life. Looking back, I realize a portion of their applause was directly for him.

Another fond memory I shared with Adam was our Glee Club performance on the first anniversary of September 11. We sang "America the Beautiful" on live television at Ground Zero as President Bush, Secretary Condoleezza Rice, Colin Powell, and Mayor Giuliani, among others, consoled the families of the victims of the national tragedy. We stood proudly yet humbly behind the group of families who displayed pictures, wreaths, and flowers in memory of their loved ones who died a year before. Unbeknownst to all of us was that one of our very own would soon commit his life leading men on the battlefield for those we honored that day. A line from "America the Beautiful" pays tribute to him: "O beautiful for heroes proved in liberating strife. Who more than self, their country loved and mercy more than life!"[1]

There were many other cadets who knew and loved Adam. While digging deeper to know him beyond my relationship with him, I found two other classmates who helped me form a more complete picture of who Adam really was. I spoke with Adam Christenson, who sang in the bass section of the Glee Club with Adam Snyder. He recalled that Adam was always cool mannered and managed to handle both compliments modestly and corrections gracefully during practices and rehearsals.

Christenson's relationship with Adam Snyder extended beyond the Glee Club to their lieutenant time at Fort Benning during the Infantry Officer Basic Course in 2004. Christenson recalled that Adam, being a physical specimen, was admired by all the other lieutenants for his performance at PT and in the gym; he tried many times to drag Christenson to lift weights, but he admitted to me that Snyder's enthusiasm proved to be a little much for him. Christenson recalled that because Adam was handsome, kindhearted, and humble, he tended to draw the attention of young ladies. During the tense and stressful moments of training, his sarcastic sense of humor added much needed levity. In the evenings while other newly graduated West Point Officers seemed ready to let loose in social settings, Adam always appeared more mature and focused than his peers. Christenson always saw a man who sought to fulfill service to God and his country before anything else. He wondered if Adam would be one of the few 2004 graduates to become a general officer.

My post-USMA encounter with Adam Snyder was also at Fort Benning. I distinctly recall seeing his face as I left to refit after my first phase of Ranger School. Having already graduated Ranger School, Adam waited in the parking lot to take the Ranger students into town and to offer advice for the grueling weeks ahead. I petitioned him for recommendations on the upcoming phases, and he advised me to not wear socks during water-crossing days in the mountain phase. A week later I took his advice and found that after a few miles I was literally unable to walk due to the hot spots on my feet. When I told our patrol leader and classmate, Dan Koban, that I couldn't walk because I wasn't wearing socks, he became very irritated and asked me what I was thinking. It was embarrassing, but I made it through the patrol. To this day I don't know if Adam was pulling my leg or if maybe I misunderstood him. His sense of humor was so dry and cynical that perhaps I took him seriously when he was really mocking some dumb things Ranger students try pulling off. Unfortunately, I never got the chance to tell him the story. He probably would have laughed hysterically and told me he was joking!

Another friend and classmate of ours, Patrick Brice, was in my Plebe year company and shared a mutual sponsor with me at West Point. Patrick, however, had the distinct privilege of serving with Adam Snyder on two consecutive deployments to Iraq after graduating. His memory of Adam is probably the most unique as he knew him in combat and was also present in the last precious moments of his life.

Patrick had originally known Adam at West Point during Beast Barracks, at chapel, and Officer Christian Fellowship (OCF) meetings. He recalled Adam as being humorous, outgoing, positive, and athletic throughout his cadet time. After USMA graduation and officer training, they both transitioned to Fort Campbell, Kentucky, where they attended the same church; Patrick found that they shared the same faith and passion for God. After some garrison training and preparation, both Patrick and Adam deployed to an area outside Kirkuk, Iraq, in 2005.

Patrick was a platoon leader in the Engineer Company for 1st Brigade, 101st Airborne Division from Fort Campbell, Kentucky; Adam was an infantry platoon leader in the brigade's 1-327th Infantry. Coincidentally, Patrick ran route clearance missions identifying and removing Improvised

Explosive Devices (IED) throughout Adam's battlespace. Adam's platoon happened to patrol the most dangerous and kinetic city within their brigade's area of operation, Hawija, but he was the right man for the job. Patrick remembered monitoring different battalion and brigade frequencies while out on missions and could easily pick out Adam's voice on the net as distinctly clear and commanding. Adam's communication with his higher headquarters always embodied undeniable responsibility as "the leader on the ground." He handled his headquarters' impatient and untimely requests for updates with poise during intense moments. Still, his foremost loyalty was always to his soldiers, keeping them safe on missions.

In one instance, Patrick's team was clearing a suspected IED when they came under attack. Patrick's men repelled the attack, but they were still not as well equipped as an Infantry platoon. Adam, hearing the report on the radio, immediately came to his friend's aid from over five kilometers away. Exuding all the confidence and duty of an infantry officer, Adam ordered a no-notice change of mission for one reason—his brothers needed help. Adam, Patrick, and all their men survived the incident thanks to their commitment. Their unit soon redeployed having successfully accomplished their mission. Patrick and Adam recounted to one another how blessed they were to bring all their men home.

All the Infantry Lieutenants in 1-327th IN were offered an opportunity to stay back from the next deployment in order to attend their Infantry Captain's Career Course. However, there was a lack of leadership in the Scout Platoon due to the reset of senior NCOs. As a result, Adam volunteered to deploy again, putting his career development on hold. He selflessly made the decision to mentor young NCOs and scouts as a seasoned and combat-proven platoon leader once again.

Their second deployment differed from the first as they did not have the same amount of communication with one another. But on that fateful December day in 2007, Patrick and Adam were reunited under dire circumstances. One day Adam's convoy was struck by an IED. He was medically evacuated to FOB Speicher where Patrick worked. Many times as cadets and officers they had shared moments of faith and worship in chapel, at OCF, and even while they attended the same church at Fort Campbell, but this moment would be different. While Adam was brought to the Combat Support Hospital (CSH) for treatment, Patrick rushed to him to provide friendship and comfort in the midst of the trauma. The doctors and nurses told Patrick that they had seen many traumatic wounds during their deployment, but they had never witnessed the perseverance, determination, and sheer will that Adam demonstrated. Patrick sat next to Adam as he lay in bed awaiting another MEDEVAC flight to Balad. Though Adam was barely able to respond, Patrick spent their precious moments together praying over him and reading scripture. Patrick remembered reading Zephaniah 3:17, which reads "the Lord your God is in your midst, a mighty one who will save; he will rejoice over you with gladness; he will quiet you by his love; he will exult over you with loud singing."[2] He also distinctly recalled reciting from the book of Isaiah: "Do you not know? Have you not heard? The Lord is the everlasting God, the Creator of the ends of the earth. He will not grow tired or weary, and His understanding no one can fathom. He gives strength to the weary and increases the power of the weak. Even youths grow tired and weary, and young men stumble and fall; but those who hope in the Lord will renew their strength. They will soar on wings like eagles; they will run and not grow weary, they will walk and not be faint."[3] In response, Adam, who was unable to speak, fought with everything he had to sit up and raise his arms. Patrick sensed that the Lord was present during their encounter, inspiring him to speak encouragement and comfort Adam. Patrick told me that Adam faced the end of his life with the same great courage, strength, and faith in God with which he lived. These scriptures were among the last words Adam ever heard.

Adam once honored fallen cadets and graduates in singing our "Alma Mater," but now I find that he is the one memorialized by those sacred words, "And when our work is done, our course on earth is run, may it be said *'well done; be thou at peace.'* E'er may that line of gray increase from day to day. Live, serve or die, we pray, West Point for thee."[4]

In the Gospels, the story of the centurion is recounted by the apostles Matthew and Luke. A military leader approached Christ concerned about his paralyzed servant at his home. When He asked the centurion if he wished for Him to visit the servant, the centurion replied that he did not deserve to have Jesus under his roof, but that His word alone would heal the servant. The centurion related the trust and authority he shared with his soldiers to the authority of Jesus and the faith the centurion had in Him. Christ's reply to this combat-seasoned leader was unique. Amazed, He declared, "'Truly I tell you, with no one in Israel have I found such faith.'"[5]

Adam received the same respect and led with authority similar to that of the centurion, but he also lived his life faithfully and under authority to his Savior. Though we despaired over the loss of a friend, loved one, and brother-in-arms, God knew what He was doing when He called His warrior Home. I rest assured in that faith, and I know Adam lived his life and died by the same.

Shortly after Adam's passing, Fran began making arrangements for Adam's remains according to his last wishes. Reading through the documents he prepared prior to his final deployment, she learned that among Adam's list of final requests, should he be mortally wounded, he did not want the traditional playing of "Taps," nor did he want a twenty-one-gun salute at his funeral. He was too humble to receive that honor.

CAPTAIN PAUL W. PEÑA, KIA IN ARGHANDAB, AFGHANISTAN, ON JANUARY 19, 2010

Paul's Song

Cory Wallace

"Dude, why did you buy a bass pedal when we don't have a drum set in our room?" I remember asking Paul this question during the first two weeks of our tenure as roommates at the beginning of our Firstie year.

"I can play it against boxes or our trash can," he responded with an air of disbelief that I would even question the brilliance of buying a fraction of an instrument that West Point didn't even allow in the barracks in the first place. Eventually, I learned not to question Paul on such purchases, for such arbitration was ultimately useless because Paul, as I would learn, was a visionary.

These exchanges took place on a daily, if not hourly, basis in our room. Our lives, no, the universe would never be the same after the legendary discoveries made by the Peña and Wallace Think Tank. With careful storage in the overhead bin, pizza bought on Tuesday still tasted delicious three days later. An entire weekend of Iron Maiden's "Rocking in Rio" on loop caused much less brain damage than "doctors" would have you believe. When we weren't challenging the basic laws of both man and physics, Paul and I painted our faces like Jerry Only,[1] showcasing our NYHC[2] style at the shows of Agnostic Front and Blood for Blood, and pondered the navigation of life's minefields on a barstool with the owner of Bennyhavens.[3] Also, Paul's Texan origins made singing the lyrics of Pat Green songs at the top of

Paul W. Peña

our lungs a default pasttime when we deemed that the rest of A2 (our Cadet Company) was worthy to hear our midnight serenade.

Paul majored in Military Science, or as we joked, he was working on his degree in Infantry. When I first met Paul in the fall of 2001, I learned he valued two things above all others: his mother (to whom we all referred as "Madre") and the Infantry. Although not mandatory, Paul took it upon himself to sport a high and tight[4] and read field manuals in his spare time. He pinned a Ranger Tab inside of his patrol cap to remind himself of the crucial "make or break" task of every Infantry career. Needless to say, we never missed a chance to bust his chops about his obsession; however, we all silently admired his drive and focus.

At West Point, the reality of Afghanistan and Iraq manifested itself in the moments of silence taken before meals in the chow hall to honor a fallen graduate. Occasionally, one of these names belonged to someone we knew on a personal level. Sadly, we were all much too young to grasp the gravity of a table commandant[5] we knew a mere two years earlier leaving this world months after graduating from the Academy. For us, West Point still sheltered us from the knowledge that the names of our own classmates would soon be read from the Poop Deck.[6]

On May 29, 2004,[7] reality hit us as if we ran a one-hundred-meter sprint in a ninety-meter room. The days of last-minute paper writing, room inspections, and parades that seemed like Herculean labors were soon to be exposed as the minor inconveniences they really were. After receiving our diplomas, West Point severed our umbilical cords and expected us to defend our Nation against all enemies both foreign and domestic.

Paul welcomed this challenge. He was one of those people who you could tell had just become the man he was born to be. Many people go through life second-guessing decisions that lead them to their current station. Paul was never one of those people. Anyone who knew Paul could unequivocally confirm that he would never have traded shoes with anyone in the world after his mother pinned his second lieutenant bars on his shoulders during his Commissioning Ceremony.

After graduation, my contact with Paul became sporadic. I went to Fort Knox to attend the Armor Officer Basic Course while Paul headed to Fort Benning to begin his journey in the Infantry. Occasionally, I'd get a call from him doing numerous Paul-like activities: going to a Hank Williams III concert, singing karaoke in some heinous dive bar, or relaxing in his room while listening to Iron Maiden. Based on our conversations, Paul appeared to be happier than I ever knew him to be. He was excelling at his craft and having a helluva of time. Toward the end of IOBC,[8] Paul learned that he was headed to Alaska to join the Army's newest airborne unit, the 509th PIR.[9] Clearly, things could not have been going any better for Paul.

Eventually, I made my way down to Fort Hood, Texas, while Paul continued to work his way through the Infantry pipeline of various Infantry schools. During training holidays, we'd always meet up in the happiest place in the continental United States: Baton Rouge, Louisiana. There, we made good friends with the LSU rugby team (led by a man who went by the name of "Chunks") who were all more than happy to show a couple of wide-eyed 2LTs a world they never encountered at West Point.

Eventually, I ended up meeting a woman who would later become my wife. Prior to our wedding, Nikki was always more than willing to play hostess to my rowdy friends who wanted to experience all that was Baton Rouge. After graduating from Ranger School, Paul stayed with Nikki and me for a weekend. Evidently, one does not get to eat a lot during his sixty-two-day experience known as Ranger School. While Nikki anticipated this whirling tempest of unbridled appetite showing up at her doorstep, she did not plan on Paul and his Ranger Buddy,[10] Brandon Kint, eating everything in her house except the flour and a couple of pieces of fruit. Before his departure, Paul and I bid farewell to each other. We both pretended to ignore our rapidly approaching deployments to Iraq.

Paul and I deployed for the first time within days of each other; he left from Alaska while I deployed from Hood. Just as all soldiers headed to Iraq do, I ended up spending a week in Kuwait waiting for my flight up North. While stumbling around Camp Buehring looking for the chow hall, I met a mutual friend who informed me that Paul was also at Camp Buehring and later showed me to Paul's tent.

I found Paul sitting on his bunk cleaning his M4. After a brief exchange of greetings, we headed to chow, during which he told me stories of his escapades in Alaska ranging from heading out into a stormy sea to going halibut fishing in a zodiac[11] to climbing a mountain in a blinding blizzard and subzero temperatures. We laughed and joked about times that seemed to occur centuries ago as well as shared rumors about what awaited us to the

North. The thought that this could be the last time we'd ever see each other never crossed our minds. Instead, we left that chow hall as if we both knew we would make it through this deployment without a scratch. After a quick handshake, we both headed back to our tents.

Paul spent the surge fighting the entrenched al-Qaeda forces in northern Baghdad. Other than an occasional "I'm alive" email, I had very little contact with Paul. Even after our redeployments, our contact remained intermittent until during the winter of 2009. While I was stationed at Fort Stewart, I received a phone call from Paul; he wanted to know if he and a couple of mutual friends could visit us over Valentine's Day. Naturally, Nikki and I were more than happy to acquiesce to his request.

Paul and crew arrived at our house on Friday night and sat down to one of Nikki's famous south Louisiana recipes: chicken etouffee. All sat in amazement as Paul demolished three gigantic plates as if he was trying to reenact his post–Ranger School destruction of Nikki's kitchen.

After dinner Paul would not stop talking about what he referred to as "the Center of the Universe." The rest of us knew this place as Fort Bragg, North Carolina. Paul was assigned to the 82nd Airborne Division's 2/508th PIR. Furthermore, Paul insisted on referring to the 82nd as "The Division" after removing his hat, putting it over his heart, and looking majestically at the sky. Clearly, he was once again in a situation he wouldn't trade for the world. Also, Paul was scheduled to assume command of Alpha Company on March 18, 2010, and soon thereafter he led his company into combat.

The next day, we loaded up and took our visitors to enjoy all that Savannah, Georgia had to offer. After having lunch at a place where you could both feed alligators as well as one's self, we headed to River Street. At the time, Nikki and I transported our two-month-old daughter, Anneliese, in a giant stroller. While Paul constantly fronted the persona of a hardcore grunt, he did a horrible job of masking his kind and gentle side. Instead of waiting for the elevator, Paul carried the massive stroller down several flights of ancient stone steps. His generosity and kindness always managed to surface despite his best efforts at bravado.

At the time, Nikki had a shih tzu that I desperately wanted to give away. Having a fluffy dog named Lil' Tony Chacherie was never a good thing for any combat arms officer's reputation. Strangely, Paul fell in love with this dog. While Chacherie spent the majority of his life barking at walls, vomiting in the middle of the night, and peeing on every carpet in our house, Paul somehow inspired a moment of clarity within the furry abomination's psyche. Chacherie loved Paul. During his final hours at our house, Paul offered to adopt my worthless shih tzu. I was more than happy to hand him over. However, Paul was deploying very soon and was unable to work the hasty logistics.

That afternoon, I shook Paul's hand before he headed back to the Center of the Universe. It would be the last time I ever saw him alive. In retrospect, our last weekend together was a perfect microcosm of Paul's life. Sure, he filled the majority of our time with Ranger School stories, anecdotes of how Bragg was vastly superior to every post in the Army, and questioned how one could consider anything besides airborne infantry as combat arms. However, there were also moments of pure, unadulterated altruism and multiple examples of what made Paul a great human being.

Fast forward to January 22, 2010. I was at my Company's command post on FOB Warrior just outside of Kirkuk, Iraq, when I received a call from Nikki. She instructed me to go somewhere by myself, and she broke the news of Paul's death. Nobody knew anything other than he died as a result of an IED blast on January 19 in the Arghandab River Valley in Afghanistan. I just stood there in the cold Iraqi night holding my phone and cigarette and not knowing what to say other than, "Goddamit."

I spent the next several days contacting my stateside friends in an attempt to find out what exactly happened. Nobody knew anything except when the funeral was scheduled to take place at the Fort Sam Houston National Cemetery in San Antonio, Texas. Several people contacted me after the service and described it as something in the exact fashion desired by Paul: a ceremony flawlessly executed by paratroopers and a wake attended by all those who were honored to know him.

After I redeployed, I went fishing with a mutual friend of both Paul and me. While he was unable to attend Paul's service due to scheduled training, he was able to ascertain the details of Paul's death. While showing a new platoon leader around the company's area of operations, an IED detonated in the middle of Paul's patrol. The blast wounded four soldiers, including Paul. As his men were preparing to request the MEDEVAC, Paul learned that they were going to evacuate him before his soldiers. He gave his soldiers a direct order to evacuate the other wounded soldiers first. While Paul would eventually die of his wounds, his sacrifice allowed two of the four severely wounded soldiers to live.

Paul's valor didn't surprise me in the least bit. As I previously mentioned, he was never able to fully mask the kind Paul who loved his friends and family more than anything else in the world. While I obviously wasn't there and don't know every single detail, I do know that giving one's life so that others may live is an action only taken by heroes whose song will live on for eternity. To this day, we still sing Paul's song, just not in a corny way—he wouldn't want that. All of those who knew Paul celebrate his memory on January 19 with cheap Chinese food (his favorite) and Arnold Paul-mers (Arnold Palmer Half & Half with Patron). We refer to this as "National Paul Peña Day." Many of the conversations between me and Paul's mutual friends are still perforated with random instances of "Remember when Paul did this?" or "Man, Paul also liked to do that." Also, our son is honored with the middle name of Paul so that he will always carry a piece of this great man's memory wherever he goes.

I remember being told as a second lieutenant that you never know the impact you had on an organization until you hear what people are saying about you long after you leave. Hopefully, Paul gets to tune into our frequency on occasion to hear how much we love him. So if you're reading this, I would ask you to honor our friend Paul on the nineteenth of January each year. If you didn't know him, that's okay, for I'm sure you know someone just like him. But if you did know Paul, you understand that he would never object to anyone eating cheap Chinese food and drinking Arnold Paul-mers in his honor. Also, there's a park named in his honor located in his hometown of San Marcos, Texas. If you're ever down that way, please swing on by and take a minute to watch all the kids and dogs running around enjoying what Paul gave them.

Daniel P. Whitten

CAPTAIN DANIEL P. WHITTEN, KIA IN ZABUL PROVINCE, AFGHANISTAN, ON FEBRUARY 2, 2010

Evoking Rapture in the Tempest: My Life with Dan

Jimm Spannagel

As I flew over the Rockies, I marveled at the striking beauty emanating from the simple contrast of white and brown. It was a welcome distraction from the blank page on my computer screen, patiently positioned on the plastic tray table. I was flying west while my friend was flying much farther east, into a land still foreign but all too familiar to me. My task seemed simple but proved to be challenging—distill the insight of my entire military experience into a single email for the benefit of a first-time deployer. As I wrestled to formulate a coherent message, the beauty of the landscape below pulled me deeper into a daydream, and thoughts of Dan led me to the familiar place of smiles and teardrops.

Unlike Dan, I did not get into West Point on my first try. I had applied to the Class of 2002, but it was on my second attempt that I was granted admission. On June 28, 1999, I walked across the fifty-yard line at Michie Stadium in the third and final reception wave for the Class of 2003.[1]

I often wish I had the ability to travel back in time to particular moments in my life for the sole purpose of observing others or myself through the lenses of my current mind-set and context. Having grown to know Dan as I have, I chuckle at how he must have handled himself on "R Day." I am entertained by the assured truth that he struggled to not laugh when being screamed at by the Cadet in the Red Sash.[2] He most certainly found that charade to be contrived, at best, but just as certainly buckled down because it was the only thing that stood between him and his midday meal. Lunch, I imagine, was a particularly frustrating experience given that his food intake was limited to a helping inconsistent with his dietary ethos. Most of us fell prey to the shock of the deconstructionist model of Beast Barracks, which loosely mirrors that of Army basic training. We became bewildered by a week of constipation, waking up to Guns N' Roses's "Welcome to the Jungle" blaring over the loud speaker, or memorizing obscure pieces of Army knowledge and West Point heritage from our Bugle Notes.[3] Dan, on the other hand, reveled in that empty space between the ridiculous and the sublime, a foot in each camp, a toothy smile upon his face.

Dan and I never crossed paths during our first summer at the Academy or during the first academic year. My first year was extremely tumultuous. I was in the midst of significant family turmoil, I routinely ran afoul of certain upperclassmen, and I struggled with core classes such as Discrete Dynamic Systems[4] and Chemistry. During our second summer at Camp Bucker, I seriously considered leaving West Point. Ultimately, I decided to stick it out, forging forward on blind faith that everything would work out. Following the ceremonial seven-mile run from Camp Bucker to the Cadet Area at the summer's conclusion, I moved into company H-2[5] on the sixth floor of Bradley "Long" Barracks. It was then that I first met Dan.

Truth be told, I could not stand him immediately upon meeting him. My cynicism and youthful penchant for thoroughly dismissing a person who rubbed me the wrong way combined with Dan's boisterous, unbridled enthusiasm were a recipe for conflict. I quietly despised him as he smiled through all of the West Point bullshit. I had not yet learned this about Dan, but he had a unique ability to thrive in two divergent spaces while remaining unconstrained by stereotypical Army sclerosis. It was as if the theatrics of an institution like West Point did not affect him. Yet even as insightful as he was, knowing the secrets of success and prosperity as a cadet and officer, he never reached a tipping point of arrogance or an air of faux humility, as is common with smart, successful Army types. As easily as he traversed the system, he was just as inclined to help others in their paths. It was not apparent to me at the time, but Dan's example in large measure reinforced my decision to stay at the Academy.

Over the following year, my scorn for Dan quickly waned as my respect for him grew in earnest. He had been selected to be an exchange cadet at the U.S. Naval Academy, and so he attended Annapolis for the fall semester of our Cow[6] year in 2001. Approximately two weeks after signing the contract to remain at West Point and commit to a minimum of five years of active duty military service, the meaning of our commitment changed dramatically.

On a brisk Tuesday morning in September, I was hurriedly walking back to my barracks room to complete a paper that was due later that afternoon when I bumped into my roommate, who hurriedly told me to turn on the news when I arrived at our room. I turned on my computer's TV application and watched in horror as I witnessed the second plane impact the World Trade Center in real time. Thirty-four minutes later another plane crashed into the Pentagon. Not long thereafter, the towers collapsed and news came of United 93 crashing in a remote area near Pittsburgh, Pennsylvania. As I sat in the Cadet Mess Hall at lunchtime, my eyes remained glued to the class lights, a visual signaling system used to dismiss classes at the conclusion of meals. We had received no further information about the attacks other than that it was assumed to be an act of terror, leaving us to wonder if an attack was planned on the service academies. With the entire Corps of Cadets dining simultaneously in one location, we reasoned that attacking at lunchtime in a similar fashion would prove to be an equally symbolic act of aggression against the United States, just as were attacks on its symbols of capitalism and military prowess. The attack never came, but the imperative to drive on with military stoicism was immediate. Teams of firefighters and police officers worked around the clock to recover the bodies of those lost at Ground Zero. Classes resumed. The Yankees were in the World Series.

The resumption of routine carried with it an air of defiance. It was as if writing my sociology paper and drilling for Saturday's parade were symbolic flip-offs to Osama bin Laden and the rest of al-Qaeda. In that, I learned a lesson in resilience that allowed me to cope with the myriad uncertainties of Army life. Life goes on, as does everything with it. There is both comfort and fear in such a realization. For those of us who were enraptured by the prestige of attending West Point as a steppingstone to a six-figure salary some five years after graduation, 9/11 served as a sobering dose of reality that deconstructed the commonly held cadet fantasy that those five years were no longer an asterisk. America became a nation at war, and we had solemnly sworn to uphold the Constitution against all enemies, foreign and domestic. In less than two years' time, the Class of 2003 would find itself in faraway cities and villages of Afghanistan and Iraq. Just days after trading "two for seven [years],"[7] the stakes grew almost beyond comprehension.

Upon Dan's return to West Point for the winter intercession and spring semester, we served as a cadet cadre together, me as the company's first sergeant and Dan as a platoon sergeant. Dan allocated equal energy to his military development and scholarly pursuits. In his example I tried to find the equally developmental value in them as well. We gravitated toward each other, rallying around this shared outlook. Mutual professional respect immediately blossomed into an extraordinarily tight friendship. For the first time as a cadet, I began to see the path to success in the Army through the eyes of someone who was already there.

Dan did everything with animated immoderation. His zeal is both what put me off to him early on but drew me ever closer to him in our friendship.[8] As a student, the sharpness of his mind was lent to the most challenging academic pursuits. He majored in mathematics with independent study projects traversing realms of mathematical theory well beyond that of an undergraduate. As we entered our Firstie Year, Dan's rank within our class was in the top fifty, or roughly the 95th percentile.

The fall semester of our Firstie year was generally as expected. We enjoyed the comforts our tenure within the cadet system granted us: we carried sabers instead of rifles, we took primarily electives, we left the gates at our leisure, we enjoyed beers at the Firstie Club with our classmates. We spent countless hours during mutual downtime in our academic schedules pontificating about life's platitudes with the characteristic hubris of twenty-one-year-olds, as we sipped flavored Godiva coffee and devoured Little Debbie's Oatmeal Cream Pies.[9] Sex, politics, war, music, the Army—no subject was beyond our intellectual mastery or immune from the privilege of our discourse. We feverishly debated our immediate future as Washington's war hawks compelled then-President George W. Bush toward decisive military action against Iraq, a country reportedly manufacturing weapons of mass destruction and providing safe haven for al-Qaeda.

Though the fall was unremarkable, the spring semester proved otherwise. Dan was serving on the regimental staff and I was the company's cadet commander, a position inconsistent with typical bouts of senioritis experienced by most Firsties. Dan labored over his capstone project as a math major as I refined my senior thesis in sociology. On March 20, volleys of some thirty-six tomahawk missiles impacted Baghdad and announced the impending invasion of Iraq by the United States. For soon-to-be second lieutenants, the outbreak of war in a second theater was sobering. Having monitored the lead up to war, Dan and I were personally disappointed by our nation's decision but equally as committed to support it. Nonetheless, we were angry at the uncertainty. Just as 9/11 grounded us with the gravity of our commitment to the profession of arms, the Iraq invasion reaffirmed it. Upon returning to the Academy following spring break, we discussed the invasion over pizza and beer at South Gate, a local bar in Highland Falls. We went about the business of completing our final two months as cadets, mentally preparing to go to war.

On March 28, H-2 had a party at the [Class of] 49er Lodge, a beautiful log cabin behind West Point's Jewish Chapel. That afternoon, the company had convened to discuss the major events scheduled over the final months of the academic year, as well as summer training programmed for the lower three classes. We intended the party to be a home stretch kickoff and had been planning it for two months. The Brigade Tactical Department approved a request to serve alcohol, but limited the amount served to one keg of beer rather than the requested two kegs. We obtained a waiver to allow the Plebes to wear civilian clothes in an attempt to build better cohesion among the four classes.[10] The H-2 party was intended to celebrate the beginning of the year's end and the impending transition contained therein.

For more than ten years I have wrestled with understanding the underlying forces within Dan and me that influenced the events of that evening. I know that I have a deeply rooted propensity to challenge authority in moments of intense disagreement or at critical points of departure. This has always been my way. In Dan's case, it is difficult to surmise the drive behind his choices other than an ever-present desire to know the exact location of a line by sometimes stepping over it. While the details of the H-2 party are not particularly relevant or flattering, suffice it to say that Dan and I stood comfortably in the eye of a storm of youthful zeal as some thirty cadets willfully broke the rules in a glorious id-driven fury, illegally consuming alcohol. We were responsible, and we were at fault. By April 9,

Baghdad was under Coalition Forces' control, and Dan and I were at the mercy of the Commandant of Cadets, our immediate future as cadets and officers even less clear than before.

For the next two months when we were meant to enjoy our vanishing time at West Point, we were fighting to keep it. For nearly four years, we were model cadets. We never walked a single disciplinary tour[11] for any of the myriad reasons cadets contravene. Yet we quickly became the Army's equivalent of an exposed double agent. One senior officer berated us with dichotomous frustration and elation, noting that our "forty-six-month deception of character" was "gut-wrenching" but celebrated having caught us "in the nick of time." During the last week of May, our classmates packed their belongings and greeted their families in the joyous preparation for graduation day, while Dan and I sat in a small conference room tenuously clinging to the privilege to be cadets. At the conclusion of our disciplinary boards, the investigating officers assigned to our cases recommended to the commandant that Dan remain at the Academy for an additional semester and I for an additional year. We were relieved to not be expelled but immediately ashamed of the fact that we were not graduating with the Class of 2003. We attended our classmates' graduation, tucked far into the upper bleachers of Michie Stadium. As our friends threw their white hats into the air, we consoled each other through choked sobs until finally retreating to our temporary barracks room. One month later, the commandant disposed of our cases with identical punishments. We were turned back to the Class of 2004 and were to spend an additional year at the Academy,[12] remediating our failures in preparation to become combat platoon leaders.

As cocksure delinquents, we had the pleasure of negotiating a most unfortunate milestone together. This event's silver lining was that we were to spend an extra year at the Academy together as students in the English Department. Having both completed our respective programs of study, we embarked upon a new academic enterprise together, ensuring that for the first of two semesters we would share every single class hour. Our study began in a senior seminar exploring the literary canon of the Arthurian myth with the English Department head. We read selections from a translation of Mallory's *Le Morte d'Arthur*, Tennyson's "Idylls of the King," Clemens's *A Connecticut Yankee in King Arthur's Court*, and Eliot's "The Waste Land." Through each piece we deconstructed, our literary world expanded into varied eras and traditions. It was here that I first marveled at Dan's academic versatility. He defied the typical student bias toward left brain or right brain. It was absolutely stunning. His depth of intellect in all areas seemed unchallenged by the usual scholastic inclinations. He could carry on discourse in theoretical mathematics and write literary criticism with equal aplomb.

Perhaps the most impressive evidence of this versatile mind is Dan's senior English thesis in philosophy, in which he explored the superempirical qualities of elegance and simplicity as legitimate selection criteria for mathematical and scientific theories. On the cover page of his paper in simple font, he included three quotes. The first is from the protagonist in the Darren Aronofsky film *Pi*, which underscores the relationship of mathematics as the language of nature, observed in natural patterns. The second quote is from French sculptor Auguste Rodin (most famous for his sculpture "The Thinker"), elevating the beauty in nature as seen through the eyes of an artist. The third is from Keats: "Beauty is truth, / Truth beauty—that is all / Ye know on earth, / And all ye need to know." Reading his introduction, one immediately felt small standing next to this intellectual giant, but inspired by his prowess.

Throughout the paper, Dan carefully laid out various superempirical qualities for theory selection—economy, coherence, simplicity, elegance—focusing on the latter two. He then deconstructed each, highlighting the critical contrasts. For example, among the various forms of simplicity there exists epistemological simplicity, syntactical simplicity, semantical simplicity, conceptual simplicity, logical simplicity, pragmatic simplicity, and informative simplicity. Throughout the piece, he explored and evaluated various titans of science, including Heisenberg, Dirac, and Einstein, all who in some manner pointed to simplicity as a selection criterion for theory.

He then turned his focus toward a similar exploration and deconstruction of elegance. Unlike his evaluation of simplicity, he looked to contemporary work for support. It is here that the reader catches a glimpse of his heart, his ethos. He carefully selected a quote by Graham Farmelo, a professor at Churchill College in Cambridge and 2012 recipient of the Kelvin Medal for his biography of Paul Dirac titled *The Strangest Man*. The quote is from Farmelo's *It Must Be Beautiful: Great Equations of Modern Science*, published in 2002, just two years before Dan penned his thesis. Concerning the existence of elegance in scientific theory, Farmelo posits:

Fundamentally, it means that the equation can evoke the same rapture as other things that many of us describe as beautiful. Much like a great work of art, a beautiful equation has among its attributes much more than mere attractiveness—it will have universality, simplicity, inevitability, and an elemental power.[13]

In his conclusion, Dan submitted this advice to the reader: "With effort and focus, beauty is observable in mathematical and scientific theories." Just as Dan saw beauty in life, he was beauty in the lives of many. To divorce numbers from words, beauty from truth, and elegance from complexity were constrained and unnecessarily limiting ways of living. Just as he appreciated the beauty of Michelangelo's *David* or guitar riffs in Pink Floyd's "Comfortably Numb," he saw similar beauty in mathematics, the order of the lockstep strictures of West Point, and the unruly nature of love. He possessed a keener awareness than the rest of us; the beauty of all things moved him. Beauty was his panacea, which inspired in him an elemental power. For me, he was the bridge to an understanding of beauty, rapture, and love.

To the great relief of our families, Dan and I negotiated our second Firstie year without incident despite the fact that we enjoyed our usual brand of chicanery. We ingratiated ourselves with our new cohort in the Class of 2004 early in the year by choosing to participate in the Ring Weekend[14] festivities, including receiving our Class of 2003 rings again as our new classmates received their rings for the first time. Dan's affinity for mischief manifested in a clever prank to play on the newly minted Plebes from the Class of 2007. The ceremony where Firsties receive their rings is held at Trophy Point, a beautiful overlook on the Hudson River. The only obstacle standing between the Firsties and the kickoff to their party weekend is the Plebes. They eagerly lie in wait, prepared to raucously recite the "Ring Poop,"[15] and politely harass Firsties about their often gaudy new accoutrements. As Dan and I walked back from Trophy Point, the Plebes clustered around us, screaming the Ring Poop in unison.

Dan garnered sympathy from the naïve Plebes by demonstrating that he was crestfallen by the fact that his ring had the wrong year on it. Rather than display the Class of 2004's crest and motto ("For Country and Corps"), it had that of the Class of 2003 ("Protectors of the Free"). Bewildered Plebes quietly backed away from the awkward situation, as our shared *schadenfreude* felt pleasantly scratched.

We endured another season of depressing Army Football, attended our second 100th Night, and even enjoyed a tip-of-the-cap from then Chairman of the Joint Chiefs of Staff General Richard Myers (USAF) at the Graduation Dinner, who commended our five-year journey over that of our underachieving, four-year classmates. On the morning of May 29, 2004, we awoke early and gathered outside Michie Stadium, poised to complete our journey as cadets. We filed into the bleachers and listened to then Secretary of State Donald Rumsfeld deliver his commencement speech. One by one, each member of the Class of 2004 traversed the stage to receive his or her diploma and revel in the emblematic achievement. As our white dress hats flew quickly into the sky and then drifted lazily to the ground, the reality of our achievement set in. We furiously scrambled through the throng of elated classmates to find each other. Whereas the year prior we embraced through choked sobs of sadness, we now embraced through sobs of relief and joy. After many minutes in a tight embrace, we separated to find our families, reconvening a short time later in our Class A uniforms as newly commissioned army officers.

Dan was bound for Fort Benning, Georgia, to attend Infantry Officer Basic Course (IOBC), and I for Fort Knox, Kentucky, to attend the Armor Officer Basic Course (AOBC). We left the Academy prepared and exuberant for our Army experience. We also left with heavy hearts. Having grown to be an inextricable unit, the time of our separation was inevitably upon us. As I departed Thayer Gate, my old Jeep Grand Cherokee laden with footlockers, I was more equipped to lead soldiers and begin my adult life in part because of the training West Point had given me, but in larger measure because of the love that Dan taught me to have in my heart for myself, my fellow mankind, and the world around me.

In the years following graduation, Dan and I saw each other only a handful of times. Our paths ran in a generally parallel fashion as we ticked off our junior officer years. In close contact via telephone, email, and letters, we eagerly compared our experiences and shared insights. Though our contact limited and we only saw each other three times in the years following our graduation, the times we did share together were epically memorable.

The first time we reconvened was a few weeks after graduation. I had moved to Washington, D.C., for the summer before reporting to Fort Knox. Dan stopped in for a night of eating and drinking on his way south along the I-95 corridor to Daytona Beach. There he spent time with his sister Sarah before reporting to Fort Benning. Always the consummate big brother, Dan would awake early with Sarah on days that she had to work to make her coffee and iron her clothes. Dan opted to attend IOBC in July so that he could complete it and begin Ranger School in the fall. It was during this time that Dan met Starr Oliver, the sister of a West Point classmate. She was a student at the University of Georgia in Athens, where Dan and her brother, Rick, spent many weekends. They began dating and fell in love almost immediately. Dan graduated from IOBC and began Ranger School. Because email and telephone contact were not possible while he was in Ranger School, I sent him words of encouragement in the mail. However, I did not write him a note or card containing clichéd messages of good luck, but rather sent him a message that only he could understand. I had returned to West Point for a friend's wedding that fall. While in the area, I visited all of the popular eateries in Highland Falls—Gray Line Eatery, Dong Fong's Chinese Restaurant, and Schades Pizza—collecting their menus. These places had been staples of our cadet diets, serving as comfort food when we were unwilling to don our uniforms to eat in the mess hall or were so engrossed in academic projects that deliberate breaks to eat were not possible. I packaged the menus neatly into a small envelope and mailed them to him. Ranger School is a grueling sixty-one-day course, the hallmarks of which are sleep deprivation and a lack of food. It is not uncommon for soldiers to lose significant body mass while completing the course. Receiving menus in the mail while at this school might send a saner person into a murderous rage. Dan, on the other hand, understood the message and took it as a challenge. Dan had completed two of the three phases of Ranger School, but his class ran over the Christmas and New Year holidays. As a result, he received time off, known as "Winter Exodus," when no training occurs. During that time, we met again in D.C., for lunch with his soon-to-be fiancée. I had just completed AOBC and was preparing to move to Germany for my first assignment. While Starr and I got to know each other, Dan repaid my gift of menus by devouring every piece of food he saw, to include those on my plate. Dan and Starr drove north to visit her family in Pennsylvania. Dan had requested the honor of Starr's parents' blessing in asking her to be his wife, and her mother bestowed upon him her mother's wedding ring. The ring traveled with him in his duffel bag through his final phase of Ranger School, at the conclusion of which he proposed. They moved to Fort Bragg, where Dan served as a rifle platoon leader with the 82nd Airborne Division. He was fulfilling his dream to be an Airborne Ranger. I moved to Germany to serve as a tank platoon leader with the 1st Infantry Division in the industrial city of Schweinfurt in the northern part of Bavaria. The unit to which I was assigned was currently deployed in support of Operation Iraqi Freedom some sixty miles north of Baghdad when I arrived. It returned approximately a month after my arrival, meaning that I was to spend at least a year in Germany before deploying to Iraq. Within a few months of arriving to the 3rd Brigade Combat Team of the 82nd Airborne Division, Dan received orders to deploy to northwestern Iraq on a short deployment of only four months to augment existing forces. While he reported that his tour was generally unremarkable, I nonetheless kept in very close contact with him and questioned him constantly about every facet of deployed life. His was my first window into that world, and the only voice I trusted beyond a shadow of a doubt. While he was in Iraq, my unit made preparations for its deployment in the summer of 2006. The reality of combat was quickly arriving for me. We next saw each other in March 2006 in Malaga, Spain. Having returned from his deployment, his father and stepmother decided to spend a week in a time-share in southern Spain. Dan and Starr accompanied them, as well as Sarah and her best friend from college. Having spent fifty consecutive days in the field for tank gunnery at the snowy Joint Maneuver Training Center (JMTC) in Grafenwoehr and a mission readiness exercise at the Joint Maneuver Readiness Center (JMRC) in Hohenfels, I jumped at the opportunity to both see my best friend (whom I had not seen in over a year) and blow off steam. In true Whitten fashion, we overate, overdrank, and overindulged in each other. Dan and I caught up, discussing his time in Iraq, his decision to marry, and my impending deployment.

Within four months, I was in Kuwait awaiting movement north into my battalion's area of operations in the city of Ramadi. Dan had asked me to be the best man at his wedding; however, our army schedules once again conflicted, and I sadly missed the event. Nonetheless, I sent several proxies in my stead, including a person to read the lengthy speech I would have delivered had I been present. Dan and I spoke often while I was deployed. I had been selected to lead the battalion's scout platoon for the deployment, and as I settled into Kuwait, I received news that a soldier from a platoon I had previously led had been killed by an IED in Baghdad. Having been in Kuwait for only four days and hearing rumors that we were going to what was called an "unwinnable province," the impact of this loss was immediate and visceral. Dan had not lost a soldier during his deployment to Iraq, but he nevertheless provided me with sound counsel and the encouragement needed to be focused and ready for what lay ahead. My first tour in Iraq serves as the pinnacle of my Army experience. I was fortunate to be at the intersection of several favorable factors. These included a platoon sergeant beyond my wildest dreams, a group of soldiers committed to the mission and always hungry for a fight, a company commander who had the utmost faith and confidence in my judgment, and being matched up with an interpreter who opened my eyes to the nuances of a foreign culture, to name a few. Over fifteen months of combat, I learned that the ethics imbued in me at West Point had a practical application beyond the illustrative vignettes in a classroom environment. I also learned that courage is easily mustered when the fate of many lie in the decision-making abilities of a few. I shared my experiences during this tour with Dan and other close friends by writing a serial email blog, detailing the ridiculous situations in which I consistently found myself. Dan always provided feedback and support; he was my touchstone.

While I was in Iraq, Dan deployed to Afghanistan with the 1-508 Parachute Infantry Regiment (PIR) of the 4th Brigade Combat Team (BCT), 82nd Airborne Division as the Assistant Operations Officer (S-3 Air). While there, he was selected to be the aide-de-camp to the Deputy Commanding General of Operations (DCG-O) of the 82nd Airborne Division. Following this, he returned to Fort Benning to attend the Infantry Captains Career Course. Having originally thought that he would not be able to return to a light infantry unit, Dan was fortunate to not only return to the 82nd Airborne Division, but to his same brigade, and later to command the same company in which he had served as a platoon leader.

I last saw him in December 2008 at the Army-Navy game in Philadelphia. It was a rare coincidence for us to have similar off cycles from deployments, so when the opportunity to see him presented itself, I jumped at it. At that time, he was at Fort Bragg and I was studying Arabic at the Defense Language Institute in Monterey, California. When we graduated from West Point, I swore off Army football altogether. I still attribute my distaste for the sport to enduring the loss of scores of autumn Saturdays at West Point as the Army team constantly struggled to win. Nonetheless, when Dan pressed me, I caved with no resistance. I bought a plane ticket and flew east into the Philadelphia winter. On the morning of the game, I met him at the Association of Graduates Alumni tailgate, which he was attending with Starr and her family. We had not seen each other in two and a half years. Our immediate embrace served as testimony to our time apart. We drank heavily to arm ourselves against the December weather and exuberantly entered the stadium. Truth be told, I do not remember anything about the game. It was not until later that I learned the score and that the players wore what looked like ACU pants. I was thoroughly enraptured by our time together, as well as the impromptu reunion with other classmates and friends, to include a few with whom we studied English in our fifth year. We even made an ill-fated attempt to take a picture with the H-2 guidon, much to the chagrin of the company's tactical officer and NCO. Later that evening, I overslept for our dinner reservation at the Melting Pot, a popular fondue restaurant. I arrived at the restaurant as Dan, Starr, and other friends were leaving. He castigated me loudly in the street for making a reservation at a restaurant where one was expected to not only cook his own food, but wait for it to be cooked. It stood in diametric opposition to his storied "scorched earth" culinary spirit. Nonetheless, we enjoyed a night of drinking and the usual carousing. As we parted ways in the wee morning hours, we exchanged generous hugs and made drunken promises to never again go two and a half years without seeing each other. I returned to Monterey and he to Fort Bragg, where he was then serving as a brigade operations planner, impatiently waiting for his chance to command a company. That summer, his unit was set to deploy to Afghanistan to the Zabul province in Regional Command South. Just weeks before the deployment, he received orders to take command of Charlie "Rock" Company in the 1-508 PIR. He excitedly called me during an Arabic lesson. We spoke of his inventory schedule, change-of-command date, and deployment plans. To me there was a sense of peace in the news that he was to command a company in combat. It nested neatly into my conception of the world being in its proper order, everything in its right place. Within six weeks, he was off.

When Dan departed on his final deployment, our communication was intermittent during his first few months, which is completely expected. The first ninety days are a whirlwind—getting one's bearings in the area of operations, understanding the threat, planning operations, and the like. Because his platoons were spread out on small firebases or joint security sites, he traveled to visit them regularly, sometimes by air and other times in a ground convoy. Our Facebook messages were terse but conveyed much. We perennially lamented missing each other and brainstormed a possible future rendezvous similar to our Malaga adventure in 2006. I joked about the juxtaposition of his two Afghanistan tours with my two Iraq tours. His first was as a general's aide, traveling around the country in relative safety, whereas my first tour in Iraq was as a scout platoon leader in perpetual contact with the enemy. His second tour was as an infantry company commander and similar to my first tour, whereas my impending second tour was to be at the corps level in the relative safety of Baghdad's mega-FOB. I last heard his voice in a Christmas morning voicemail in 2009, two weeks before my arrival in Baghdad. He was merry and warm, genuinely happy to celebrate the holiday even if not with Starr, Sarah, or his parents.

Our last exchange came just a few weeks later and was of a much darker tone. A fellow company commander in Dan's brigade and West Point classmate—Paul Peña—was killed in action on January 19. The loss affected Dan deeply. There was a subtle intimation in his tone that the randomness of combat and the irretrievable path of one's fate were to be his end, imminently. He changed his Facebook profile picture to a simple, black box and shared with me a moving quote from Colonel Joshua Chamberlain's Gettysburg dedication speech about sacrificial service. In a *New Republic* article written by our former West Point English professor, it was highlighted that the only message contained in Dan's yearbook profile was a simple, yet cryptic, line from "The Burial of the Dead" in T. S. Eliot's "The Waste Land": "I will show you fear in a handful of dust." It was as if he knew, and had always known, that in fourteen days' time an improvised explosive device would claim him. And so it did.

The morning we lowered him into the ground, there were no clouds in the sky. It was February 12, 2010, ten days since he was killed in the town of Qalat a world away from West Point. Well over a thousand people gathered first in the Cadet Chapel to memorialize him and then in the Cadet Cemetery for his burial. Six of us spoke forcefully about him, failing in turn to capture his essence. Starr exhibited amazing widow's courage in recounting their love story, her "favorite love story." A family friend read a poem written by Dan's father[16] about the casualty notification officer's visit to his home. Three friends spoke of their love for him and his love for them. The general to whom Dan was assigned as an aide spoke about his time with him.

Just days earlier as I flew home from Iraq, I found myself on a Lufthansa flight from Kuwait City to Frankfurt in what has become a familiar scene: a blank computer screen patiently waiting for my feeble attempts to memorialize and honor my best friend.

> Good morning. I would like to extend the sincerest thanks to everyone in attendance this morning. It is not only a tribute to what a great man Daniel was that you are here to honor him, but it is also a deeply personal gesture that means more to Daniel's family than you may know.

As I sat at my computer in Baghdad in the days following Daniel's death, I found my mailbox flooded with messages from friends, loved ones, and even strangers expressing their sorrow, sympathies, and recalling some fond anecdotes. To me, Daniel's influence is so ubiquitous and so penetrating that to capture his spirit or essence with words is a fool's errand, for the man's influence spoke and will forever speak for itself. Nonetheless, I will try to share with you the piece of him that gave me refuge.

Simply put, Daniel was a force of nature. Few people are so arrogant as to live with such vision, to conduct themselves every day with an unbridled inertia on a course that settles for nothing short of excellence. Be not mistaken; his hubris was neither offensive nor prideful nor selfish. In demanding perfection of himself and those around him, he exhibited the greatest measure of humanity. Whereas Daniel firmly put a finger in someone's chest to remind him of the path from which he strayed, Daniel would overpower him in the embrace of his great big arms as he helped this person find his way. In our younger days, that someone was often me.

For Dan and me, our early twenties were our true childhood. During this time, we learned how to live in the world, despite the microcosmic nuances of West Point. We found one another ten years ago as newly scrambled yearlings. I was going through a phase deliberating whether or not I should stay at the Academy while Dan was feeling particularly inconvenienced that three years stood between him and actualizing his dream of becoming an Airborne Ranger. As one friend recounts, it was a perfect match. Daniel spurred me on, motivating me to stay and commit to developing myself as a young Army leader, while I helped to reign in his unbridled enthusiasm. And so it went. We lived the same challenges, learned the same lessons, and dreamed the same dreams. Yet even under intense adversity and in error, Daniel demanded excellence from us both. I am fairly confident that he remains the only person in the Academy's 208-year history to be turned back but never walk a single hour on the area throughout five years as a cadet. Daniel did not allow us to let up for a second. As another friend recounts, our partnership generated electricity, as we continuously gave each other verbal alley-oops for the other to slam dunk, always perfect in timing and creativity, but generally delivered at less-than-opportune or appropriate times. Daniel inspired me to remain true to our shared vision: that no one could be more amused by ourselves than us. Who else could go to Ring Weekend for the second year in a row, receive the same ring, and then convince the Plebes to feel sorry for him because it had the wrong year on it? The man's spirit was pure magic.

Today, through tremendous sadness and grief, we honor that spirit. Sadly, the last conversation Daniel and I had before he was killed in action was a brief and somber one reflecting on the death of a classmate, another company commander who fell two weeks earlier. In moments of despair, even the best of us question our roles as military officers in a time of war. We give more of ourselves than we know we had, much less were willing to give. We succumb to the overwhelming feeling of anguish. However, Daniel, true to his intellectually and emotionally stalwart form, shared with me a comforting quote from Joshua Chamberlain of the 20th Maine Infantry delivered during a dedication of the Maine monuments at the Gettysburg battle site.

In great deeds, something abides. On great fields, something stays. Forms change and pass, bodies disappear, but spirits linger, to consecrate ground for the vision-place of souls. And reverent men and women from afar, and generations that know us not and that we know not of, heart-drawn to see where and by whom great things were suffered and done for them, shall come to this deathless field to ponder and dream. And lo! the shadow of a mighty presence shall wrap them in its bosom, and the power of the vision pass into their souls. This is the great reward of service. To live, far out and on, in the life of others.

To our brother, husband, son, paratrooper, leader of men, our hero: we know that in your deeds, freedom abides. We miss you and love you and implore you to wrap us in your bosom, that we might muster the courage to drive on with the same fearlessness and unwavering vision that guided you daily. After all, if I have learned anything from you over the years, it is that a person needs ten hugs a day to be healthy.

As you leave us to join the ranks of the ghosts of yore, may it be said, "Well done, be Thou at peace." And as always, Big Bites.

Plato's *The Symposium* is a magnificent opus that contributes perhaps one of the most famous and recognizable discourses on love to the literary canon. The piece of this work that I find most poignant is the speech of Aristophanes, who emphasizes that in order to appreciate the power of love, one must first understand human nature and its origins. Aristophanes posits that there are not two but rather three genders—male, female, and "androgynous"—the latter being an antiquated combination of the two former genders. The three genders were the progeny of the sun, earth, and moon, and as such were large, round forms with four legs, two sets of genitalia, and other features. They represented a grave threat to the gods in both strength and vigor. In order to weaken the human being without destroying it, Zeus and Apollo conspired to split it into two equal forms. Once split, the two halves clutched one another desperately, attempting to remain as one. As the story goes, they died of starvation because they spent all of their time trying to become one. Furthermore, their genitals were in the rear of their new form, making reproduction impossible. As halves began to die away, Zeus took pity on them, and rearranged their genitals in such a fashion that they could easily procreate. The meeting of a man and woman produced offspring. The meeting of two men or two women produced sexual gratification and social union.

The physicality of reproduction and implications of sexual orientation notwithstanding, Aristophanes' metaphor is profound in its demonstrative value for explaining a possible origin of love. Every human being is descended from a whole being divided in half, and thus its imperative—biological, social, emotional, spiritual—is to be whole again. Human duty, as it were, is to love.

That's how, long ago, the innate desire of human beings for each other started. It draws the two halves of our original nature back together and tries to make one out of two and to heal the wound in human nature. Each of us is a matching half of a human being, because we've been cut in half like flatfish, making two out of one, and each of us is looking for his own matching half.[17] The utmost urgency is to locate and fuse with the perfectly complementing moiety. The prevailing assumption derived from this concept is the love between a man and a woman, a man and a man, or a woman and a woman as romantic mates, or life partners.

Yet during my education of love under Dan's tutelage, I learned that one person can serve as the perfect complement to many in varied forms—son, brother, husband. Dan's legacy is simply that "to live, far out and on, in the life of others." In Jungian verbiage, Dan's archetypal self could be seen in varied forms—hero, herald, mentor. Just as the hero is a story's protagonist and the character to which an observer most closely identifies, the hero cannot exist with the herald.[18] Similarly, the mentor equips the hero for his quest with inspiration and the tools necessary to bypass the threshold guardians.[19] For me, Dan has represented all archetypes of *Unus Mundus*.[20] While he left me as my hero, his example in love has been my herald and my mentor. In this, I find refuge.

An evaluation of Eliot's "The Waste Land" grants me further comfort. I had a mild appreciation for this work as a cadet reading it within the context of the Arthurian myth, but as it emerged as a text associated with Dan following his death, I wrestled with its opening salvo, "The Burial of the Dead." In a way, I forcibly apply the metaphor to the experiences of loss, grief, and coping. Eliot tells us that

> April is the cruelest month, breeding
> Lilacs out the dead land, mixing
> Memory and desire, stirring
> Dull root with spring rain.
> Winter kept us warm, covering
> Earth in forgetful snow.[21]

His implication is that the resumption of life after a long, cold, snow-swept winter is violent and exists at a point of divergence. One path remains rooted in memory and its familiarity, albeit painful or dreadful. This, in its own right, is comforting. The other path desires renewal and a return to vivacity. The experience of loss demands a choice between decomposition and growth. Dan reminded us all of the difficulty in this choice by using Eliot's words, "I will show you fear in a handful of dust,"[22] while equipping us with the love necessary to drive on.

On a Christmas evening a few years ago, I stood arm-in-arm with my brothers before Dan's final resting place. We silently passed a flask full with bourbon between us—each experiencing the moment through his own lens. Salty teardrops pierced the weeks-old snow; the only sounds uttered were those of sniffling noses. Context defines loss and grief—a long bout with cancer that terminates in a merciful close, a life cut short by a traumatic accident, or a full life having consummated its full course. Coping remains an unconstrained individual labor from which there must be a redefinition of something integral to life, as one knows it. Through this alone one finds solace, closure, and meaning. The epiphany in meaning enables us to renew, to move on.

One form the epiphany takes is inspiration. It is as if loss must undergo a metamorphosis into something positive and lasting, a reassurance that wraps us in the warmth of knowing that there is some cosmic score tallied for each individual. It also provides a fitting memorial to the person lost—a way to "carry the torch" as is common counsel rendered to the grief-stricken. For me, there is an unholy trinity that defines inspiration: unbridled intellect, the romanticism of struggle, and unconditional love. Inspiration is not merely an attention-grabber or childish admiration, but rather a force so moving that it demands constitutional change in my worldview, in how I dispose of my numbered days. Daniel was unconditional love. In his legacy, I know my charge. I am duty bound to love, to counsel, to bear witness.

Jason E. Holbrook

CAPTAIN JASON E. HOLBROOK, KIA IN TSAGAY, AFGHANISTAN, ON JULY 29, 2010

Texas Drawl, Keen Wit, and a Heart of Gold

Jim Wilson with contributions from Cassidy Dauby

Our Cadet Basic Training, aka "Beast Barracks," culminated with a fifteen-mile road march back from the training area on a sunny August morning, which was ironic given the amount of rain the previous week. My excitement for the end of summer training mixed with an anxious uncertainty about what plebe year would bring. A few miles short of the finish, we stopped to change into clean uniforms to make us presentable and help hide some of our "field stench." As we arrived on campus, thousands of parents and local community members lined the streets to welcome us. I was proud to have completed the first part of our training, but I did not fully appreciate that this was just the beginning of our "forty-seven-month experience."

After a quick lunch and a good-bye from our summer cadre, we moved to our academic-year companies where upperclassmen waited to "welcome" new members.[1] I entered a dark hallway lined with glow sticks and a gauntlet of seventy-five upperclassmen yelling as I made my way to sign into my new company, the H3 Hurricanes. My feelings of excitement and accomplishment gave way to stress, disorientation, and questions about my decision to attend the Academy. After reporting to the company commander, I received my room assignment and moved quickly to escape the hallway. There I met my roommates for the first time, Adam King (Long Island), Nathan Strickland (Illinois), and Jason Holbrook (Texas).

Jason and I bonded quickly. We were both from small towns—he from Burnet (population 6,084) and me from Waupaca (population 6,069). We were also both determined to become members of the 2% Club, or those who made it through the four years with their high school sweetheart. (Neither of us did.) Throughout that year, I learned a few things about Jason as a person. He was quiet, but very smart, reflective, and someone you knew would always be there for you.

On one occasion, I was in hot water with our company first sergeant and became involved in a series of uniform drills, which required me to change into various uniforms and report back to him for inspection.[2] I was the textbook definition of a "spazzing plebe"—sweating, frustrated, and struggling for confidence. It was a Friday evening, and Jason could easily have left the room to avoid the drama. Instead, he stuck by my side, prepared different uniform combinations for me, and researched additional news articles for me to recite while the first sergeant inspected my uniform. Early on, Jason demonstrated calmness under pressure and that he would never leave a fallen comrade.

While Jason was quiet, he had a great sense of humor and playfulness once you got to know him. As you might imagine, the stress of plebe year and the proximity of four men living together led to tensions at times. Jason instituted the time-honored "door knob game." In the event anyone in the room let one rip, the other roommates could beat that person until the offender was able to touch the doorknob. He also declared that all who entered our room were to be held to our standards. While the game led to a number of great wrestling matches between us roommates, the best were the unsuspecting visitors who found themselves being attacked by all four of us!

Jason and I changed roommates for the second semester and then moved to different companies for the last three years.[3] We did not hang out often, but we did try to grab dinner together once a month. The army forces a strange dichotomy, where you learn to quickly form new friendships while maintaining strong bonds with past colleagues. After graduation, we left our rockbound highland home to join an army at war: Jason in the infantry and me as an intelligence officer.

Our paths crossed next when we met up at a chow hall in Kuwait. We were both preparing to move north to Iraq with our units in the fall of 2006, and it was great to see a familiar face. Jason hadn't changed much. He remarked how much he loved being a platoon leader and how proud he was of his men. The meal ended quickly and we bid each other adieu, unsure when we'd meet again.

The fifteen months we were deployed proved to be a watershed period for Iraq. Violence was at a crescendo in late 2006, before brave Iraqis, a change in tactics, and a surge of U.S. forces helped to stymie attacks and bring a relative calm to the country. This time period, unfortunately, also claimed the lives of six of our classmates. It was a solemn reminder that the gains were not without cost.

Amid the grueling schedule of a young infantry officer, Jason managed to find himself a beautiful woman, Heather. Cassidy Dauby, a mutual friend who served in the infantry with Jason, recounts a story that captures both the deep empathy and intellect that helped Jason as a leader and how he wanted to share himself and his experiences with others.

As Jason was about to permanent change of station to Fort Bragg from the Career Course (late 2008), he called to say that his (then) fiancée, Heather, was at Fort Benning and he wondered if they could stop by.[4] He was interested in introducing her to other military families and to try to show her something besides the single young officer lifestyle. We lived in the White Elephants on Running Avenue, the classic, white, four-family homes from the late 1930s, with the physical training fields across the street. It was actually a pretty ideal setting for that kind of "developmental" outing. It was a sunny day, and he and Heather showed up punctually around 12 o'clock in his pickup truck. They came inside, sat down, and my wife offered them chai, or if they preferred, she would whip up some Turkish coffee. Jason had recently returned from deployment and got really excited about the chai and launched into stories about drinking chai in Iraq, and the different types and customs involved. His interest went well beyond the chai, and he was proud to be able to use it as a starting point as he continued to branch off on other aspects of Middle Eastern culture for Heather. They had already begun making plans to travel through the Middle East together and assured us that Turkey would be high on their list of places to go. His visible excitement and true appreciation for the Iraqi culture and the differences between theirs and his, in the Texas Hill Country, were truly inspirational. The light in his eyes and the smile on his face as he remembered those times were in sharp contrast to the then very common disregard for local customs and traditions and the often-heard comments regarding the population. It was a picture-perfect example of the counterinsurgency manual and the subsequent four years of intense training. Jason's intense desire to become a Special Forces (SF) officer was derived from just that sort of passion about learning of other cultures and people. Even with its extreme difficulty and ability to stand alone as a lifetime achievement, his identity as an SF officer did not necessarily take over who he was. It was simply a derivative of the internal passion, goodwill, and genuinely honest character that made him who he was.

I would soon receive an invite to his and Heather's wedding. I was honored to have made the invite list, excited to meet Heather and to see Jason for the first time since Kuwait. Unfortunately, I had to miss it due to a training exercise in Korea. I did not know at the time how much I would later regret missing his wedding.

Jason was killed on July 29, 2010, along with SSG Kyle Warren when their vehicle struck an improvised explosive device (IED) near Tsagay, Afghanistan. He had just recently deployed, but he was where he wanted to be—again leading soldiers, this time as an Operational Detachment commander with 1st Battalion, 3rd Special Forces Group.

The turnout for his funeral in Burnet was amazing and a testament to his character and the impact he had on others. Despite the town's small size, thousands lined the street as his body was moved from the local airport to the church, in some ways reminiscent of our march back from "Beast Barracks" almost ten years earlier. Friends and family from all different points of his life shared wonderful stories and memories of Jason, and they all fit a central theme—he was compassionate, smart, driven, and possessed a great sense of humor. He might kick you in the butt, but you always knew he would be there for you.

Jason, I miss you, but it comforts me to know that "ya'll are home in Texas" (said in my best Burnet drawl) and that you and Davy Crockett are probably out shootin' armadillos or the like. Heather and your family remain in my thoughts and prayers, and I look forward to the time when we can again grab a beer together. Well done, my friend . . . be thou at peace.

CAPTAIN DAVE HORTMAN, KILLED IN A TRAINING ACCIDENT ON AUGUST 8, 2011

The Palmetto and the Crescent Moon

TJ Root and David Strickler

Years ago when I was in flight school, a helicopter went down. As confident, young student pilots, we sat in the classroom the next morning speculating about what had happened. We wondered aloud about the crash, and more than once we speculated as to why the crew hadn't managed to save themselves or their passengers. After a few minutes of our collective guessing and armchair critiques, our salty old instructor—a retired Vietnam Huey pilot—interrupted us. "The only thing we know is that they did the best they could with what they had," he said. "That's all that matters."

I have always remembered that bit of advice from that wise old Huey driver. I've had to call on it far too many times. Not long ago, I again found myself as a student pilot, training for a new airframe in a very challenging unit. As we sat in the classroom, grinding out our plan for the next night's training mission, an instructor poked his head in the door.

"Do any of you guys know Captain Hortman?" he asked.

I'd known Dave for years. We were classmates at West Point, though we ran in different circles. We found our friendship on funeral detail at Fort Rucker, and then went through the OH-58D Aeroscout Aviator course together. We'd gotten so drunk on a tubing trip we had to crawl onto the shore at trip's end. We worked on our identical Triumph motorcycles. We were sent to Fort Drum together. He met my wife on our third

Dave Hortman

date. He'd preceded me in joining our special operations unit, and when I assessed for a spot he helped me through the process and cheered me on. I'd sat in his truck with him—the same truck he'd had since we were cadets—just a few weeks prior and caught up on our respective lives. Of course I knew Dave Hortman.

"Yeah, I know him really well, why?" I replied.

"There was an accident last night," the instructor said. "He was killed. I'm sorry." He walked out of the room.

If our lives are our own mythologies, Dave Hortman was a Titan. While it's natural to elevate and exaggerate the virtues of those we've lost, Dave needs no help from me, or anyone else. He was that good. At everything. If you take nothing else from this, take this fact: if Dave Hortman tried it, he was good at it. Accordingly, his death was a knockout punch. After losing so many classmates in such tragic ways, losing Dave—a man I judged to be invincible by his sheer abilities—in a training accident seemed, and still seems, among the cruelest of fate's tricks.

He was a southern gentleman of the variety rarely seen any longer. To know Dave was to know his home: South Carolina. He had a pride in his birthplace that is usually only seen in Texans and zealots. The Palmetto State was where his heart lived. No matter where the Army sent him, he kept his South Carolina license plates. When he bought his truck, his first official act as its new owner was to emblazon it with the familiar moon-and-palmetto sticker on the window. He believed in where he came from, and in the people there who'd molded him. He went back as often as he could.

After his death, I helped another officer gather his belongings from his beloved black Ford. As we carefully cleaned and inventoried the vehicle, I couldn't help but laugh at the specialty South Carolina plates he'd gotten, commemorating the South's use of a submarine during the Civil War. Of all the people who ever ordered such an odd plate, I'm sure none was prouder to slap it on his car than Dave.

He was a good son. I say that because it is true, and because so many of us are often not. He was a good uncle to his niece. He gave freely of himself to his family and friends, which after years of deployments and long absences is harder than most can admit. The Army doesn't lend itself to a great family life—at least not over the past decade—and special operations is even worse in that regard. Nevertheless, Dave found a way. That was his nature. He always found a way to be a good son, even in death. Years prior, he left instructions in a letter that declared that should he die in the discharge of his duties, a family friend should inform his mother of his passing so she wouldn't be met by strangers with bad news.

He was a great pilot. A natural. Even the grizzled thirty-year veterans of the unit said so, which they don't say about any commissioned aviators. It was no accident that Dave ended up where he did. He thrived on the challenge, and thrived in the cauldron of training and deployment to execute the most difficult missions.

He was an adventurer, and a stalwart one at that. In another life, he might have been a Sir Edmund Hillary. He found a way to smile through the worst times—the tough times, the times when it didn't seem as though there was much to smile about. Six months before he died, Dave took a snowboarding trip with a group of old West Point friends. He and Dave Strickler (in a moment of typically brave decision making for which they were known) took on the challenge levied by two buxom Canadians to meet them for a day's run into the wilderness off the ski slopes, an area known locally as the Minturn Mile.

In the words of Dave Strickler:

> That evening at a local Vail bar, Dave and I met two pretty Canadian grad students who claimed to be pretty good skiers. The moment they showed interest in an attempt at The Minturn Mile, Dave's interest piqued, and he was in. So it was settled, the following morning we would meet the Canadians, warm up on the resort's runs, and head off into the wild for the Minturn Mile.
>
> As Dave and I slept nervously, some nasty weather moved in to the area. While it did dump the fresh snow we were seeking, it also brought chilling temperatures and a rare rise in humidity. We woke to dismal conditions, but decided to pack extra clothes and food, and go for it anyway. The Canadians, who proved to be far smarter than two Daves, decided to renege on the attempt at the last minute. They reasoned that the snow wasn't right, and that the wind and cold would make for a miserable day of skiing in the backcountry.
>
> Undeterred, Dave and I exited from the backcountry access gate and hiked through unusually heavy snow to the large bowls where we would begin

our journey. After an obligatory fist-bump, we were off, charging through wide-open bowls of waist-deep powder. Slashing turns through the bowls, I noticed a definite heavy feeling in the snow. Turns that should have felt effortless were challenging, and at times the cold snow stuck to our boards like paste.

Dave joined me at the bottom of the bowls, and we began to navigate the steep chutes. I must have fallen a half dozen times, and Dave also had a tough time in the heavy, sticky snow. We paused, absolutely exhausted, and reconsidered if we would be able to finish the journey. While we had already ridden the technically difficult portion of The Mile, it would take hours to navigate the remaining terrain, which on a normal day would be casual. We decided to continue, but I had a feeling that we were only doing so because neither of us wanted to be the one who proposed we turn back.

Within a half hour, Dave Hortman showed the good judgment to say, "Dude, this is stupid. We should hike back, and ride down the resort side." Of course I agreed, and we began the arduous hike back to the security of the resort. I was relieved that we decided to turn around, but knew we had hours of tough hiking through deep snow ahead of us.

I must have wanted to quit a hundred times, but I followed Dave's steady footsteps up the mountain, one step at a time. We ran out of water, ate all our food, and were drenched with sweat in freezing snow and wind. Surely this was one of the more physically miserable days of my life, but I got the feeling that it wasn't too bad for Dave. We finally arrived at the backcountry gate, and slumped over in the snow, approaching exhaustion. When we arrived at our hotel, our friends said that we looked like frostbitten Vietnam Vets, complete with the "1,000 meter stare."

The next day, as we parted ways at the Denver airport, I shook Dave's hand; through shared suffering on the Minturn Mile, we had become much closer friends. I had no idea that I would never see Dave again.

A few months after that epic, soul-sculpting trek, I found Dave Hortman sitting in his truck outside the gate to our compound. The gate was closed, and as I approached, I saw his familiar black truck, unmistakable with its Oobe sticker and palmetto tree beneath a crescent moon. I stopped my car and hopped in with him. I hadn't seen him in months, but that's common in busy units, and we picked up as though only a week had passed. I had just started training, and he was deep into his new job at the flight line. We talked and laughed, and when the gate opened, we parted ways with a handshake. I had no idea that I would never see Dave again, either.

The aftermath of Dave's passing has been as intense as his life. In that way, his death has been like the fall of a mythical legend (and I recognize the gravity of saying that). Something about Dave's . . . spirit—something I can't put into words for you—touched people. People loved Dave. They just loved him. As a friend, as a man, as a son, as a peer, as a leader—however people came to know Dave, they loved him. Women he dated loved him long after they parted ways, even if they broke up with him. Soldiers and superior officers alike were proud that he was in their unit. His personality transcended the simple acquaintances and strictures of life. For reasons I cannot fully divine or define, that was the magic of Dave. He belonged to everybody.

Over and over, I find myself wondering about the last moments of his brilliant life. As all pilots do, I second-guess the situation. I wonder what might have been different, what minute difference in airspeed or altitude might have changed everything on that bright August afternoon. But in the end, I know that Dave could do anything. I've always known that about him. If he couldn't save that aircraft, and himself, then it couldn't be saved. Like the legions of aviators before him who found themselves in peril in the sky, he did the very best he could with what he had.

He always did. That's all that matters.

> *I serve with the memory and pride of those who have gone before me, for they loved to fight, fought to win, and would rather die than quit.*
>
> —Night Stalker Creed

II

INTERLUDE

CLASSMATES

Joe Myers

"Ok, nobody's looking. Quick. Put it up there, Gary."

Dressed in a red T-shirt and his trademark cargo shorts, Garrison Avery took the screwdriver and screw out of his pocket and began to secure a proper hanging spot for a special photograph into the wall of the First Class Club. Matt Schutte, Brian Hanrahan, and I kept watch on the nearly empty Firstie Club in the booth with Garrison, as he quickly and nervously fastened the screw under a large photograph of a 1950s-era West Point runner.

It was graduation week, 2004. Weeks earlier, as I worked on my share of a pitcher of lager, I noticed an awkward bare spot on the wall of the Firstie Club. It occurred to me that the spot should be filled with a handsome photograph of some of the newest members of the Long Gray Line. I informed my classmates. We jokingly called it Operation Urgent Legacy and set out to leave a small mark on the institution that brought us together.

Once Garrison, known as MacGyver for his propensity to carry tools with him at all times and his uncanny ability to fix anything, finished his phase of the operation, I opened my bag and pulled out a framed "old corps" photo we had taken a few weeks earlier on the steps of the old First Division Barracks. The sepia-toned 8 × 10, featuring eleven of us posing in mock pretension with late-nineteenth-century cadet collars, fit snuggly in the unoccupied spot on the wall. The four of us posed proudly with the product of our successful operation.

The Firehouse Plebes, or "FHP" as we called ourselves, were now a small part of West Point's history. Classmates on the wall.

When I was growing up, my grandfather, West Point Class of 1941, used to talk about his classmates. The word *classmate* was often tinted in a reverent tone. It had a resounding kinship associated with it that made an impact on me. My yearning to experience this camaraderie of "classmates" as my ears heard the word as a child fueled my decision years later to pursue a commission through West Point.

Our journey together began in August 2000 when we marched into Old South Area, or Grant Barracks, to the sound of Darth Vader's "Imperial March." I'm sure the words "oh, shit" went through many of our minds when we saw the imposing vision of all of 2nd Battalion, 1st Regiment's upperclassmen standing at parade rest, ready to welcome us to the start of Reorganization Week. They made it perfectly clear that we would have to earn our place as cadets in company F-1, the "Firehouse." It would not be an easy week.

Reorganization Week pitted us against the upperclassmen in nearly every task, making even the most simple act, such as walking down the hallway, challenging. Laundry, phone calls, and table duties were made more difficult than Beast Barracks for the simple fact that our "enemy" now outnumbered us three to one.

The induced stress of that week had the intended result of bringing us closer together. The personalities of the individuals in the group began to emerge. There was Frank Aburto, the pugnacious kid from Jersey with a strange fascination with all things Chinese. There was the soft-spoken and wise beyond his years Erik Wright. There was the ever-likeable cheesehead from Wisconsin, Matt Schutte. Rick Hawkins was rarely seen without a big, infectious grin on his face. Jorge Orlandini was a prepster and a wild man. Lori Bigger's southern charm and sense of humor helped brighten up the day. Mark Reid was the congenial, if not slightly loud, Texan. Jay Dallas was the gentle big man from Minnesota. Burt Eissler was the athletic farm boy with a delightfully sarcastic wit. Jered Dacosta had a Pooh Bear personality and the shiniest shoes in the regiment. Dan Strangio was the best storyteller in the group. There was Brian Hanrahan, the tough Irishman from Boston who was equally friendly as he was vicious in a fight. Dave Howald's ability to parody any situation kept us laughing. There was the always dependable Oklahoman, Matt Bandi. Finally, there were my roommates and fellow "Duty Rangers" Randy Tau, a southerner with excellent taste in cigars and the finer things in life, and Sam Wilbourn, a shy man who only revealed his sharp wit to those he trusted and knew best.

As we moved into the academic year, the pressures of a demanding curriculum added an additional struggle to our continuous "battle" with upperclassmen. Optional dinner in the evenings became one of the only escapes for us. Ten of us would march silently together to the mess hall and find an empty table so we would not have any upperclassmen to disturb us. There we would relax, laugh, and plan future weekend adventures. We continued this tradition throughout the four years, designating my room as the meeting spot at 6:15 p.m. to eat and laugh together over a plate of pizza pockets and potato-cheddar munchies, among other sumptuous dishes.

We met the academic challenges of West Point, not as individuals but as a team. The stronger among us helped the weaker. I remember sitting in my room with Garrison Avery and Dan Strangio during Dean's Hour reciting Rupert Brooke's haunting World War I poem, "The Soldier" back and forth to each other in preparation for our English recitation that afternoon. I remember the discomfort we felt thinking about standing before a group of our peers and reciting poetry. For science courses, we used our wardrobe doors as dry erase boards for our resident "Star Men" to instruct those of us less enlightened. The common struggle of those coffee-infused late nights strengthened our already durable bond.

On September 11, 2001, we were just beginning our Yearling year. I watched the towers fall and the Pentagon burn on a television during Spanish class. Erik Wright watched as well, wondering whether his father, a colonel working at the Pentagon, was wounded or dead. I remember asking Erik at a Dean's Hour brief that afternoon whether he had heard from his father yet. He had not. Luckily, Colonel Wright survived despite being close to the impact. We were honored to have him administer our commissioning oath on graduation day three years later.

Randy Tau received news of his parents' divorce after arriving at Brian Hanrahan's house in Boston during a weekend road trip Cow year. Brian looked at his classmate, who was clearly shaken. Without hesitating, Brian said,

"Get in the cah." He drove Randy back to West Point, never mentioning how disappointing it was to miss a fun weekend in Boston. For us, the one in need was the only one that mattered.

With graduation, as with all the members of the Class of 2004, came deployments to Iraq and Afghanistan. Matt McKee was the first of us to deploy, serving with the 3rd Armored Cavalry Regiment in Iraq. I deployed in mid 2005 to Mosul, Iraq, as a Fire Support Officer in the 25th Infantry Division. While I was in Iraq, Garrison Avery and his wife, Kayla, stopped in to visit my parents in Pennsylvania. He was getting ready to deploy with the 101st Airborne Division south of Baghdad. I spoke to him on the phone shortly before he deployed. I was on my way home.

On February 1, 2006, I received the call from Kayla. Her husband was gone. I wept. When I composed myself, I told her I would fly immediately to Fort Campbell to help. Then I called Brian Hanrahan, who was stationed with me at the time in Fort Lewis, Washington. He was on a field exercise, but luckily had his cell phone on him. He said he would come with me. Together, we did what we could to help Kayla through the pain and arrangements that needed to be made. She decided to have him buried at West Point. Garrison had told her he did not feel worthy to be buried there. Kayla and his classmates thought otherwise.

I escorted Garrison's body from Dover Air Force Base to West Point. Kayla gave me the single greatest honor of my life by allowing me to eulogize him in the Cadet Chapel, where only months before he had been married while I was deployed to Iraq. I was to be his best man that day. Instead of a toast to future happiness, I would deliver a eulogy for a life well led. He was laid to rest wearing his FHP T-shirt my mother had made for all of us shortly before graduation. Weeks later, as Kayla was going through his things, she found a napkin inside of a safe where they kept important papers. On the napkin were notes Garrison and I had scribbled together about counterinsurgency techniques in Iraq, as we sat over a pitcher of lager in the Firstie Club. I was touched that he treasured our conversations as much as I did. The napkin is framed and hangs on my wall today.

The year 2006 ended as sadly as it began with the death of Ryan Dennison on November 15. He was killed by small arms fire in Iraq. Denny lived life with a vigor that each member of FHP admired. None who ever saw his smile will forget it. When Erik had knee surgery Plebe year, Denny insisted on carrying his dinner tray in the mess hall. While doing some research in the library, Denny found a picture of one of my role models, General James Gavin, commander of the 82nd Airborne Division in World War II. He had the photo laminated and gave it to me as a birthday present. It was the same 82nd Airborne Division with which Denny was serving when he died in Iraq.

After his death, Denny's wife and classmate, Haley, found the final entry in the journal he kept in Iraq. It read:

> I am so thankful that God has blessed me with so much. If catastrophe strikes in Iraq, I will still feel so very blessed because I have lived the equivalent of four men's lives in my short 24 years on this planet. I owe it all to God, my father. He blessed me with wonderful friends, family, parents to adopt me. And most of all with my beautiful wife, my companion, my very best friend.

Denny's life was a blessing to each member of FHP.

I was stationed with Brian Hanrahan in Diyala Province, Iraq, briefly. We would link up and go on runs together with other classmates on the FOB. I had the privilege of listening to Brian beautifully eulogize soldiers he lost in his platoon to an IED. The blast wounded Brian, but he quickly made it back into theater to take charge of his platoon once more. Randy Tau and I met up in Baghdad during my second deployment in 2007. He and Jered Dacosta, also wounded in Iraq, would talk to each other in the evenings over the secure phone lines to check on one another. Brian and Matt McKee have most recently kept up the dinner tradition while serving in Afghanistan.

I recently returned to West Point with my girlfriend at the time just to visit and enjoy an Army baseball game on a nice, spring day. We went to the cemetery to visit Garrison's grave. A blue infantryman's cord and a weather-faded Bronze Star lie atop his marker, along with other offerings left by those he touched.

On our way back to the plain, I saw the door to the Firstie Club open and decided to stop in. A band was setting up in the corner, and the bartender was attending to the beer taps. They had not opened yet. My girlfriend uneasily asked me whether we should be in here now. I said, "Of course," and made my way over to the picture. It was still there. Eleven classmates standing together, whole.

As I stared at the photograph Garrison and the rest of us hung there in May 2004, I thought of a letter I received as a cadet from Dick Winters, commander of "Easy Company" of *Band of Brothers* fame. It was a reply to a letter I sent him as a Second Class Cadet asking for leadership advice. I wrote the letter as I watched the Iraq war invasion on television in March 2003, knowing that my future and that of my classmates was linked to what I was seeing. He attached to his very gracious letter a photocopy of an interview he gave to a historical magazine. With a yellow highlighter, he marked a passage he felt was important. It read, "As I look back over the past 57 years, I find that as I meet, deal with and socialize with other men, I realize that I've always been looking for and hoping to find men like those in Company E."

Looking at the young faces of classmates on the wall, some dead, some living, some still serving, I now know exactly what he meant.

"A PLACE IN THE FIGHT"

Nick Horton

Men, women, boys and girls
Recruited out of their homes
Running into an inescapable freedom
Leaving home with only a few tears
A few tears of those who love them
Conditioning of these men, women, boys and girls
Takes place at Forts, Bases, and Camps
All emerge as warriors
Some will become heroes
Sacrifice is the price to become a hero
Bursting waterfalls of sorrow take their place in the parade
The future promises to reopen painful scars
Time and faith can fill these holes, heal the scars
Men, women, boys, girls fill reopened scars of the Earth
Loved ones become the new warriors
Conditioned to endure the daily battles
Gunshots and explosions continue to maim
Warriors at home are casualties of a mobilized media
Warriors afar sustain injuries that feed this other battle
Men, women, boys and girls

They are all at war
In time, all will emerge as heroes
Not all heroes return home to the sound of a drum
Not all heroes left home at the beckoning of a drum
Battles rage in distant lands
While casualties continue to mount on American soil
A homegrown insurgency of network media and ignorant robots
They do not know the price of their freedom
Mortal wounds will serve to heal the scars of the Earth
While every day the heroes fight
In order to preserve their right
To assume our place in this struggle

THE WAR

The first round fired by an enemy that snaps over a soldier's head creates a supernebula of emotions that changes everything about that individual's character within a nanosecond. Where there was once blissful ignorance, there is now a clarity regarding one's mortality and the very real possibility that he or she may have to take another human being's life in order to survive this ordeal. The taxonomy of emotions associated with combat is not unlike what an individual experiences on a daily basis in a peacetime environment; however, the magnitude of these feelings and the manner in which they blend is almost something akin to the supernatural plane of existence. They complement and obliterate each other in a dynamic emotional Tao that permeates the human psyche to the very core and forever distances the veteran from a perception of the world that was familiar, if not unappreciated, to him or her before their chaotic enlightenment. Back when the world was familiar. Back when it was once innocent.

HOPE

Of all the emotions inspired by combat, hope is the most sublime. It channels a Kantian sense of the word with respect to elevating an individual from their current surroundings and connects them to a level of understanding devoid of the sweat, fear, and metallic taste of blood. Hope silences the cacophony of the flapping of the black and soiled wings of the past and allows us to gain traction, albeit tenuous, on the belief that tomorrow will be a better day.

HAVE YOU PASSED THROUGH THE NIGHT?

Joey Nickel

The likeness of old friends.

The car came to a stop. Through the glass window I could hear children laughing nearby. Their voices were so strong and distinct that I barely noticed the sound of a distant hammer or the idling engine of my own car. Such an odd reception. It is not often that we appreciate how short-lived the laughter of children really is.

There was no color, only the dead stalks and twisted limbs bleak and somber patiently waiting for spring. The drive from Baden-Baden was short but pleasant. This was a brief, but deliberate, stop in my travel to Salzburg for R&R. As I inched gracelessly out of the car creasing the hardened crust beneath me, the icy air filled my lungs and I thought: I want to remember this when I am old.

Hundreds of bodies wandered about the welcome center: bodies in motion, bodies hushed by the frozen air spilling over from the mystic voids we all sought to consume. Restrained by steel links of reverence, we tested and retested the tensile strength in our efforts to breathe, drink, eat as much of our surroundings as the natural world could allow. Rubber soles grating against fine gravel and the chip-chip flutter of camera shutters opening and closing were all that accompanied our foggy breath as the winds whipped us forward to be engulfed by an iron gate inscribed "ARBEIT MACHT FREI."

And then he appeared, a shade really. The image moved too quickly in and among the other tourists like a caged bird released into a skylight. Strong, round face. Close-cropped hair. Lean and sinewy. The kind and curious look of a man who knows full well the dark behind the door and knocks anyway. Suddenly my legs cemented to the earth while the rest of my body swayed weightlessly, a tethered and fragile likeness of myself. It was Ben. Benjamin Britt. He had been dead for almost three years, killed by an IED in Iraq.[1]

I followed the man awkwardly through the crowds wanting to believe it was somehow Ben. That maybe the newspapers, the reports, the world had gotten it wrong. That perhaps it was all a mistake and Ben was alive doing all the things he had not gotten the chance to do before. Same brisk step. Careful in observation. The urge to reach out and touch his shoulder almost overcame me, to touch and know that he was flesh and blood; to pick up from our last conversation four years ago in the gym at Fort Benning when I had just completed Ranger School and Ben was about to start. And if he was real and not Ben, then I could tell him about the man he so strongly resembled, how lucky he was to have that likeness, to be mistaken for a good man with natural warmth and faith in his brother.

But it was not Ben.

I never spoke to that man who looked so much like Ben. I stood and watched as he disappeared down the old prisoner formation area, the sides of the path lined with poplars quietly and appropriately at attention. That was how I remember my cold, January day at Dachau on midtour leave in 2008.

Similar experiences would happen over the next several years, at times elliptical and overexposed like a madman's film negatives and at others, painstakingly lucid. Dan Whitten studying the nutritional value of Capn' Crunch in the commissary at Fort Bragg. Paul Peña walking with a friend down Ardennes Road heading back to the brigade area. A familiar laugh echoing in the company CP[2] or friendly voice muffled by a closed door. The silhouette of an Indiana Jones hat complete with smoking pipe. Faces and bodies suspended in time. A catchphrase or style of speech. It is never how they could or should be—older, wiser, better—but how I saw them last. The airbag impact of that first encounter lessened with each meeting after. I admit there are times now when I secretly hope for them. There are some lies I will always be thankful for.

I want to know others as they grow old.

Green among gray.

As our bus eased to a halt outside Michie Stadium that June day in 1999, not one of its passengers could have predicted our Nation would soon be fighting a war spanning over a decade. Even as American Airlines flights 11 and 77 and United Airlines Flight 175 crashed into the Towers and the Pentagon, most of us experienced seemingly violent emotions illuminated through the pixel eyes of the media's lens, an anger not fully understood and hastily constructed from papier-mâché. And two years later, when gathered quietly in formation preparing to enter the mess hall, our world masked by gray, enveloping stone, the intercom made an announcement followed by the resonating toll of the Cadet Chapel bell sounding "America the Beautiful." We sang along in the windowless corridors of our minds, chests inflated, shoulders back, standing on legs that could give any minute, but would not. We were at war.

The truest definition of that word would remain intangible and gritless even as we sprinted toward it as innocent and ignorant as children wandering toward the smoke of a fatal car crash. Hands still clean. Fingernails devoid of soil.

War. I will do my best to be truthful to a term that has many faces covered by many masks.

Departure, drinking from floodgates, and bloody noses.

A young wife, maybe nineteen, holds her husband tight with their unborn child between them. Brightly colored confetti litters the floor around them. Inverted night sky. Torn paper stars. Our history of constellations erased. A tattered road map. Later, he will say he hopes to meet his son. She is thinking the same, but afraid to say it aloud. The band plays something patriotic, and the man behind the curtain says it is time to go. Andromeda disfigured.

The harrowing burst of PKM[3] fire cracking overhead. Dirt and gravel whipping the ground around you. An RPG[4] detonates twenty meters left, striking a young sergeant to the ground momentarily before he vomits, shakes his head, grabs his M4, and continues to engage the enemy as blood pours from his nose and ear before a five-hundred-pound JDAM[5] eliminates the threat.

Bodies tense in step. The smell of human waste and garbage, sour, burns inside my nose. Alleys flooded with the stench. A hard-nosed team leader yells out like he won the Powerball Lotto as he yanks up command wire hand over fist to uncover daisy-chained 155 mm rounds.

Cursing Hollywood for all the movies where you can hear indirect rounds whistling in before the ground erupts. Like waking in the middle of the night only to find your father eating the Oreos you had put out for Santa.

Loving your soldiers more than yourself. The weighted knowledge that you will make a decision that will cost at least one of their lives. The raised, purplish scars across Atlas's back were no more profound.

Accurate and effective enemy fire. Three platoons and mortar section in contact. Black on water. Intimacy with a Katyusha Rocket.[6] Mortarmen hanging 81 mm rounds so rapidly they can hear only the sounds of the fire commands above their own thoughts. Aircraft overhead releases three two-thousand-pound JDAMs in a triangular pattern. A ridgeline of fire.

Vulnerable. Exposed on a flank as security collapses. RPGs detonate around you and airburst overhead. Like dropping the needle on a worn record, the music plays on cue. Team leaders and squad leaders turn and lean into the fire without hesitation or fear for their own safety.

Ground Battle Damage Assessment. Wet blood on wet grass. A grotesque attempt at modern art. Someone finds an ear. Another, an unidentifiable appendage. Blood trails where most of the remains were already recovered. Keen shadows.

Benzene and filth hang in the air. Soldiers barely on their feet. Running on Red Bull and Zam Zam.[7] Local adults of all ages begin to swagger by. Few at first, followed by many. The proud presentation of purplish-blue index fingers. The temporary tattoo of the voters. Rejuvenated, soldiers laugh and offer high-fives. A quick "how-to" class ensues.

Awake from the dead. Lazarus. Eye-sockets pools of sweat that burn as you reenter the world just as you had left it, choking on the sun.

Cold mountain. Freezing rain that shudders your core. Your e-tool fights it out with the frozen earth. You dig deep because if you do not, it might not be enough. The warm shoulder and short laugh of your RTO[8] as you both avoid the obvious.

Trapped in a wadi.[9] Mud walls fifteen feet high. Three trucks immobile. Security established on near side. RPGs somehow clearing the defilade. The unbroken concentration of an NCO as he rigs up the trucks for recovery. The air silent around him. A mortarman exposes himself and switches to handheld. Three 60 mms in the air before the first impact. Willy Pete followed by HE. Shake-n-bake. The earth becomes still. Quiet. Fingers shaking. Naswar[10] from reflective tin to mouth. The simplest movement a labored task.

The first time you hear the words *shaped charge* and *EFP*.[11] Terms understood only when you see the remains in the truck.

A taste of home, the flood, and what no one can teach you.

Dallas. A.M. Stop over for midtour. Wishing for anonymity as you make your way to your next flight. Still worried about your boys left behind. The guilt settles high around the shoulders. As a group of you pass through an elevated, glass corridor, citizens stand and clap. A few at first, then almost all. The few still absorbed in their cell phones are directed by their neighbor to turn them off and get on their feet. Moments pass before the entire terminal is in chorus. Embarrassed, you hasten your pace to get out of view. You sigh and are proud of your fellow man.

Security running the ridgelines. Soldiers foot it ahead of the trucks, metal detectors in hand. Intel supports that any step may find a pressure plate. All ranks fight to take the task, PFC to CPT. The rotating responsibility of shared risk. Many even refuse to hand it off. No one wants to be the guy who does not take part. Everyone willing to give himself for another.

Holding ground as enemy 82 mm rounds walk in on your position. Eyes excitedly scanning the ridgelines for the observer. FO knows he only has a brief window to call as many 120 mm rounds as he can for the adjacent security element on the hilltop. Impact within forty meters. One more. Displace.

A-10 low overhead. No PID.[12] Someone runs out for a long sprint to draw enemy fire. Hill-foot-shuttle-sprint-backstop. Incoming tracers streak the air around him while support by fire laughs and engages targets of opportunity. Apaches come on station. Twenty minutes of playtime. PID. A great thundering of hooves that briefly leaves the body hollow.

The quiet and long overdue discussion with your NCO counterpart. Dawn edging in. A cool slant of light candy-caning your worn and dirty faces. The echoing bark from Frank, a connection to the world beyond this room. I don't hate them. They're men just like me, like us. Fathers and sons and husbands. I will kill them. You nod and agree.

Heavy in your arms. The lifeless body of a seven-year-old boy. You hand him to his father. Hand on his thin, heaving back. Bone through coarse brown fabric. A wordless exchange. Loss. An elder puts his arms around me. In this land, children die, he says.

A young medic and soldier drag their dying friend fifty meters. Chests heaving with exhaustion. The taste of iron and dirt in the backs of their throats. Lungs burning, exploding. Can't stop. Enemy fire still filling the spaces in between. CASEVAC[13] just at the base of the hill. I can do more. You did everything.

You count the rings. Maybe no one will answer. Hello. Hi. Your hope that the Casualty Notification Officer has done his job is confirmed through the strained voice, rasped by years of crying. You want them to understand, to know. An elusive day defeated by pervasive night. Drawn shades.

Taking confession from a thousand-year-old E5. The hardest one, he says almost like a question. The one that stays with me, he pauses and takes another breath. The one that stays with me was an eleven-year-old boy who picked up his father's AK after I put him down. I hoped the kid wouldn't be able to fire it. There was nothing I could do differently. You pull him close, closer than you ever thought you could pull anyone. It's not your fault. It's not your fault.

Your shoulder swells with salt and quiet sobs as you hold one of the toughest men you know. He has lost a faithful friend, violently. There are no quiet or easy deaths. Only deaths, noble in our knowledge they did their best and gave all for their brother.

Loving an Iraqi platoon leader or Afghan leader as your brother. You have shared so much. Eyes filled with tears, he touches your chest and says, my friend, I love you my friend, as you board the aircraft for the last time.

Homecoming, harvest of the flooded plains, and the road.

The roar of families cheering for their soldier. Bright, handmade signs made in the backseat en route to the reception area. Fathers greeting their children. Some for the first time. A sense of uneasy relief. We expect the world as we left it, unchanged and familiar. The father and mother you never met before. Their son absent. His laughter will never fill their home again. Hands shake and you thank them for coming wondering if they hate you, resent you for not dying instead. As if it were that easy. Sometimes, you wish it were. At other times, you are thankful it is not you and hate yourself afterward. Again, the floor speckled with confetti, no measured design, a reckless windfall. The pieces we either ignore, frantically pile and gather, or recover periodically as we need them. Perhaps, still a tattered road map in a sense. In the end, balance.

The crisp, starched press of fabric carefully folded. A blue triangle of night with stars shining in formation. So heavy. An eight-year-old girl reaches for it. Your eyes meet and swell. Her hand briefly pressed on top of yours. A breeze carries the scent of freshly cut grass and vanilla soap. You salute. Her memories of her father will always be poured through the stained glass window of the words and sighs of her mother.

No. It is not as we would have imagined on that June day in 1999. We failed to see the road too clearly. Nonetheless, it found each of us, and we traveled it by the light of our NCOs and soldiers who taught us more than we could ever have hoped to teach them. All we have to do is listen. They will forever be my favorite people.

> In the desert
> I saw a creature, naked, bestial,
> Who, squatting upon the ground,
> Held his heart in his hands,
> And ate of it.
> I said, "Is it good, friend?"
> "It is bitter—bitter," he answered;
>
> "But I like it
> "Because it is bitter,
> "And because it is my heart."
>
> —"In the Desert" by Stephen Crane

"WALKING THE LAST MILE HOME"

Lay Phonexayphova

NEAR THE MEKONG RIVER BETWEEN
THE LAOS-THAILAND BORDER

The sounds of crickets chirped in the night and the slow, steady tides from the river touched the muddy embankment, as six small bodies of a mother, father, and four kids scurried west along an abandoned path that led them toward their freedom.

While my father stared into the night, intent on finding the right path for us, I gripped his firm, rough hands. My stomach was nearly empty. My legs were tired. Mile upon mile, we had walked most of the afternoon in silence. Feeling the heaviness in my legs, I looked across at my mother with half-open eyes, pleading for her to pick me up but knowing she could not since she carried my little brother, who was asleep in her arms. Her gentle eyes peered down at me, and she whispered in a hush, "Just walk one more mile, son."[1]

Keeping my word, I walked one more mile, then another, and another until we reached a predesignated location on the river's edge. My father had arranged for a canoe to taxi us across the Mekong River and, from there, we would make our journey to the refugee camps in Thailand. As we stepped into a small, wooden boat, I gripped its sides and, not knowing how to swim, I sat in the middle of it and became fixated on the notion that at any moment our little vessel would capsize.[2] I remember the cold water splashing onto my legs, quickly accumulating inside the boat's bottom, and a sinking feeling swirled inside me.

BAQUBAH, DIYALA PROVINCE, IRAQ

The same feeling swirled in my stomach after the Chinook, carrying my ten-man military training team, touched down on the pavement of FOB Gabe in Baqubah, Iraq. In the excitement of exiting the helicopter, my wedding ring slipped off my finger and rolled into the abyss. I frantically searched my pockets and every crease in my uniform and equipment to see if my precious ring would miraculously reappear, but no luck. It would never be seen again. Jenny was going to kill me, I thought. A month before, I had to say the usual tearful good-byes to her and our three-month-old son, leaving them in her hometown; and now, I would have to tell her that I had lost the very symbol of our commitment to one another. Although I knew she would eventually forgive me, I could not easily shake the feeling of unease as I began my second deployment to Iraq.

It was early March 2008, and Baqubah (like much of the country) was in transition.[3] During the 2007 troop surge operations, the city and its surrounding villages and towns had been the sites of some of the most violent sectarian killings and fighting between insurgents and Coalition Forces.[4] Once the team hit the ground, as the intelligence officer I worked hard to gather and filter out as much information about the area as possible so as to prepare the team for the worst. And from initial intelligence preparation we should have expected it, but I felt confident that our team could handle the challenge.

Similar to others, my transition team was a hodgepodge of six officers and four noncommissioned officers (NCOs) with differing experiences and skill sets and from diverse assignment histories.[5] Meeting three months before our deployment, we trained at Fort Riley, then at Camp Buehring, Kuwait. At one moment the cold and unforgiving wind of central Kansas battered our faces and, at another moment, Iraq's desert sand and oppressive heat welcomed us to the Middle East.

Despite the situation, we gelled together, as best as we could, and became a team. Given the size of our team and the risk associated with training Iraqi forces in remote outposts, we depended on each other. The threat of insurgent attacks loomed at every corner that we turned. There were reported incidents of ISF members, who were double agents for AQI, who would help or participate in attacking their military trainers.[6] We would operate hundreds of miles from other Coalition Security Forces, and if we got into trouble, we understood that no one would come to our rescue but the very person next to him. While we knew that we would get on each other's nerves and have the occasional blowups that men have when they live too close to one another, we realized that having a strong team bond was something that these squabbles could not weaken too easily. Though the Army brought us together, we worked to stay together as a team and trusted each other without exception.[7]

As is customary for military units, even for a ten-man team, we conducted a handover of equipment, responsibility, and information with the team we replaced. Though they were gracious enough to give us their rooms since (unbeknownst to us) they were leaving in a few days, they were not willing to share much else with us. They gave us a brief intelligence assessment of the city, conducted a couple of mounted patrols, and drove us across the guarded base to introduce us to our Iraqi battalion in the 5th Iraqi Division. In less than a week, every single member of their team had caught convoys back home.

A week later, we received orders to change our mission and to assume responsibility for training a newly formed Iraqi army battalion, located near the city's western outskirts in the town of Kanan.[8]

MEMORIES OF A FRIEND

While most members of the team had grumblings about having to travel to work, we all understood that this was part of the mission. I sat down that afternoon to read the significant events of the last week and to study our travel route to the IA's headquarters. Combing through a PowerPoint report, dated March 10, 2008, I immediately recognized a name on the slide: Torre Mallard. While leading a patrol near the area that my team would travel to the very next day, Torre's vehicle hit an improvised explosive device (IED), and he died from his wounds.

Memories of Torre's large smile, his wife at military balls, and their sons at a family barbecue flashed through my brain. Though he was two years ahead of me at West Point, we were in the same academic company and, when my unit relocated to Fort Hood, Torre joined the unit to wait his turn at commanding a cavalry troop in a time of war, the epitome of a young combat arms officer's career aspirations. It was a dream that would come true for him.[9] The last real conversation I had with Torre, strangely enough, was about how much we loved the smell of the arms room, because it reminded us that we were soldiers in the Army.

As I breathed in the dusty air of our team's makeshift operations center, I called Jenny to hear her kind voice. For almost an hour, with our infant son wrapped around her, she sacrificed sleep to talk to me about everything except for Torre's death—that conversation would wait.

Like many wives of deployed soldiers, Jenny has suffered the hardships of war. During my first deployment, she made friends with a group of wives whose husbands were in my regiment. They lived in the same neighborhood, hung out together, and were a source of strength for each other. Within a few months of the unit's return, a sniper killed our friend's husband and, on the same day, insurgents killed our next-door neighbor's husband.

Jenny would later describe to me the events that unfolded upon hearing the news. While in a conscious fog, she stumbled over to her friend's house. As she and another friend approached their home, another white van, full of soldiers in dress uniforms, circled the neighborhood to give their condolences to another family. My wife broke down in the middle of the sidewalk, while her friend held on to her. They sobbed together in the open. As my wife suffered the worst moments of her life, I was on my tank, perched on top of a hill, leading my platoon and preparing for Operation Restoring Rights in Tal Afar, Iraq. I had not spoken to her in almost a month. I didn't learn about that day until I redeployed.

"Good night, honey, have a good day. See you in a little bit," Jenny whispered to me when our son's screams abruptly ended our conversation. I said a quick prayer and thought, one more mile.

LIEUTENANT AMAR

After a slow ride along the winding highway to Kanan, my team arrived at our IA battalion and, as soon as we stepped out of our armored HMMWVs, a group of IA soldiers swarmed us. The unusual sight of a gray-haired, rotund man in tightly fitted camouflage caught my eyes. He looked like a bald Iraqi Santa Claus and, grinning from ear to ear, he presented himself as Lieutenant Colonel Hathem, the unit's battalion commander. After I introduced myself as the team's intelligence officer, he quickly grabbed my arm and led me into his headquarters, which was once a police station.

Entering the tiny, dark room, the musty air intermixed with sweaty bodies and mold to make the space feel even smaller. In the half-lit corner stood a lanky figure of a man with a pronounced smile on his face; he marched toward me with a soldier's purpose and greeted me with a warm (but manly) hug.[10] "Molazim Amar,"[11] he sharply announced to me. Then, Hathem pointed out in his excited baritone voice that Amar was my intelligence counterpart.

In a matter of seconds, Amar brought me a white plastic lawn chair to sit down in and a cup of steaming chai to sip. Instead of discussing the mission at hand, we talked about the most important things in our lives: our families. He told me about how much he loved his kids, wife, job, and country; the deaths of his brothers in the Iran-Iraq War; and his hope for the future, which was simply to have a better Iraq for his children.[12] Conversely, I talked about my family, my history, and the reasons why I was in the military. We formed an instant bond.

Within the first two weeks of training, Amar absorbed the basics of intelligence preparation of the battlefield. Using lessons learned from my first deployment, Amar and I created an information tip line for suspicious activities, distributed flyers throughout the town, and became teammates, running a small Iraqi intelligence section in a former prison cell converted into an office. At the same time, Amar taught me about the area: where the sectarian fault lines were, the names of tribal leaders, and suspected locations and activities of insurgents. I felt that by the end of the first month in Iraq I knew a good amount about our battlefield; moreover, I was optimistic about collaborating with and training our Iraqi battalion.

Inarguably, the battalion's most successful section was Amar's. At the latter half of the month, almost every time we came to train the battalion, using the tip line, Amar's team found new caches of weapons, artillery rounds, or other types of explosives. Also, there were always suspected insurgents in their holding cell, waiting to be questioned and processed through the Iraqi judicial system. Hathem gave him almost free reign to take action on intelligence. Hence, within minutes of receiving a tip, my counterpart formed and led assault teams to capture insurgents and to find caches. Amar was making Iraq a better place for his family.

THE DEATH OF A FRIEND

Sitting in front of me, sweating and wide-eyed, were two teenagers. They were no older than sixteen years old. With jet-black hair and peach fuzz on their tight upper lips, they stared at me with deep black eyes. They hated me, I affirmed. The smell of dirt, sweat, and blood on their clothes settled into my nose and caught me in stride when I walked closer to them. They had their hands zip tied behind their backs, and they appeared docile, almost innocent, in the corner of the room. However, two hours before, our IA unit raided their home and detained them for killing Lieutenant Amar.

Earlier that day, Amar had received a phone call from the tip line about a possible weapons cache in the southern villages of Muqdadiyah.[13] He grabbed a group of soldiers, loaded them in the back of pickup trucks, and raced off on Highway 5 to confirm or deny the report. Less than twenty minutes from the city, Amar's truck hit a command-wired IED, which flipped the vehicle upside down. While the IA reported to us that they pulled security around his vehicle after the blast, we later learned that Amar and another soldier died from gunshot wounds. This discrepancy in the story made me believe that the other vehicles left them when they were in contact.

It was a cloudless, bright day, and the sun momentarily blinded me as I walked out of the detention cell. I staggered over to our vehicle, sunk into my gunner's hatch, and gulped down a warm bottle of Gatorade. Amar was dead. I failed. A rush of guilt, anger, and confusion swirled inside of me. But as soon as those feelings appeared, for some reason, my thoughts returned to Jenny, to my son, to my parents, to West Point, and lastly to Amar's family. "One more mile," I whispered.

COMING HOME

Working with Hathem and Amar was the highlight of the deployment. In the next six months, my training team would be assigned and reassigned to four different IA units and then spend the last two months working with the Diyala Provincial Police Headquarters. With the constant changes in battle space and responsibilities, we were never able to build the same type of relationships and training successes as in the first two months. For the rest of the year, we banged our heads against the wall.

In February 2009, at last, the team prepared to redeploy. Before leaving Iraq and flying home to my family, I went to a memorial in the middle of FOB Warhorse. I read the names of soldiers who had died fighting in Diyala. Most of them were strangers, but there were those whose names and faces brought back memories of better times. Torre Mallard, Michael J. Medders,[14] and John Ryan Dennison.[15] And, in my mind, Lieutenant Amar. I stood there, thought about the greatness of their lives, ultimate sacrifices, and love for their families. I said a prayer, "Be thou at peace," and walked another mile toward home.[16]

IN GOD I TRUST

Jerry Eidson

W hile I knew Iraq was going to be completely different from my Jamaican honeymoon from the previous year, I had no idea how dissimilar the two places were actually going to be. I tried to prepare myself mentally for the upcoming deployment, but I knew that there is nothing that can prepare you for the true nature of combat. My First Sergeant even warned me in a private conversation before we left that our unit was going to lose many good soldiers. His understanding of war rested in years of experience and previous deployments. Unfortunately, my First Sergeant's outlook on the tour was very accurate; I never expected that eleven men from our company would make the ultimate sacrifice. Further, I could not have possibly imagined that one of those eleven men would be a West Point classmate. The greatest oversight, though, is that I never dreamed that spending only three months in combat would take such an emotional toll. Those three months in Iraq were hell. They had to be hell. What else could they be since God was nowhere in sight. At least, that was what I thought.

Bravo Company occupied an old potato processing plant in the southeast corner of Yusufiyah, Iraq, in late September of 2005. The factory previously housed a company of National Guard soldiers from Georgia. While it did offer few creature comforts, it was very lacking in defensive positions. Our primary mission in Yusufiyah was to disrupt the enemy by conducting presence patrols in the city and surrounding villages. Additionally, our company had the responsibility of overwatching the Jurf Kas Sukr Bridge (JSB) from an abandoned hydroelectric power plant that served as a remote patrol base. Located approximately ten miles from the potato factory, the mission at the JSB was to both guard the bridge and prevent movement across the Euphrates River. Second platoon, led by my classmate Ben Britt, was the first to cover the JSB while third platoon started patrolling Yusufiyah. My platoon began the deployment by improving the potato factory's defenses. Each platoon rotated between guarding the JSB, patrolling Yusufiyah, and defending the potato factory.

It didn't take long to make contact with the enemy. Shortly into the deployment, an IED severely injured the leader of third platoon during a dismounted patrol. He survived the attack but suffered permanent damage to his face and was immediately MEDEVAC'd[1] back to the United States. Days later, another IED completely destroyed a third platoon, M1151. My platoon served as a Quick Reaction Force[2] and met the disabled vehicle at the infamous intersection of Route Peggy and Route Sportster. Route Sportster was rightfully nicknamed "The Gauntlet." Multiple IED craters every one hundred meters confirmed the apt moniker. As we came around the corner onto Route Sportster, I could see through a rain-soaked windshield what was left of the vehicle, and I remember thinking, "This shit just got serious." From that day forward, the IEDs started getting bigger and bigger. It was as if our presence patrols stirred a hornet's nest.

While at the potato factory, we did our best to learn about our area during supply trips to the JSB and traveling Route Fat Boy[3] to the battalion TOC. During that time, we encountered IEDs almost daily, as did other elements in our battalion. On November 2, a massive IED struck the CSM's convoy. The blast claimed the lives of two Bravo soldiers: one from my platoon and one from Ben's. Needless to say, it was a very rough time for everyone. In the past, I turned to God to see me through hard times. But now, things seemed so bad that they were beyond His help. The following day, we left the potato factory and headed south for a month's rotation at the JSB.

The JSB's facilities were in better shape than the potato factory, but they still needed some work. Ben walked me around and gave a detailed description of his platoon's improvements of the living quarters and defensive positions. In addition, he took me to two manned checkpoints outside the compound for which we would also be responsible. One position overlooked an Armored Vehicle-Launched Bridge (AVLB)[4] that crossed a canal and connected the only route to the other checkpoint. We called the AVLB position "The Alamo" because our platoon could only spare a three-to-four-man team to man the position at any given time. All in all, it seemed as if our turn at the JSB would be a fairly easy month.

Our rotation at the JSB ended in late November. This meant that we would spend Thanksgiving huddled around our grill longing for the traditional feast. On the morning of Thanksgiving, I received a call over the radio from a military police (MP) unit. Their convoy was in our area to investigate a claim about a cemetery with unmarked graves. The MPs needed assistance locating the site on Route Caveman. Earlier in the month, my platoon was part of a route clearance mission down Route Caveman, so I knew the exact location of the cemetery. With no other missions on the docket for that day, I volunteered to jump in a truck and lead their convoy. The MP convoy commander agreed, but at the last minute I backed out. I can't say why I decided to opt out of the mission other than I had a bad feeling. Instead, I marked the location on the MPs' map and sent them on their way. Around lunchtime, we heard a huge explosion from the direction of Route Caveman. I radioed my commander to confirm that no platoons from our company were operating in that area and concluded that the MPs made contact. About an hour after the explosion, we received a call that the MPs hit an IED and needed support to recover their vehicle. My platoon sergeant and I grabbed a squad and made our way to their location. There was no mistaking which way we should go. Shortly after leaving the gate we could see a pillar of black smoke leading us to the site of the attack.

By that time in our deployment, we had witnessed multiple IED attacks and the various levels of destruction of which they were capable. The IED that hit the MPs on Thanksgiving was the worst that we ever saw. When we arrived on the scene, we were greeted with the gruesome sight of the remnants of an up-armored Humvee spilling black smoke into the sky. The burning vehicle lay on the opposite side of a canal running parallel to Route Caveman. A medic met us on the road and informed me that there were a total of five people in the vehicle—two of whom were missing. I gave my squad leader the task of finding the missing soldiers while my platoon sergeant, our medic, and I swam across the canal to verify the status of the driver.

I leaned over the driver trying to catch my breath from fighting the swift current in the canal. One of his legs was gone with a tourniquet wrapped tightly around the stump. My pulse was beating in my ears, but I didn't need to hear the medic to tell me that he was dead. His inert form and lifeless face told me everything I needed to hear. While lost in thought preparing the body for evacuation, the MEDEVAC helicopter landed one hundred meters from our position. As we transported the driver's remains to the helicopter, I remember surreally thinking, "This is the first dead body that I've ever seen." I wasn't quite sure how to process the scene, but it didn't matter—I didn't have time to reflect upon the incident.

After the MEDEVAC left, we swam back across the canal to look for the two missing personnel. In an explosion that big, I didn't expect there to be survivors, but miraculously, there were; the interpreter survived with a broken back and the gunner lived but lost both of her legs.[5] I also did not expect that one of the dead would not have a single scratch. We found the body of one of the missing passengers, an Iraqi colonel, sprawled along a ditch, and from the road we could see that he was completely nude without a scratch on him. My best guess is that the colonel died from the concussion of the IED rather than the bomb itself. It was strange to see the nude body lying in the ditch, but at the time, I didn't have time to reconcile the strange and horrific scene. We still had one more body to locate.

My squad leader solemnly followed a trail of body parts to the resting place of the convoy commander. When we pulled the soldier out of the weeds, the medic, who until that point had everything under control, broke down emotionally. The body of the convoy commander was in really bad shape, and as we waited for another body bag, a group of my men formed a wall around the soldier to keep the MPs from seeing their leader in such a condition. While they blocked the scene, the rest of us did the best we could to secure the remains inside a body bag.

We spent the rest of Thanksgiving cleaning up the site. We discovered more remains that had to be accounted for, and we also scraped the bottom of the canal recovering ammo and weapons. A general from the MP's parent division arrived with an EOD unit from the Navy, who estimated the IED to be approximately two thousand pounds. I still remember the smell of smoke and scorched flesh, and to this day I cannot spend Thanksgiving without replaying the day's events. That day also served as a turning point in my relationship with God. Standing there loading what was left of the convoy commander into the body bag, I cursed God and told myself that there was no way He could give a man life with the sole purpose of meeting such a brutal demise. I gave up hope in God that day. I wanted so badly to still believe, but all the evidence pointed me in the other direction. My platoon left the JSB at the end of November as different soldiers. Having faced the harsh realities of war, I feared that I would meet the same end. Instead of turning to God to provide support through these emotions, I handled them on my own and turned them into hatred.

Third platoon replaced us at the JSB, Ben's platoon moved to man the traffic control points at Peggy and Sportster, and we did as best we could to assume responsibilities in Yusufiyah. On December 10, we were gearing up to conduct a presence patrol in Yusufiyah when a call came in to the FOB that two soldiers from First Platoon were shot—SSG Travis Nelson and SGT Kenny Casica. Nelson was the squad leader in charge at a TCP down the road from Peggy and Sportster, and Casica was one of his team leaders. A trusted confidential informant opened fire on the checkpoint, shooting Casica in the neck and Nelson in the back of the head. When I heard the news of Nelson and Casica, I rushed to the aid station to see if I could help. Ben was there standing over Casica and was visually upset with the situation. Nelson, who served during Desert Storm, was a favorite of the entire company and a father figure to the young men of the unit, including Ben. Casica and Nelson were an unstoppable pair. I could tell that Ben wanted to help, but couldn't muster the emotional stability to do so. I took Ben's place and assured him that I would do what I could to help. Ben left the aid station, and the physician's assistant handed me Casica's I-V bag and told me to squeeze. I stood there and squeezed the fluid into Casica with all my might while Nelson lay on a table next to him in even worse shape. While standing there in the aid station, squeezing as hard as I could, I watched as Nelson and Casica passed away.

The entire company felt the loss of Nelson and Casica. Once again, I had the disheartening task of loading soldiers into a body bag, but this time it was different. I knew Nelson and Casica very well and admired them just as much as everyone else in the company. I became increasingly angry about the death of Nelson and Casica, and to me it was more proof that if God did exist, He was inept and didn't give a damn. The situation was also tough on Ben as he had to put his men back on the checkpoint where it all took place. I didn't get a chance to speak with Ben after seeing him in the aid station. In fact, I never had the chance to speak to Ben again. An IED killed him twelve days later.

On December 17, half of my platoon was tasked with pulling convoy security for dump trucks transporting gravel to the battalion FOB. The battalion commander wanted gravel displaced throughout his base, and he called on our company for support. The mission required just two squads, and since my platoon was on standby at the FOB, we had no choice but to accept the inglorious assignment. While half of my platoon escorted the gravel trucks, I led the remaining squads on presence patrols in Yusufiyah. After spending the evening of December 19 pulling a stuck M1114 out of a field, we called it quits and returned to the FOB. Shortly after returning, my commander called me into the TOC to inform me that the other half of my platoon was finished escorting the gravel trucks and needed to return to our FOB. The procedure in our area of operations mandated that all convoys consist of at least three vehicles. At the start of the mission, my platoon sergeant took two vehicles and jumped in a resupply convoy on the way to the battalion FOB. Now, he had only two trucks and was unable to secure his section's movement back to our base. Since we were not going on a mission and the route to the battalion FOB was cleared regularly, I felt that minimal disruption of my men's evening was worth the risk of only taking a total of nine soldiers, including myself.[6] I am proud to say that I had more than eight volunteers, but I chose the first bunch, loaded up a driver, gunner, and TC in each truck, and moved out.

We made regular trips to the battalion FOB in the past three months, so I knew the route like the back of my hand to include the rear entrance to the base that most convoys miss. Because of my understanding of the area and the fact that it was nighttime, I decided to put my vehicle in the front of the convoy. Along Route Fat Boy, there sat an abandoned Iraqi National Forces checkpoint that still housed a serpentine of concrete barriers in the road. It was a pain to get around, but the checkpoint served as a handrail for letting me know how far we were from the next turn. Passing the last barrier, my truck was just getting back up to cruising speed as we rounded a curve in the road. I traveled that road so many times by that point that I developed a sixth sense that pinged when something was out of place. As we came around the curve, I noticed a large, uprooted bush off to the left side of the road. Without time to react, I remember thinking, "That's not supposed to be there. I bet that's an IED." Then came a bright flash followed by an enormous explosion.

After the explosion, many things were going on inside that truck. I remember very explicitly the flash, the explosion, glass in my face and mouth, and the immense heat—all in that order. What I do not remember, however, is our vehicle launching off the road and tumbling into a canal. From my best guess, given that my Kevlar helmet was destroyed, I was hit with a piece of shrapnel and knocked unconscious. When I regained consciousness inside the vehicle, I could not see a thing. It was also eerily quiet given that we were just hit with a five-hundred-pound roadside bomb. As I sat there in the dark, I could tell that the truck was shifted sideways, and I could also hear the swish of water in the floorboard as I moved my legs to regain composure. My first instinct was to check on the status of my driver and gunner. I could hear the moans of PFC Ryan Davis coming from the gunner's position behind me, and I asked if he was okay. Davis said he was fine except that his leg hurt, but I could tell by the sound in his voice that nothing major was wrong. I then asked my driver, SPC Noah Galloway, about his condition. "Galloway, are you okay?" No response. "Noah? Noah? Are you okay?" No response. Only silence that brought with it a deep fear for the worst.

I tried to open my door, but it wouldn't budge. The only way out, then, was through the top of the truck by way of the gunner's hatch. I pushed past Davis and felt my way out into a cool breeze that granted some relief from the heat of the explosion still lingering inside the vehicle. Once outside, I could tell by the moonlight that we were off the road and about fifteen feet down in a canal. Still wondering about the status of Noah, I jumped off the top of the truck and landed in waist-deep water. I turned to face the vehicle and, due to its current angle, I was eye level with the bottom of the driver's side door. As I pulled out my flashlight to assess Noah's condition, I could see that the door was completely blown off and Noah was in really bad shape.

Nothing that I say can ever fully describe the carnage that my flashlight revealed. The entire left side of Noah's body was mangled, and it was impossible for me to properly assess his wounds due to the enormous amount of blood. Since I was eye level with the lower portion of the door opening, I was staring right at what was remaining of Noah's left leg, and I could not see much more. I kept scanning with my flashlight, frantically searching for any sign of life until I finally saw what I was looking for. Looking past the carnage and beneath all the blood, I saw Noah's Kevlar vest move up and down, up and down. Although erratic, the rhythm of Noah's vest sang a song of life and gave me hope that he might survive.

When I turned away from Noah, I expected to see my men coming to pull us out of the canal and evacuate us to the safety of the FOB. Instead, I was met again with that eerie silence that I awoke to moments earlier. I thought surely that the vehicles were parked up on the road while my squad leader was establishing security and my team leader prepared a group to come to our aid. They were waiting for me to pop my head out of the fifteen-foot ditch and point them in the right direction. Without hesitation, I scrambled up the slippery slope of the canal to meet the assumed-to-be waiting cavalry and lead the charge to safety. As I came over the top of the ditch, I found the source of that eerie silence. Nothing. Darkness. Not one vehicle. Not one soldier. Only darkness and silence. To say that I was scared would be an understatement of my true emotions. I was terrified. It was as if the darkness represented the imminent outcome of this horrible situation and blanketed the remaining hope that we would survive.

The noise of Ryan Davis following me out of the gunner's hatch broke the silence. I slid back down to his position, hopped on the truck, and helped him the rest of the way. Ryan's leg was still in pain, and upon examination I noticed a hole from a piece of shrapnel. Compared to Noah, the wound appeared very minor. I left Ryan and once again headed to the driver's side of the truck. I pulled my flashlight out and confirmed that Noah was still breathing.

By then I regained trust that whatever was keeping my two trucks from reaching my position was no longer a factor and they were waiting for me at the top of the hill. I climbed the slippery slope once again, only to be met with the same disappointing result. I could no longer hold back my emotions; I had two wounded soldiers in a vehicle fifteen feet down in a ditch. I had no weapon; it was lost in the explosion. I did not even have a helmet. Every soldier who has served in combat can tell you how helpless you feel without a helmet, much less your weapon. I remember thinking that I needed protection and I needed it quick. Ironically, I looked down at the edge of the road and found a helmet. As I reached down to pick it up with my left hand, I realized that my arm would not work. I came to find out that there was a bone protruding from my wrist that I could not see under the sleeve of my ACUs. I switched hands and picked up the helmet to find that it was badly chewed up and full of blood. It was Noah's. As I tossed it aside, it seemed as if I was tossing away my expectations for a rescue. My two trucks were still nowhere in sight, and I thought for sure that an enemy element was now moving in the darkness to ambush our position and take advantage of our vulnerability. It was at that moment that I expected to die.

At other times during the past three months, I had witnessed death and had come to grips with the fact that I could meet the same fate. For the sake of my men, though, I could not afford to dwell on such things. This time it was different. This was not some small IED that blew up outside our truck only for us to laugh about like we had so many times before. I was stuck in the moment for quite some time that night, and I knew for certain that I was about to die. I had time to think about what was to come in the next few moments. I even had time to picture how it was going to play out. The more and more I thought about it, the more and more I became fearful. I did not want to die. So in the middle of that road, under the darkness and silence of that night, I did something in which I had given up. I got down on my knees and I prayed.

It was a simple prayer confessing to God that I needed Him. Looking back it is clear that although I quit on God, He never gave up on me, which is how it always is. Despite my repeated efforts to curse and criticize Him, God remained strong as a warrior for my soul and did not turn His back. Not one second after I finished the prayer, I could hear in the distance the sweet roar of a diesel engine; my trucks returned. I flagged down the lead vehicle in the moonlight, and before coming to a stop, my squad leader SSG Leslie Fuller was out. I could tell by the confused look on his face that Fuller didn't understand where my vehicle laid to rest after the explosion. I pointed down the steep, slippery slope and told Fuller that Noah was stuck down there and was hurt badly. With six men left between the two trucks on the road, Fuller grabbed three additional men and headed for Noah. I stayed up top with two men manning the gunner's position in each truck and called back to my commander for a MEDEVAC. Four men trying to pull a soldier missing an arm and leg out of steep canal was not going to happen, and we needed more help. My commander ingenuously reminded me that I had taken the last vehicles from the FOB and there was no QRF available. His advice was to get to the battalion FOB any way that we could. I knew that was impossible. I briefly thought about running the final two to three miles to the battalion FOB to get help, but that just goes to show how desperate I was. While Fuller and his group worked hard to pull Noah up the ditch, I prayed again. I thought, "It worked once. Hopefully it will work again." It did. I prayed to God again and this time He sent a large convoy. Led by my classmate Ryan Ciovacco, the convoy consisted of three to four U.S. vehicles along with a truck of Iraqi National Forces soldiers. I met Ryan on the road, gave him a status report, and allowed him to take control of the situation. I radioed back to my commander that we would be en route to the FOB and to have a MEDEVAC on standby.

Noah survived the extraction from the ditch and was put in the lead vehicle. I followed behind in one of my trucks and met up with Noah at the same aid station where Nelson and Casica passed away. I'll never forget the look on the PA's face when I entered the room that night. I asked how Noah was doing, and his look was very uncertain. Like the others before, I prepared myself to load Noah into a body bag and once again push those emotions deep down inside. My train of thought, however, was interrupted by the MEDEVAC helicopter and the rush of the medics to get Noah on board. I was close behind them, and before getting onto the bird, my commander looked at me with tears in his eyes, and having no words to comfort, he gave me a hug. That was the last I saw of the potato factory and the final mission of my abbreviated military career.

While I still live with pain in my arm from the blast, the emotional injuries far outweigh the physical. When I came home, I searched long and hard for the reason I survived but so many others died. It wasn't fair that I never had the chance to say goodbye to Ben or to hear him call me "Dude" one last time. I also became depressed for leaving my men in combat after just three months, for in my mind, I was never the leader that I spent four years training to become. I often regret accepting a medical discharge a year later because my decision to do so deprived me of a career in the Army, something that I dreamed of since I was young. To deal with this, I turn to the life I have now and understand that coming home to my wife and children each day is something that I am thankful for and will never take for granted. I found peace in knowing that God is in control, and from that night in December, I learned to trust in Him. I can't explain why things happen the way they do, and it's not my job to do so. I can only rest on God's promises and remember that when we cannot trace God's hand in our lives, we must simply trust His heart. While my experiences in Iraq were a personal hell, it's clear now that God had His reasons.

ANGER

Anger is different from hate. While hate demands that we offer an equal and opposite malevolent action to right the scales of fate, anger offers us the chance of gleaning a cathartic moment from our past experiences and reconciling the future without doing additional harm to our surroundings. Arguably, it is the most basic of human emotions and operates on an infinitely complex and dynamic scale of magnitude. However, anger is an evanescent sensation and will only manifest itself as long as we deem its presence necessary to justify our next course of action.

HIER KANNST DU NUR KRIEG FUHREN (HERE YOU CAN ONLY WAGE WAR)[1]

Bradley R. Vance

I write this for my wife, Katie, daughter, Lillian, and son, Abrams: the reason I came home. I will never forget the great men behind these stories, especially those who gave their lives in places most will never understand. Vincit Amor Patriae.

The United States was not at war when I first entered West Point in the summer of 2000. September 11, 2001, the "Day of Fire," changed everything. The fighting that followed in Afghanistan, coupled with the invasion of Iraq in 2003, dissipated any doubt within the minds of combat arms officers that they would soon deploy to either Operation Enduring Freedom or Operation Iraqi Freedom. It was the Class of 2004s turn to, as Stephen Crane said, "see the elephant." Graduation couldn't come soon enough as Donald Rumsfeld addressed our class at graduation on a cloudy day in May of 2004.

In the years that followed, I deployed three times in support of Operation Iraq Freedom. My experiences in Iraq were a combination of rolling desert, urban jungle, and everything in between. I arrived to join the 2nd Brigade, First Cavalry Division in Baghdad, most of whom had already been deployed for eight months. Stepping off the back of the C-130 for the first time at Baghdad International Airport (BIAP), I saw nothing but the endless combination of destroyed Iraqi military bunkers and squatter villages. The air perpetually smelled of something burning, or the stench of fuel hung in the air. It seemed remarkably warm for December, and we jumped onto a five-ton truck for a ride over to our new Battalion CP. The Battalion Commander assigned me to a M1A2 Tank PL. I met my platoon for the first time in the motorpool at Camp Striker; my brand new uniform made me stand out from their battle-worn fatigues. They had tested their mettle in urban combat and were battle hardened by eight months of heavy fighting all across central Iraq. I glanced over at my M1A2 tank and the name stenciled in black spray paint on the bore evacuator of my tank's dust-coated main gun: "Blood and Guts." We patrolled the streets of Baghdad, and they were significantly different than what I had thought they would be—a large amalgamation of all-sized buildings, trash almost everywhere, and civilians who covered the streets, in tanks that, not surprisingly, provided a significant overmatch against dismounted insurgents.

Our battalion was reassigned in December 2004 to spend the remainder of the deployment at COP Dogwood in Anbar Province. COP Dogwood, which consisted of nothing more than some abandoned Iraqi army two-story buildings surrounded by a six-foot dirt berm, substantiated what I thought combat was—an austere living environment with a mission of finding and killing the enemy. Our mission became a combination of patrolling and COP force protection. The Euphrates River jetted through our AO, giving life to large palm groves and some fields near two vehicle bridges. As we overwatched the area, my driver remarked, "This would almost be a nice area if only it wasn't in this shithole."

Patrols found caches containing RPGs, IED-making materials, home-made explosives, and shoulder-fired weapons in small- to medium-sized villages. Daily, the enemy emplaced IEDs outside the COP or on main supply routes (MSRs) attempting to disable or destroy our vehicles. They also engaged our static security positions with small arms or RPGs. The first time I saw an RPG fly across the sky, it reminded me of a basketball on fire streaking above the horizon. My gunner grabbed me by the leg and yelled, "Maybe you want to get the hell down, sir!"

On January 25, 2005, our entire battalion conducted a screen line to prevent insurgents from entering Baghdad and disrupting the elections. Most were enroute to intimidate or conduct suicide attacks on election sites;

however, over two hundred were instead captured or destroyed by our battalion. After our relief in place (RIP), we began the long trip south to Kuwait, moving in company-sized convoys along MSR Tampa, the I-95 equivalent in Iraq. Crossing the Iraq/Kuwait border was a significant emotional event. Soldiers rejoiced, most huddled for a celebratory cigarette, and some even kissed the ground after surviving over fourteen months of intense combat. Flying home to Texas, we bused from Hood Army airfield to the Division Headquarters and reunited with friends and family on the parade field. The only thing I remember from the guest speaker was a concise yet fitting statement: "Well done; mission complete."

I was honored to receive a second platoon, this time with five HMMWV gun trucks and three Bradley Fighting Vehicles. After nineteen months back at Fort Hood, we redeployed back to Iraq. By 2006, Baghdad was flooded by sectarian violence, and a fledgling Iraqi army and police forces were nearly powerless to stop the violence. We arrived at the International Zone (IZ), or "Green Zone," which was almost too eccentric to describe. The IZ was a combination of U.S. FOBs, tall apartment buildings occupied by Saddam's flunkies, and shantytowns filled with squatting Iraqis. We stood in awe under the famous saber arches carved from the outline of Saddam's hands— this seemed to be the most famous photographed spot in the whole country. Watching Iraqis enter the Green Zone was similar to following the yellow brick road from the Wizard of Oz. People brought in everything—from Jack Daniels whiskey and livestock to AK-47s—to the "Emerald City."

The urban fight our squadron encountered in Baghdad was unlike anything for which we could have fully trained. We were caught in the middle of widespread sectarian violence. Sunnis and Shiites sequestered themselves into neighborhoods in Baghdad and attacked any outsiders on their turf. Our average patrols consisted of focusing on one section of a neighborhood and trying to talk with any local powerbrokers willing to speak with us. Most of the time, nobody wanted to be seen talking to us. The sectarian violence caused endless strife, and most Iraqis blamed the U.S. forces for being unable to stop it. Unfortunately, things only got worse in the spring of 2007 when the Secretary of Defense announced that all U.S. forces in Iraq and Afghanistan would be extended from twelve- to fifteen-month deployments. This was crippling to morale, painful for the families, and hard to explain as a leader. At the "one-year-deployed-mark," maintaining standards and discipline became increasingly difficult. I watched a soldier hold himself hostage because he wanted to go home, eventually shooting himself through the chest with a M9 pistol. In January 2008, after two consecutive Thanksgivings, Christmases, and New Years, our replacements from the 4th Infantry Division arrived at FOB Prosperity. After fifteen months of a long, hot, and complex deployment, our squadron arrived home at Fort Hood.

In 2008, after the completion of the Maneuver Captains Career Course at Fort Knox, the Army assigned my wife and me to Grafenwoehr, Germany. We didn't have time to savor most of the sites, as the 172nd Infantry Brigade was less than thirty days from deploying back to Iraq for OIF 08-10. I was assigned as the assistant operations officer in TF 2-28 Infantry, which was responsible for Babil and Karbala provinces. Just to the east of Anbar Province, Karbala Province was an endless rolling desert dotted with towns. Babil Province, located just south of Baghdad, contained the Babylon ruins, large- to medium-sized towns, and a few major highways. OIF 08-10 was inherently different than any other deployment to Iraq. The theme of every operation was to put the Iraqi Security Forces (ISF) in the lead. The highlight of this concept was the summer of 2009 transition of operations to the ISF, which included the Iraqi Army (IA) and the Iraqi Police (IP). They were to take the lead in all planning and execution of operations within the cities. While this was briefed on PowerPoint well, there was a significant gap in the capabilities of the ISF after the handover. Our battalion labored for the remainder of the deployment in an attempt to make the Iraqi military internalize their duties and responsibilities. By the end of twelve-month rotation, the IA was improving, and we greatly improved the performance and infrastructure of two IP academies in our area of operations. In November of 2009, we were replaced by the 3rd Infantry Division and arrived home in Germany to eagerly awaiting families.

By mid-2010, a deployment to Afghanistan was imminent, yet unannounced. By October this became reality, causing the modularization of my tank company into a rifle infantry company. Tankers, scouts, and infantryman comprised the new team as we prepared for the yearlong turn to Afghanistan. We happily removed in mostly ineffective Army Combat

Uniforms and replaced it with OCP, or commonly known as Multicam. Arriving at Bagram Air Field (BAF) was like being in a small city surrounded by vast mountain ranges. Apart from the occasional indirect fire, it is a place far removed from actual combat and occupied by a plush accoutrement full of large DFACs and coffee shops. It took about seven days to arrive by helicopter at COP Tillman. Established in 2005, it was named in honor of Pat Tillman, who became famous in 2002 for leaving a lucrative NFL contract to join the U.S. Army Rangers but was tragically killed by friendly fire on April 22, 2004. I stepped off the helicopter and surveyed the jagged mountain ranges that surrounded me on all sides. The temperature was 107°, and someone had spray painted the altitude of 7,100 feet on the side of a HESCO bag. Immediately, the altitude combined with the heat was overwhelming, and breathing became a difficult task. I glanced toward the East, assessing the terrain between the COP and Pakistan (PAK). Like most of East Paktika province, I saw dominating mountain ranges spilling down from the Hindu Kush and undulating wadis rolling through the uneven base terrain. COP Tillman had the dubious honor of being the closest U.S. forces to the border of PAK at a little less than three kilometers to the "zero line." We lived and slept easily within the indirect fire range of our enemy, which could fire with near impunity from the PAK side of the border.

I glanced over toward a vehicle that looked as if it used to be a HMMWV—the doors, rear, and most of the major components had been removed—and this was my first indication that vehicles weren't much good in this neighborhood. A lieutenant from Dog Company, 2/506 PIR, called in my direction, "You the incoming commander?"

"Roger," I replied.

"Welcome to Rocket City, hop in."

A short time later came my first of many foot movements between Tillman to OP1, a permanent observation post that sat on the high ground to the east of the COP. I trailed behind the company XO, who moved with the speed of a deer as he trekked the beaten earth toward the OP. Halfway up the 60° incline, I took a knee. Breathing heavy, it felt as if I was sucker punched. The hot temperatures and increased elevation seemed to make me work twice as hard to draw a breath. "This is going to be a long freaking year," I cursed to myself as I arrived last at OP1. A soldier manning a M2 .50 caliber machine gun smiled in my direction and quipped, "Welcome to Afghanistan, republic of sir." I stood next to him and gazed at the view below. My first thought was this would be a beautiful country if only it weren't Afghanistan. The geographic embedding of Tillman became instantly obvious; without this COP, the Taliban could move vehicle after vehicle full of weapons and insurgents from PAK unopposed. I must have gotten lost in the scenery because I heard another soldier flatly offer this advice: "If you like your head where it is, don't stand up too long. Snipers know we are here." About ten days later, the last of the Screaming Eagles departed the Tillman LZ for the last time. As I bid farewell to the departing company commander, I noticed the Pat Tillman memorial sign. A sun-scorched, well-worn picture of Pat Tillman solemnly stood watch over the area. Surrounding Tillman's somber photo were the unit patches of those who had come before us—Special Forces, the 173rd Airborne, 10th Mountain Division, and more. Now it was our turn: the former Tank Company turned Rifle Infantry Company had to "move the football" further down the field in order to defeat an insurgency.

The first and most critical move was to understand the environment and the enemy. The locals mostly support the Taliban, either actively or as a result of intimidation. If we left the COP during the day, usually within a few hours the Taliban were within direct observation of our movements. The fall "fighting season" was in full force by the time we arrived in the country. As we entered the month of August, the company slowly began venturing further out from Tillman on foot, encountering the local tribal leaders and small villages. Every operation was dismounted, except for recovering supplies dropped by the Air Force. It was difficult to target our platoons when we walked countless directions over different approach routes to avoid dismounted IEDs. In short, we walked everywhere; this wasn't an easy task as the mountains of eastern Afghanistan are steep, rigid, and unforgiving. The only trees in the area are bare and sit along the rocky slopes of the sun-scorched mountain ranges. My first key leader engagement (KLE) in the small town of Zhangi reaffirmed what I had read about this country. This part of Afghanistan was mired somewhere in the seventeenth century in culture and existence. There are no paved roads, cell phone towers, Internet service, and very few running civilian vehicles. The literacy rate is estimated at somewhere around 10 percent, the nearest hospital is forty-five kilometers away, and anyone looking for a sense of Afghan national pride might as well look on the moon. The majority of people don't even know they live in Afghanistan—being a Muslim and a Waziri tribesman is paramount to being an Afghan.

Enemy contact with the Taliban came in all forms. But COP Tillman earned its unfortunate reputation of being called "Rocket City." The 107 mm rockets or mortars fall almost daily on infrastructure, vehicles, and sometimes personnel. During my second week at the COP, the Taliban launched a rocket that could best be described as a "one in a million shot"; the round landed in the doorframe of the DFAC that belonging to the private Afghan security company that provided a guard force for the COP. Three Afghans were killed instantly by shrapnel, and seventeen others sustained wounds requiring MEDEVAC. The first time I met their commander, a man named Sarwa, he was kneeling silently over his three dead soldiers. Without standing up, he quietly told the interpreter next to me, "I would shake your hand, but I am covered in their blood." On patrol, contact was generally small teams of insurgents attempting to place effective small arms fire (SAF), RPGs, or mortars on our dismounted forces. After one such engagement, I heard a soldier joke, "Afghanistan is like the luge; lie flat and try not to die." In September 2011, I was honored to award most of my soldiers their first combat patch on the ten-year anniversary of the 9/11 attacks. As we stood on top of the OP at approximately 7,500 feet, I never felt prouder of my soldiers and what they had accomplished. The enemy reminded us that they remembered 9/11 as well; we received thirteen effective rockets on the COP in the span of a few hours.

The fall fighting season never seemed to end. One morning, First Sergeant John Orbe and I were walking up to the HLZ to meet the battalion commander. We walked out of the inner gate and started up the sun-scorched ground that resembled a dirt road that led toward the landing zone. I suddenly stopped dead in my tracks—I heard a high-pitched whistle noise coming from the east.

Three seconds. I turned and yelled, "Incoming!" over my shoulder to the soldiers manning the inner gate.

Two seconds. The First Sergeant echoes the same warning as we both simultaneously dive to the ground.

One second. No cover here at all, just dirt and mud. "Maybe today is the day," I think to myself. The whistle now sounds like a jet engine screaming toward us. With a thunderous clap, the round strikes the ground forty meters away from us near the HLZ, kicking up rocks, dirt, and cutting a few HESCO bags into shreds. I was wrong—it was not "my day."

In October, our third major air assault operation was to conduct a direct attack against one of the historic firing points that constantly launched effective rockets into the COP. As we waited on the LZ for a ride in the "school bus in the sky," the CH-47 Chinook, I couldn't help but survey my soldiers as they waited for the mission. Some smoked, some slept, and some just stared off into the darkness. Radios crackled, and the metallic clicks from soldiers checking their weapons occasionally broke the silence of the night. The aircraft touched down onto the HLZ, spraying its awaiting passengers with dust and gravel. Shortly after we were airborne headed north toward OP4. Anticipation builds as the Chinook crew chief yells, "Thirty seconds to wheels down!" The wheels come down hard on the Afghan rocks, NODs flip on, and soldiers shuffle their way out of the aircraft and establish a hasty perimeter near the rear of the aircraft. All in now, no going back.

As the aircraft depart, I glance up at the mountain we must crest to put eyes on OP4—it never seems to end in the blackness of the night. Affectionately, this menacing mountain is known as Big Nasty. The darkness is silent as a slow approach to the objective begins save for the occasional profanity that follows someone busting his ass as we ascend the mountain. Tension builds as we crest the ridgeline, and everyone quietly wonders what is waiting for us near the top. There it is, finally—OP4. It is hard to identify at first, but finally the remnants of bunkers and friendly-fighting positions appear in our NODs. We reoccupy the position for the first time in years, and just as dawn breaks we are dug in for the Taliban attack that is sure to come—we just set up camp in the enemy's front yard. We are 450 meters to the border of Pakistan. To my west on top of Big Nasty is Lieutenant Justin Lujan's White Platoon set in with their machine guns scanning from the high ground. I scan toward the south and make out COP Tillman with a naked eye. OP4 is a historic hotspot to engage the COP with mortars and 107 mm rockets. The close proximity to the border allows the enemy to quickly escape the launch site and return to the safety of the Pakistan side of the border. Right before dusk, Lieutenant Andrew Brundson, the platoon leader of Blue Platoon, is south of our location in an OP when he breaks squelch on the radio.

"Pain 6 this is Blue 6, my terp is picking up a lot of chatter on his radio. I don't know what it is, but it sounds fucking close."

Just after dusk, I am crouching toward my Fire Support Officer, Lieutenant Chris Shaffer, to discuss our fires plan for withdrawal. As I near him, I hear the unmistakable zip of a small arms round cutting through the air. The radio screams to life in my ear.

"Contact, contact east of the OP. Small arms fire . . . holy shit!"

The horizon erupts with enemy tracers, and the volume of fire increased instantly. My first thought is we're gonna be OK, we have relatively good cover and own the high ground. Seconds later an enemy mortar round lands approximately ten feet from me and my RTO. I stand up to identify the heavy weapons engaging us. A RPG screams to life from the low ground, striking some rocks to my left and knocking me and another soldier to the ground. Before I can ask him if he is OK, he is rapidly returning fire with a M249, screaming "Fuck you!" at the top of his lungs between machine gun bursts. I return fire with my M4, attempting to hit anything in the low ground with a muzzle flash. I notice movement thirty meters to my northeast. Whether is it enemy or shadows moving, it is worth the grenade to find out as I pull the pin and throw it as hard as I can toward the location.

"Chris, give me something!" I yell toward my FSO.

"Rounds on the way right now," he screams back, mostly inaudible because of the gunfire.

With the cacophony of small arms and mortars exploding, it is hard to pinpoint whether the fire is coming from the low or ground direct across from us. There is a Pakistan Military (PAKMIL) checkpoint on the high ground. Not surprisingly, rounds are coming at us from all elevations.

"White 6, Pain 6, confirm that you identify fire from all locations to our east," I yell into my handmike. No answer. Someone gets on the net and yells, "The fire is coming from everywhere!"

I didn't take me to tell anyone to fire back. Soldiers are firing back with everything from machine guns to M203 grenades. The unmistakable sounds of rocket-propelled grenades (RPGs) cut the air, impacting on old sandbags and against rocks. PEQ-15 lasers from U.S. weapons look like something out of a light show, scanning the horizon and placing a bright beam on any static muzzle flashes. Suddenly, as if we had an angel on our shoulders, friendly artillery strikes the earth, creating a brilliant flash between us and the enemy.

I suddenly realize that the best weapon I have for this fight is not a rifle, but a radio. I call the Task Force Commander, Black Lion 6, who is already pushing close air support (CAS) to our location. No one in the TOC seems to care about the arbitrary border between PAK and Afghanistan at the moment. The intensity of the fire begins to subside after approximately ten minutes, which I swear felt like an hour. Black Lion 6 clears two F-16s, and about twenty seconds later, something that sounds like thunder begins to streak from the sky. Two five-hundred-pound guided bombs land perfectly on the enemy's locations; the flash and explosion are brilliant to watch in the green glow of night vision goggles. The combination of Chris Shaffer's artillery strikes and the Navy's fine work from the sky causes the enemy to swiftly disengage and move back further east into PAK. Despite a few "pot shots" from the retreating enemy, the night suddenly becomes eerily quiet. Soldiers survey the area around them—brass shell casings cover the floor, and the ground is still smoldering from enemy munitions. A few soldiers discover holes in their rucksacks and equipment from enemy fire. The movement to the pickup zone (PZ) goes smoothly—the enemy doesn't have the combat power to follow us at the moment. The flight back to Tillman seems to last forever. In the pitch black, we stand up after the wheels touch down in the gravel of the LZ. I disembark the aircraft and sit heavily against the side of an old HESCO bag. I light up a cigar I was saving for a special occasion and stare off into the distance. Quietly, I thank God that no soldiers were killed in the most intense firefight of my life.

In mid-November, a decision at an upper-echelon forced the first mounted convoy to approach Tillman in over two years. The last operation was plagued by ambushes, broken down vehicles, and unfortunately two soldiers killed in action by a deep-buried IED. Our role in the battalion operation was to occupy the high ground and provide overwatch as a forty-vehicle convoy slugged its way to Tillman from FOB Orgun-E, the location of the Battalion HQs. With only our luck, the operation occurred in a four-day window, with Thanksgiving Day falling right in the middle. We stepped off from the COP, each soldier carrying upward of eighty to one hundred pounds of normal equipment plus cold weather gear for the cold nights ahead. The march through the night was grueling; just as the sun was coming up, Red Platoon and I arrived at the top of the rigid mountain, and we dug in for an overwatch mission. I glance at my GPS: 8,149 feet elevation. White Platoon occupied a mountaintop to our east, allowing them a similar overwatch of the route. Staring back at us is Steyr Gayan Valley, easily the most heavily Taliban-populated area in our battlespace. The convoy passed through our locations with less contact than expected; however, we and the enemy knew that they had to come back the exact same route. As the vehicles were one hour away from our location, the Taliban engaged both Red and White platoon locations with small arms fire and RPGs. I sat near a sheer cliff, surveying the valley with binoculars. The unmistakable sound of small arms fire opened up to our northeast. White Platoon, who is closer to Steyr Gayan, receives the blunt of the attack. A small enemy team attempts to probe Red Platoon, but it prematurely begins firing approximately one hundred meters from the perimeter.

After the intensity of OP4, the task force commander was ready for this likely enemy attack as we were in a fixed location tied to a route. He unleashed the 155 mm howitzers from FOB Orgun-E in conjunction with 105 mms from Tillman against the enemy dismounts. Over a hundred artillery rounds slapped against the mountainsides and created a deadly combination of flying shrapnel and rocks. As the enemy tapered off, two F-16s and a B-1 bomber came on station to finish the job. In conjunction with the artillery, five-hundred-pound GBUs (guided bomb units) rained down from ten thousand feet in the sky. The sound was so loud that it was almost deafening. The only way to distinguish the artillery from the aircraft strikes was by the height of the exploding ordnance as it struck the earth. The coup de grace arrived in the form of AH-64 Apache aircraft that engaged the last of the fleeing enemy as they limped back into Steyr Gayan valley. There is something to be said for the expenditure of ammunition—it works. My RTO remarked, "Damn sir, I thought you were joking when you said we had to fight for our Thanksgiving meal this year!" After four long days, we collapsed our positions and began our foot movement back to Tillman. Even with the high spirits, the move was taxing—the last mile to the COP may have been the hardest physical task I have ever accomplished. Exhausted, we crossed the gate and collapsed against HESCO bags. Red PL, Lieutenant Chris Gehrels, came over and proudly announced, "Fifty-four!"

"What the hell do you mean?" I asked him.

"I had my GPS running from when we stepped off—we just walked fifty-four total kilometers."

Our dining facility was small, serving only one hot meal a day. Still, our austere Thanksgiving dinner of 2011 is still one of the best I have ever eaten.

"ECONOMY OF FORCE"

My View of Hell from Deep within the "Triangle of Death," Kargouli Village, Iraq, 2007

Doug Livermore

In the period following the invasion of 2003, Kargouli Village[1] served as a major conduit and safe haven for Sunni insurgents and their materiel traveling to and from Baghdad. However, even within the insurgency, there were three main groups that vied for control of Kargouli Village. Jaysh-al-Islami ("Army of Islam") was the smallest group, comprised almost exclusively of members of the minority al-Janabi tribe and maintained closer ties with the al-Janabis in Rushdi Mullah. Next was the 1920 Revolutionary Brigade, which was mostly a secular and nationalist insurgent group that took its name from the 1920 Iraqi revolution against the occupying British.[2] And finally, the most radical insurgent group in Kargouli Village was al-Qaeda in Iraq.[3] While al-Qaeda did not possess the greatest number of fighters, their ruthlessness and resources allowed them to heavily influence the insurgency in Kargouli Village and throughout our area of operations. These groups would alternate between fighting each other and occasionally cooperating to attack Coalition forces.

The population of Kargouli Village maintained a deep-seated loyalty to Saddam Hussein specifically and the Ba'ath Party in general. Homogeneously Sunni, there were no competing sects to complicate the human terrain, and the only real conflicts seemed to come from tribal influences. Prior to the arrival of the 2nd Brigade Combat Team, 10th Mountain Division in

August of 2006, there had been no attempt to permanently place Coalition troops inside Kargouli Village to disrupt local insurgent operations. The 2nd Brigade, 101st Airborne Division had previously been responsible for the area, but had succeeded only in constructing and occupying positions around the periphery of the village in an attempt to contain the effects. The 2/101 division had many competing objectives during their tenure, and their inability to occupy Kargouli Village was more an indication of how thinly spread they were than a criticism of their efforts. Unfortunately, the event that most marred the reputation of 2/101 and set in motion events that would terribly impact both them and us occurred on March 12, 2006. On that night, soldiers from 2/101 raped a fourteen-year-old girl and murdered her family just south of Yusufiyah,[4] providing the rallying cry and excuse that the insurgents used to justify many of their future atrocities.

On June 20, 2006, insurgents captured two soldiers from 2/101 from one of those battle positions (BP) located on the periphery of Kargouli Village. Generally, battle positions are fortified locations designed to control some piece of terrain and deny its use to the enemy. Unfortunately, the battle position then occupied by the 2/101 soldiers was very vulnerable. The soldiers were dragged all the way up the main road of the village (identified by Coalition forces as Route Malibu), until they reached the Yusufiyah Thermal Power Plant. There, the insurgents continued to mutilate the bodies before finally booby-trapping them and leaving them for Coalition forces to find. The insurgents claimed the March 12 rape as justification for the attack. With the exception of short duration searches, usually inserted by air assault, no Coalition forces dared to venture up Route Malibu into Kargouli Village. When we arrived in Iraq to replace 2/101 in August of 2006, we were told in no uncertain terms to stay out of Kargouli Village and remain always on our guard whenever we operated around that area. The village was described as a veritable "Heart of Darkness" into which no sane man would dare travel, much less attempt to subdue. Of course, being the "new guys" on the block, we naively took these warnings as a challenge that drove us forward on a great quest to succeed where others had failed. No one, neither the previous unit nor the insurgents themselves, was going to tell us where we could or could not tread in our own area of responsibility.

From August to early November in 2006, I served as the Assistant Battalion Operations Officer and was intimately involved in our battalion's efforts to first move from Mahmudiyah to Yusufiyah and then make our rapid expansion throughout the greater Yusufiyah area. With breathtaking speed our Companies thrust out from Yusufiyah in all directions to establish patrol bases throughout the area, using lightning-quick air assaults followed by with rapid ground clearances to bring in the materiels to build our forts deeper and deeper into "Indian Country." However, Kargouli Village still remained outside our grasp for the first few months. In November, I participated in both the planning and execution of our first probing raid into Kargouli. We assaulted into the village aboard helicopters from the famed 3-227 Aviation Regiment, the same unit that carried LTC Hal Moore and 1-7 Cavalry Regiment into the Ia Drang over four decades previously. In a postmission press release that I now only barely remember, I said, "We were air assaulting into an isolated and alien environment, far from possible help from our comrades. We had to rely on each other and our training to accomplish the mission and get everyone home."[5] And we did accomplish the mission, patrolling a large swath of Kargouli and conducting valuable reconnaissance before departing a couple of days later. Armed with the intelligence we gathered during that mission, we planned for the occupation of Kargouli Village and the establishment of the first permanent U.S. presence. Summarizing the intent of this occupation, I was told that Delta Company would conduct an "economy of force" mission in Kargouli Village, blocking the flow of fighters and weapons across the Euphrates and providing relief for the other companies trying to pacify the larger villages nearer to Yusufiyah. The people of Kargouli Village were too hostile and Delta Company too small to ever hope to make an immediate impact toward bringing the Village "into the fold" of Baghdad's legitimate authority, but our presence there would disrupt the ability of the insurgents to continue operating in areas where there was a more significant Coalition presence.

After serving on the battalion staff, I was assigned as the executive officer for D Company, 4th Battalion, 31st Infantry Regiment. The Company was, at that time, responsible for a handful of battle positions and a patrol base in an area several kilometers south of the town of Yusufiyah. In that month, D/4-31 IN moved from Patrol Base Jufr-al-Sukr Bridge to Patrol Base (PB) Bataan, which D/4-31 IN established in the nearby (and completely inoperative) water treatment facility. Patrol Base Jufr-al-Sukr Bridge was transitioned over to the 4/4/6 Iraqi Army Battalion, and the Iraqis assumed full control of the bridge barricades that controlled all traffic across the Euphrates River. Immediately, the battalion began building up the facilities (such as fuel and food storage, maintenance facilities, and living quarters) to support the requirements of the Company. To protect the northern perimeter of the patrol base, the company permanently positioned vehicles near the same spot on Route Malibu from which the 2/101 soldiers were kidnapped. From this position, our soldiers could see a few hundred meters down the road, but the claustrophobic effect of the surrounding jungle forced them to remain constantly vigilant for possible insurgent attacks. No one wanted to suffer the fate of our predecessors who were dragged from their vehicles in the middle of the night and horribly tortured by insurgents before being executed.

Recognizing the importance of Kargouli Village as both an insurgent safe haven and resupply route, the battalion drafted plans to move D/4-31 IN into the village in mid-November 2006. In the third week of November, D/4-31 established Battle Position (BP) 151 approximately three kilometers west of the PB Bataan stationary vehicle observation point (by then renamed BP 154), effectively installing the first permanent U.S. presence in Kargouli Village. Insurgents engaged BP 151 with mortar, rocket, RPG, and small arms fire from multiple directions on a daily basis for the first month of U.S. occupation. The heaviest fire, consisting of rockets, mortars, and rained heavy machine gun fire, originated from insurgent fighting positions on the other side of the Euphrates. Our soldiers would constantly shift between defending their position and improving their position's defensive capabilities.[6] The Company conducted a series of operations in December to clear north along Route Malibu, which established one more battle position (Battle Position 152) and PB Inchon in Kargouli Village. Delta Company handed PB Bataan over to A/2-5 Cavalry, a company attached to our battalion and equipped with both Bradley Fighting Vehicles and Abrams tanks.

Our area was hotly contested, as insurgents attacked patrols with a mix of antivehicle and antipersonnel improvised explosive devices, small arms, mortars, and rockets on a daily basis. For a few weeks, insurgents struck Inchon nearly every day at dawn with very precise mortar fire. These attacks decreased after a few weeks in both accuracy and frequency after snipers from our battalion scout section found and killed the mortar team's spotter shortly before their "scheduled" attack. As a heavy weapon unit, Delta Company had significantly fewer soldiers than a standard infantry company, giving us just enough people to patrol Route Malibu and maintain the battle positions. On December 23, an IED struck a resupply convoy in which I was traveling along this route, killing SPC Charles Norris and permanently affecting our control of the route. Without control of Malibu there was no way to either reinforce or resupply Inchon.

The insurgents in Kargouli Village continuously tested our positions and patrols throughout the month of January 2007. These well-coordinated attacks killed multiple soldiers and damaged or destroyed multiple vehicles. The IEDs used in these attacks were devilishly simple affairs using mortar and artillery rounds initiated by the use of a simple electrical wire delivering a strong charge directly to the detonator. On December 27, a dismounted patrol clearing Route Malibu was struck by such a device, most likely costing of several mortar rounds suspended at chest level among the thick foliage initiated by a nearby pressure plate.[7] The blast mortally wounded SGT Christopher Messer and PFC Nathaniel Given. Both died before the rescue helicopter could reach them. In many ways, we wished that the insurgents would come out and face us in the open, en masse, as they had during November and December.

As if hearing our naïve prayers, the insurgents massed their efforts in a simultaneous coordinated attack against a U.S. patrol and PB Inchon on the twenty-fourth of January. The insurgents ambushed 4th Platoon while they were traveling south along Route Malibu, approximately eight hundred meters south of the Inchon. All four vehicles in the patrol were disabled, and three soldiers were wounded, although 4th Platoon managed to counterattack and repel the enemy ambush. At the same time, insurgents engaged Patrol Base Inchon from three different directions, again using machine gun, RPG, and mortar fire with deadly precision. Luckily, a suicide truck bomb approaching along Route Malibu from the north was engaged and detonated before it could cause serious damage. After almost thirty minutes of sustained contact, the insurgents broke off their attack and the company began the long and difficult task of recovering the destroyed vehicles and wounded men back to Inchon and the FOB Yusufiyah.

IED attacks began to decline toward the end of January, as the colder, damp weather coupled with our increased patrolling discouraged the insurgents from launching any major attacks. In early February, CPT Jamoles relinquished command to CPT Gilbreth, who then departed on his midtour leave. This left me as the acting commander for the majority of the month and, as many very junior (and inexperienced) officers are wont to do, I made every attempt to "win the war" in Kargouli Village before CPT Gilbreth returned. While we lacked the strength to actually clear or hold any terrain, we planned and executed ambushes and raids almost nightly. If there wasn't a planned target for the evening, then I was out with a patrol laying in ambush or beating the bushes to find insurgent supplies. Our efforts paid off, as Delta Company recovered sizeable caches of munitions while driving the major insurgent leaders deeper underground as we killed or captured a number of their underlings. Several insurgent attacks yielded casualties and destroyed vehicles, but each attack consisted of smaller and smaller quantities of munitions. The larger plan to relieve pressure on the other companies by employing Delta Company as an "economy of force" effort in Kargouli Village certainly seemed to be paying off as attacks throughout our battalion area of operations declined considerably.

However, by the end of March, Delta Company had no more than two of the four required vehicles per platoon. We were competing with the other companies for priority of the very few replacement vehicles that arrived to our battalion at an agonizing pace. Only by constantly juggling functional vehicles between platoons and spending every free moment in the maintenance bay were we even able to keep the Company operational. The strain on men and vehicles was considerable. While progress was gradually achieved, the constant strain and tension of combat, combined with the unceasing requirement to literally bend steel and vehicles back into operational condition, ground down the morale and energy of us all. By far my greatest challenge was keeping up the morale of the men as whispers grew into grumbles that grew into outright conversations accusing the battalion of haphazardly casting us into Kargouli-like sacrificial lambs.

Our offensive efforts to root out suspected insurgents and seize their supplies helped morale greatly, giving us an opportunity to "take the fight to the enemy" versus simply waiting to be attacked. At an intellectual level, the battalion's "grand strategy" of using Delta Company to disrupt insurgent efforts in Kargouli Village, thereby relieving pressure on the rest of the battalion, made perfect sense. Indeed, our sister companies were making huge advances in their respective areas, spreading the rule of governance and gradually handing over security operations to partnered Iraqi army and police units. Our offensive focus kept us going while operating in the mud and blood of Kargouli, crawling through rice paddies and tropical forests fighting an elusive enemy that preferred to ambush and leave explosive booby-traps. Faced with the near-inevitability of being attacked each day, in which death or dismemberment seemed randomly probable, the only reliable motivation that I found to leave the relative safety of Inchon on each patrol was to tell myself that we were taking the fight to the enemy.

The cool, calm, predawn darkness along Malibu was shattered right before five on the morning of May 12. Soldiers at Inchon heard heavy small arms fire rattling and multiple explosions coming from the vicinity of our 1st Platoon, then manning a static patrol located on Route Malibu approximately one thousand meters south of Patrol Base Inchon. The reaction force encountered multiple IEDs just a few hundred meters outside the patrol base, forcing them to dismount and continue on foot for almost a half kilometer to reach the location of the stricken patrol. Encountering this delay, the Company mustered a second force from BP 152, south of the attack, but they also found IEDs and had to continue on foot for the last five hundred meters. Both elements arrived at the scene of the attack at roughly the same time and found that insurgents had overrun their comrades' position. The two Humvees were burning fiercely in the middle of the road while the onboard ammunition exploded randomly from the heat. Eventually, once the fires died down, the patrols determined that there were four dead U.S. soldiers, one dead Iraqi soldier, and three U.S. soldiers missing.

Within the hour, I flew from Yusufiyah with the battalion scouts directly to PB Inchon. I reported to CPT Gilbreth for an update on the situation and then immediately moved with the scouts to the attack site to assist with the ongoing search of the immediate area. SFC James Connell, SGT Anthony Schober, PFC Christopher Murphy, PFC Daniel Courneya, and Jundi Salah Mahad Azeus were presumed killed (and later confirmed through DNA testing of the bodies), and SPC Alex Jimenez, PFC Joseph Anzack, and PVT Byron Fouty were missing. The only indicator of where the insurgents had fled was two bloody drag trails that left the area heading east down an unimproved dirt road. We knew that three of our brothers were missing and that time was of the essence. Thoughts of the brutal executions meted out by the insurgents to the captured 2/101 soldiers shortly after their own capture drove us forward.

Our other patrols searched the village for our missing comrades. Every military-aged male we could get our hands on was detained on the off chance that they could provide a crucial piece of information that would allow us to save our comrades. These detainees were shuttled back to Patrol Base Inchon for further questioning. In the late afternoon, with the trail cold and all the military-aged males we could find already detained and being questioned, I returned to Patrol Base Inchon with the scouts to report to CPT Gilbreth and coordinate additional support for the massive operation that was already beginning.

Kargouli Village was divided up into several zones, and our platoons received orders to clear each one of them. Starting with those zones closest to the site of the attack and working outward, our soldiers meticulously searched the houses and fields of Kargouli Village daily for several weeks. For days at a time we went without sleep—searching, raiding, detaining, and desperately searching for any sign of the men we'd lost. We continued to detain any local men that we encountered, who in turn provided the interrogators a wealth of new information. While our actions would certainly fail any constitutional assessment, the results were undeniable as the majority of the men we detained had some connection with the insurgency, either directly or through association. Several of the men independently identified one man who was responsible for organizing and leading the attack, as well as many of the key participants. Either by witness testimony provided by other detainees or their own admissions, more than twenty of the men we had detained were identified as insurgents. We transferred these men to the main Coalition detainee facility at Camp Cropper for further processing and trial as soon as our interrogators had completed their questioning.

Based on some of the information received, we launched several missions into the Village, killing or capturing key insurgents and allowing us to gather more information on the insurgents who participated in the attack. We systematically destroyed all of the ramshackle bridges across Caveman Canal in a series of nighttime raids in an effort to control the flow of people and materials into Kargouli Village. With the destruction of the bridges, all vehicle traffic was forced to move through the checkpoint controlled by A/2-5 Cavalry at the southeast end of the Caveman Canal. This greatly reduced the ability of the insurgency to move heavy materiels between Kargouli Village and the rest of the battalion area of operations. Finally, we cleared north-ward up Malibu toward the Thermal Power Plant, planting our flag and establishing BP 153 as the furthest outpost in the battalion. The insurgents resisted half-heartedly but were unable to prevent our occupation.

Prior to this attack, Patrol Base Inchon regularly housed only fifty to sixty soldiers. However, the influx of detainees and additional forces supporting the search saw that number skyrocket to somewhere between five hundred to six hundred individuals. The Forward Support Company increased deliveries of water, fuel, and food dramatically, and regular aerial resupply ensured that adequate stocks of supplies were maintained for continuous operations. For over a month, every available asset in theater was focused on our area, which broke the back of the insurgency in Kargouli Village and brought several of those responsible to justice. PFC Anzack's body was re-covered from the Euphrates River by Iraqi civilians several kilometers south of our area a couple of weeks later.

June saw the arrival of the "Sunni Awakening" in Kargouli Village, in that our efforts in May destroyed the ability of the insurgency to resist the spreading public resistance to their violent methods. With the major in-surgent leaders in Kargouli Village either dead, captured, or in hiding, the mullahs and traditional tribal leaders approached CPT Gilbreth with offers of cooperation. Rapidly, we stood up a local security militia, the so-called Sons of Iraq. The irony was not lost on us as we saw hundreds of newly minted "security personnel" patrolling the streets of Kargouli Village, carry-ing Kalashnikovs that had most likely been aimed at us just a few short weeks previously. But the relative peace was a welcomed respite and finally allowed Delta Company the opportunity to solidify our gains. The local council of elders met with Iraqi government officials from Baghdad, and Iraqi security forces could now patrol the streets of Kargouli Village with relative certainty of local approval and support. Efforts were even undertaken to register and enlist the "Sons of Iraq" into the Iraqi Army and National Police. The Bat-talion Headquarters moved from Yusufiyah to the Thermal Power Plant, rapidly shifting emphasis toward the Euphrates River.

In August, tribal tensions flared between the al-Owesi and their north-ern neighbors, who remained loyal to al-Qaeda in Iraq at the same time the al-Owesi chose to come over to the government as part of the "Sunni

Awakening." As a result, pitched gun battles erupted on the west bank of the Euphrates River, and the battalion seized the opportunity to deal a further deathblow to the insurgency to prevent their reemergence. Delta Company crossed the Jufr-al-Sukr Bridge in September carrying all of the materials necessary to build and occupy BP 154. This tiny fortress on the other side of the Euphrates was, again, the outermost outpost for the battalion, and Delta Company once again led the way. For weeks at a time, a platoon of Delta Company soldiers would hold the fort, conducting patrols to engage with key leaders in the al-Owesi tribe and applying critical pressure to ensure the elimination of the insurgency.

Al-Qaeda in Iraq again claimed that they attacked our patrol, killed these soldiers, and took Jimenez and Fouty prisoner in revenge for the 2006 rape and murders committed by the 2/101 soldiers, stating, "What you are doing in searching for your soldiers will lead to nothing but exhaustion and head-aches. Your soldiers are in our hands. If you want their safety, do not look for them." Despite these claims, we continued searching for Jimenez and Fouty, following up on every clue and report trying to find them. Sadly, we did not find them before redeploying to Fort Drum at the end of November. The hardest thing that we had to do was leave Iraq knowing that we still had soldiers missing. The unit that replaced us in November 2007 vowed to continue the search, and we had every confidence that they would pursue every lead with the same tenacity that had driven us. Acting on a tip from locals in July of 2008, U.S. forces found the bodies of Jimenez and Fouty in a shallow grave near the town of Jufr-al-Sukr. Their remains now rest together in Section 60 at Arlington National Cemetery.

I left Iraq with terribly mixed emotions. On the one hand, I had played my small part in a great undertaking, helping to bring peace and stability to a region that previously had been a den of insurgency and animosity. Notwithstanding the far larger strategic discussions (well above my pay grade) regarding the justification for the initial invasion of Iraq in 2003, I took pride in my two combat deployments. I departed a country substan-tially more stable than I'd found it. Yet, on the other hand, I witnessed firsthand the awesome sacrifices made by our nation's precious sons and daughters in some of the most horrible conditions imaginable. Though memories of my days in Kargouli Village still haunt me, like many warriors before me thoughts of my fallen brothers are far more troublesome. The horrible randomness of war inevitably leaves the survivors wondering why they were allowed to live while others, perhaps more worthy, were taken. I eventually made peace with this conundrum, endeavoring to prove myself worthy of the sacrifices of my comrades. With that motivation in mind, I have sought opportunities to serve at the utmost of my abilities and to honor the memories of my brothers.

LOVE

Regardless of our situation, love is the one emotion that prevents us from degrading to our base state of nature. The compassion we feel for another person enables us to discern what helps and what harms another individual. Without love, we become a being akin to Nietzsche's *Ubermensch*—a solitary predator preying upon those weaker than ourselves within the margins of morality. Love grounds us. It reminds us that we are human and that if we are to maintain our humanity, we must find a way to love both our neighbor and ourselves.

CLEARING BARRELS

Iraq's Amusement Parks

Chris Fierro

Nobody gets a Purple Heart for being shot at a clearing barrel. Sadly, I had to learn this fact first-hand during an afternoon patrol in the face-melting heat of an Iraqi afternoon in August. There will be no need to bore you with the details of the patrol my platoon conducted on the evening of August 21, 2006, because the mission was typical and "almost" concluded without incident. I will, however, tell you a story of what occurred at the end of the mission and the years to follow. When someone says, "It ended with a bang" in the business world, you can always assume that something great happened. In the military, it is the polar opposite. So let's begin with, "It ended with a bang!"

You can't imagine the plethora of foul language that ran out of my mouth, and through my mind, after I had been shot by a negligent discharge from a U.S. Army medic while at a clearing barrel site on FOB Justice in Baghdad, Iraq. The pain was inexplicable at first, and it didn't dawn on me that I had been shot until I took my third step away from the clearing area and then collapsed to the ground. You would think I stepped barefooted into a pit of fire with the way I was screaming and carrying on, but no, it was just your everyday 5.56 mm round right through my left ankle and foot. The damage was not clear at first, but believe me when I tell you this, "GETTING SHOT IN THE FOOT IS NOT AN EASY TICKET HOME!"

Let me paint a better picture of the lay of the land on FOB Justice. Justice was actually a small Forward Operating Base within the walls of a much larger Iraqi Training Compound. Essentially, it was the nucleus, and the clearing barrel site was located a quarter of a mile away from the walls of the U.S. Army Compound. Now, the clearing barrel site, let's just say that when you have the Iraqis copy certain military procedures from us, they should probably know what is going on internally, and by internal I mean the systems within. They, the Iraqis, do an excellent job of creating the shell of a solution. Their clearing site appeared to be like every clearing site the U.S. Military establishes within its perimeter; however, they forgot one key component . . . the stopping mechanism inside the barrel (sand, gravel, or ANYTHING). Needless to say, this key omission caused some issues.

After getting shot, I could not sit down in my vehicle to get into FOB Justice due to gravity and its nasty push of blood (pain) to the injured area. Logically, the solution was to place me on the hood of my vehicle and transport me this way. Hey, it worked, don't judge!

Inside Justice was our unit Aid Station and physician's assistant. Once I arrived inside the Aid Station, medics as well as the PA immediately began working on my leg. I don't remember every detail, but I do remember the PA saying, "You're going to be OK, the wound is not that bad." I was then transported to the Combat Support Hospital (CSH) in Baghdad's Green Zone where I was to be treated at Saddam Hussein's former hospital. The ride there was with some of my favorite soldiers, who smoked, joked, and laughed the entire way. Maybe it was the morphine, but I actually enjoyed that part of my evacuation. I remember the hospital being nice, but that could have been Mr. Morphine putting a shiny face on everything yet again. It was comforting to be in the hospital because the nurse who received me, Captain Reyes (the reason I remember his name was due to the fact that one of my roommates at West Point also had the name Reyes), prepped me for my first of many surgeries.

The extent of my stay at the CSH in Baghdad literally felt like a couple of hours, but in reality it was more like a complete day. There were some important highlights that occurred while in the hospital that first night. The head surgeon asked me if I had contacted my wife, who was in Germany, to let her know about the injury and my condition. I told him I had not spoken with her that evening. He reached into his pocket and allowed me to use his cell phone. The following is how my conversation went with my wife (mind you, I was administered a hefty dose of narcotics during this call):

Me: Hey baby, how are you?

Jess: Ok, how was your mission?

Me: I got shot. Don't worry though, it was in the foot, so I am OK.

Jess: What!? Are you coming home? Are you OK? How did this happen?

Me: Yeah! I should be home soon.

(The head surgeon overheard this conversation, and in the background my wife heard him yelling, "Get that damn lieutenant off the phone!")

Me: Well, I have to go now, see you soon.

Later in the evening, the surgeon asked if he could contact my wife in order to put things in a less drug-induced perspective. That call, according to my wife, went down as follows:

Surgeon: Hello, Mrs. Fierro?

Jess: Hello.

Surgeon: This is your husband's surgeon here in Baghdad. Mrs. Fierro, are you driving? If so, you may want to pull over. I understand you are a registered nurse, so I wanted to clarify your husband's condition with you, since he painted a not-so-accurate picture of what is actually going on here.

Jess: OK.

Surgeon: The gunshot wound he sustained is traumatic. The exit wound consumed a good portion of his ankle and caused some extensive nerve damage. He will most likely have to amputate below the knee.

Jess: That is crazy! He sounded like everything was fine!? Oh my God, this is horrible!

Surgeon: He sounded fine because he is on a ton of drugs.

Jess: So, what is going to happen now? When is he coming back to Germany?

Surgeon: He should be there very soon, two to three days from now. We have to start surgery on his leg now, but you will be informed on his arrival to Germany.

Narcotics tend to degrade one's ability to provide a good description of certain events. I would get to experience this fun for a very long two and a half years. The next few days were a complete blur and completely awful as far as pain goes. I learned many lessons that night: 1) narcotics are not as fun as they sound; 2) never borrow a medic you know nothing about for missions outside the FOB; and 3) my wife is an incredibly strong and loving woman.

RECOVERY: STAGE I

Ahhhh, Germany! I missed the smell, but most of all I missed my wife. Even though I was receiving morphine regularly every two hours, I still remember the excitement of arriving back to the comforts of home. The bus ride, however, was brutal! Germany, in case you don't know, is extremely hilly and has wonderful cobblestone roads throughout many of its cities. Being a passenger with extensive nerve damage and half of a foot is not fun while traveling on such pleasantries! Despite these minor setbacks, I arrived at Landstuhl Regional Army Medical Center. My first round of surgeries was about to begin.

My wife and her older sister were both at the hospital waiting to greet me as I got off the bus. I arrived on a litter and was carted off the bus by two female medics who proceeded to drop me because they could not properly handle the litter. It hurt, let's just leave it at that, and yes, my wife was not happy, as it was her first sight of me in months. A quick hello was what we were allowed. Once I entered the hospital, it was time to start prepping for surgery number two. I was starting to realize that it would be the first of many. I would receive three more surgeries during my stay in Landstuhl, each lasting a little more than four hours. Doctors began to lose hope for any chance of salvaging my lower left leg. After my fourth surgery, I had a very unpleasant discussion with my orthopedic surgeon regarding the possibility of having to amputate my leg. He stated his case for amputation and told me that the facilities at Walter Reed had to perform the procedure as the hospital in Landstuhl had exhausted all of its resources.

Jess and I had mixed feelings about having to go back to the States for an undisclosed amount of time. Luckily, we had family also stationed in

Germany who could watch over our house and animals while we were state-side. The flight across the Atlantic was miserable, to say the least. Military transport on a litter stacked below another litter is not first-class travel. The pain was unbearable and morphine was not cutting it; in fact, it was giving me hives. My hat goes off to my wife, though; she was awesome during the flight and throughout this ordeal to this point. She dealt with my almost impossible attitude and me and managed to get our affairs in order for this very impromptu relocation. Once we arrived at Walter Reed, the medics managed to get me inside without dropping me this time. After surgery number five, I began to just grin and bear it. Jess, after much conflict, was able to get a room at the hotel on post that resided a block away from the hospital. It would be years after this string of events before I could fully appreciate the sacrifice that my wife made to be by my side every day I was in the hospital. To all my friends and classmates who called or emailed me during my stay at Walter Reed, I apologize—I promise that was not the real me you were talking to. Hell, I don't even remember half of the phone conversations. Also, I apparently liked to make random calls to friends and family during the hours of sleep for normal people. Sorry.

RECOVERY: STAGE II

After surgery number twelve, I began to wonder if things would ever improve. I had been at Walter Reed for approximately one month. My orthopedic surgeon was optimistic about salvaging my foot, which at the time sounded fantastic. My wife (RN) and my sister-in-law (who is an MD) had their doubts, but I did not share their concerns. I was focused on doing anything I could to save my leg.

I began physical therapy while in the hospital, and it was awful. A small Filipino woman was my physical therapist, and she never let me off easily. She could have doubled as an interrogator in a bad 1980s POW movie. Every morning, she would arrive at my room after breakfast, and every morning I would pretend to be asleep, hoping that she would leave and never come back. It never worked. Physical therapy was torture, but it did get me out of my room and around a group of guys in similar circumstances.

The next groupings of surgeries were similar in nature, but I did have a variety of visitors that will never be forgotten. My most memorable visitor, while at Walter Reed, was the professional wrestler Mankind, Mick Foley. He was a giant of a man, who wore Chuck Taylors, jeans, and a sports coat, but much to my chagrin he was incredibly intelligent. He spoke with my wife and me for over an hour. We talked about West Point, to which he applied but did not receive admission. We discussed his charity work in Latin America and his love for culture and people. He was nothing like I expected, and to this day it is still one of my most memorable encounters.

My other celebrity visitor that I remember most was Donald Rumsfeld, Secretary of Defense; he was everything that I expected. He was coming into the hospital that evening for a personal appointment and decided to come see the troops on my floor. He was brief and stern, but I still had all the respect in the world for the man. I like to think he was getting a root canal after we had our encounter, but I guess I will never know.

THERE'S A TUBE UP MY BUTT

"Jess, is there a tube up my butt?" These were the first words I uttered to Jess after a lovely twelve hours in the operating room and first-class trip to the ICU one evening. She told me that there was not a tube up my butt and that I was just feeling the effects of the anesthesia from the lengthy surgery. "Jess, I know there is an F(*&ing tube up my A$$!" She again assured me there was not a tube up my butt. This went on for about twenty minutes, until Jess proved once and for all that there was in fact no tube up my butt but in fact only a tube (catheter) in my penis. I then directed my attentions to the monstrous pain in my arm. You see, during surgery, the technical team assisting the surgeons is supposed to switch the blood pressure cuff from arm to arm every couple of hours to prevent any damage to a person's extremities. In my case, this did not happen, so my arm felt like it was broken, and I made sure that every ICU nurse, doctor, and Jess knew it. I pissed and moaned . . . I cried, OK, I cried and cried. It hurt so badly and all because of a stupid blood pressure cuff.

My stay in the ICU was short-lived, and after a day or two I was returned to my hospital room.

FAREWELL WALTER REED!

After three months and over nineteen surgeries, the time had come to bid farewell to Walter Reed. Jess and were so excited to be heading back to Germany with hopes of rehabilitation and recovery from this experience. My leg still looked pretty terrible. The doctors tried numerous techniques to salvage my devastated lower limb, but it still looked like a bad Frankenstein movie after all was completed. I still had incredible pain, and every time I lowered my leg, the sutures would pop off and blood would shoot everywhere.

Nonetheless, we were ready to leave, which in the end was a hasty decision. I was still on crutches and with a massive cast on my leg. In Germany, this would soon warrant a return to the States.

HELLO AND GOODBYE GERMANY

Germany was a huge roller coaster of emotions. We arrived back in the country approximately at the same time that my unit was redeploying to Iraq. I had felt so guilty for the longest time being in the hospital while my soldiers were still deployed. It was nice to be able to see them again. The reunion was great and sad at the same time. I found out that two days before redeployment one of my soldiers was killed by an IED while doing their handoff ride with another unit. We were a very close platoon, and this loss devastated us. I also would discover that my job was still waiting for me, even though I wasn't physically able to become a platoon leader again. I didn't care, really, I was just happy to be back with the guys.

Germany, like Washington, D.C., had urban terrain that proved to be incredibly difficult to navigate with crutches. In D.C., someone actually put some loose change in my coffee cup while I waited for my brother outside of a Barnes & Noble in Georgetown. The store's wheelchair lift was being used by myriad stacks of unwanted crappy books, so I waited outside the store with my cup of coffee filled with dirty change. In Germany, my command sergeant major, who I will not name, scolded me one day for parking in our battalion's visitor parking instead of the regular staff parking lot down the hill and stairs. That situation made me reevaluate my future as an artillery officer.

After three months in Germany, my orthopedic and division surgeons recommended that I consider the process for amputation again. They informed me this would require a PCS to Fort Sam Houston in San Antonio, Texas. The idea did not fare well in my head, but I knew that I was not getting better, and my dependency on narcotics increased monthly. My wife, doctors, and liver all knew that it was time to make the tough decision.

Goodbye Germany, hello San Antonio.

RECOVERY: FINAL STAGE

Fort Sam Houston really should change its name to Mecca of Military Medicine. They have everything under the sun to care for our wounded. Not to mention the support base that lies in San Antonio. For the first time in a long time, I was not the only guy crutching his way around post. We were among so many others like us; it felt good.

The excitement of San Antonio life was short-lived. My newly assigned orthopedic surgeon decided that my best course of action would be continuing the limb salvage process. He explained different extensive procedures that would require large amounts of recovery time. Expectations of being able to walk or even jog without pain were set, so of course I was game for this once-in-a-lifetime opportunity. My wife was not game for this, as she was almost six months pregnant and for almost a year had dealt with Zombie Chris. I was also assigned to Brooke Army Medical Center's (BAMC) newly formed Warrior Transition Unit (WTU). After being assigned to this unit and agreeing to the limb salvage process, I began physical therapy for eight hours a day at the state of the art Center for Intrepid (CFI) located on the hospital's campus. The opportunity to rehab at the CFI was incredible and eye opening. There was not a day that went by that an amputated soldier familiar with my case didn't say, "You should really cut that leg off; it is not going to get better until you do." This pissed me off so much! I was so angry, and I wouldn't understand what that anger was about until a year later.

My first surgery at BAMC happened three months after my arrival to San Antonio. This surgery would also occur one month before the birth of my first daughter, Laci. The operation fused my ankle and foot, limiting my range of motion, and therefore creating less opportunity for breakdown and drop foot, and pain. The surgery was extremely long. Once completed, I found that one of my classmates, Michael Patzkowski, was a resident doctor at BAMC. He would visit me frequently after this surgery. It was comforting to have a friend who knew the business talk to me as a friend and inform me of certain outcomes and procedures.

Eventually, we decided to amputate my lower leg. Enough was enough, and it was time to move on with my life. Through all the surgeries, all the pain, all the gross bedpan situations, I always knew that I could count on one person waiting for me at my bedside. While the outcome of the surgeries was always ambiguous, I knew that Jess's love was not. Looking back on that time in my life, I realize that I could not have managed that burden without Jess's love and patience. When I say she is amazing, I am truly understating the true characteristics of who she is! And while life did throw me a curve ball, it really doesn't matter because I know that she will always be there for me. And hey, it didn't turn out that bad for me. At least I got a sweet prosthetic leg with a painted likeness of Rainbow Dash from *My Little Pony* (courtesy of my girls' artwork choice). So there you have it—I'm still here minus a part of one leg, but plus one awesome wife and two beautiful little girls (our second daughter was born a few years after Laci). By my math, I'm doing pretty well. Love that woman—always will!

ALL THE THINGS
I DIDN'T KNOW

Courtney Waid

The story of my deployment is not one of heroics. There were no fire-fights, no daring rescues, and no epic tales of valor. My story is one of emotion, connection, and the great pride that comes with standing among the very best of men. West Point didn't prepare me for it, though. Well, not all of it anyway. At twenty-three, enthusiastic and idealistic, I was ready to be an officer during a time of war. But as a newly married kid suddenly living in the adult world, I was not prepared for the emotional toll. West Point didn't teach me to deal with the realities of death in a far-off place, the fear for my husband's safety, or how to play the role of both the wife and the one going to war. I struggled with this dual role throughout my deployment; further, this struggle continued for years after I hung up my uniform. In fact, despite leaving the Army in 2010, it is only in the last year that I can meet a new person without feeling the need to tell them about who I used to be. I can finally recognize that the role of wife and mother may not be as exciting as that of Army officer, but it is critical, fulfilling, and challenging in its own ways.

I deployed to the area around Tikrit, Iraq, from September of 2005 to September of 2006. I spent half my time as the battalion intelligence officer (S2) for the 626th Brigade Support Battalion (BSB) and the other half as the Signals Intelligence platoon leader for the 3rd Special Troops Battalion, both part of the 3rd Brigade Combat Team (BCT), 101st Airborne—the

"Rakkasans." Being a Rakkasan was an amazing experience and more than I could have hoped for as my first unit. The organization was like a cult in almost every sense. The pride and esprit de corps was palpable. Our standards were high. We were better than the other BCTs, and we told them so. Constantly. The enthusiasm and vigor was what I imagined "the real Army" to be like. It was the kind of group I wanted to be in, a gang I was proud beyond words to go to the war with, and a place where I could thrive as an officer. At the helm of this great unit was Colonel Michael Steele. Just like the Rakkasans as a unit, Colonel Steele fulfilled my every expectation of the infantry brigade commander archtype. I felt like a rock star for the sheer fact that he even knew my name. The man was larger than life, with a physical presence and aura to him that would fill a room. At one moment he was a crude infantryman complaining that the BCT operations center stunk of "FAB" (feet, ass, and balls), and the next he was a thoughtful intellectual, firing off questions during a briefing full of words whose definitions escaped me. Colonel Steele was my hero.

The third portion of the trifecta—and just as West Point told me it would be—was my platoon sergeant, Sergeant First Class Scott Peck. West Point said I would have one, that he would be my right hand, and that we would be a team like no other. I love Scott. I love him in a way that I don't think a person can understand who has not stood side by side with somebody in a place that is lonely, foreign, scary, and where many people are trying to kill you. Scott was that person to look you in the eye and tell you, "I'm here to help you with this. We're going to be OK."

And then there is the unexpected part of my story—what it's like to be an Army spouse. West Point didn't provide me with any advice in this regard except for warnings about staying away from upperclassmen and threats of harsh punishments should you be caught in a room with girls and boys sitting on the same horizontal surface. There was no resiliency training for the bleak stretches of the long-distance relationship characteristic of the Army wife, and there were no manuals handed out during Military Intersession on how to help him cope with the stress of deployment while concurrently dealing with my own. Not once did anyone ever even hint to me that the road of the dual military couple would be complex or tell me how much I would struggle defining and redefining my own identity as our family grew and changed.

Joseph "Buck" Waid and I met at West Point and sort of fell in love on accident. He was graduating soon, and neither of us went into the relationship with the expectation of anything serious or long term. We had been friends for a few years, but I never thought more of him than that until I casually invited him to a class banquet. I had to sit at the head table with the guest speaker and his family, an experience that could be awkward and nerve-racking. A few days before the event, I dislocated my shoulder and was unable to move my right arm at all. Buck sat with me in front of a decorated Command Sergeant Major and made brilliant conversation while nonchalantly cutting my meal into pieces for me. I think that was the first time I saw him for the kind and compassionate man that he was rather than just another guy I would see around the company area. The lack of any goal for a relationship let me really fall in love with him with no attempt to make him fit some mold or preconceived notion. I loved him for him, because he was my best friend, and because my life was truly better with him in it. Right now as I sit to write this nearly eleven years after we first began our relationship, he is in Afghanistan, and the one thing I miss is simply his presence in my day and being able to talk to him. But West Point didn't prepare me for that. West Point prepared me to be the one who goes to the fight, to be the strong and confident leader, to write fancy speeches I would give to my first platoon. Nobody ever talked to me about what it would be like to play the other side, to send someone you love off to war, to worry and struggle with the fear.

The day I left for my deployment was my first taste of this struggle. Buck was with 2nd BCT, so we deployed to different areas of Iraq a few weeks apart. I left first. I had to be at the BN HQ very early that morning, and I spent the night tossing and turning, catching glimpses of the clock and trying to stop my mind from counting down the hours. I tried to focus on the feeling of the heat of him lying there next to me. I don't know if he was sleeping or not. I was up before the alarm, pacing about, getting ready. I still recall the feeling of the floor of our living room against my bare feet. I told myself to remember that feeling because there was the chance I would not ever be back to that place. Or worse—that I would be back to that place alone.

Buck drove me to post that morning still in the predawn dark. We didn't talk much; I tried bravely to hold it together. We got about halfway there, and I lost it. I broke down. I clutched his arm, and I sobbed. He told me it would be all right, but I don't know that he believed it. I think maybe he knew too that if something was going to happen to one of us it would very likely be him rather than me, and that gave him the easier burden to carry. We made it there eventually, got out of the truck, and he helped me with my bags. We kissed quickly, and he drove away. We talked about it later, that he wished he had stayed a little longer just in case that was the last time. It would never have been enough.

And then it began. We waited, we staged, we waited and staged again. We got on an airplane, and it took off. We arrived in Kuwait who knows how many days later. The flight was long, crammed alphabetically between my comrades and our gear, and the Ambien the doc was handing out wasn't entirely the best for helping me keep track of time. But it was just as well. That's how the year would go anyway. Time always seemed to pass in the aggregate but never day by day. One day would blend into any other, and then all of a sudden it was July somehow.

With my job as the S2, I was with the small group from our unit that got to move to our base in Iraq before the bulk of the unit in order to spend some time doing a handover with the unit we were replacing. While I was nervous to go without Scott and some of the other officers I had come to rely on, I was eager to get started. I would be lying if I said a part of me didn't feel somewhat special being on the advance party. All those years preparing for "the war," and it was finally time. A bumpy and jarring middle-of-the-night C-130 ride took me on the last leg of my journey. Iraq was a startling place for me. We complain a lot in the United States about how bad things are but really I didn't know what bad was. I encountered a place that looked like it was out of centuries ago. The Tigris River Valley. The first place God created. The desert of Abraham. And it didn't look like much had happened since. Hovels with no doors, no sewer, not enough electricity for everyone. Just men standing around or squatting in the dirt. That was squalor in all senses of the word.

Besides the landscape, the early days of my deployment took me by surprise with their intense emotion. In hindsight, I'm not sure why I didn't expect it, but I was so consumed with fear about Buck that I could hardly function. It snuck out of nowhere; it crippled me as I went about my work poring over route maps and threat briefings. I suppose it didn't help being an intelligence officer and spending all day reading reports of enemy activity. But I almost couldn't breathe at times when it would hit me that he was there in that place too yet still so far away. He was one of "those guys" out there, patrolling, getting shot at, getting blown up, getting killed. Who died and who lived had nothing to do with how smart you were or how good you were or how careful you were. War is a series of independent instances of violence strung together by either luck or tragedy. It didn't occur to me until then, until we were there, that there was nothing I could do.

My battalion commander with the BSB was Lieutenant Colonel Dan Reilly, another amazing man whom I had the great fortune to work with. I think I would have been a different officer if he hadn't been my first boss, and I wouldn't have been able to see so clearly the decisions that would need to be made for my family later in my career. LTC Reilly taught me what it means to really be the kind of leader who cares about people. His greatest lesson was that family was the most important thing. Even with only days to go before deployment, LTC Reilly would leave work early in the afternoon to go to his son's Cub Scouts meetings. He never stayed late when there wasn't a need, and he never expected us to either. And I think he knew the way I was feeling. He never said anything, but looking back I know he knew how scared I was about Buck, how sometimes I could barely keep it together when he asked if I had heard from him. One day a few months into my deployment I found out there was a helicopter going to Buck's base. I had absolutely zero professional reason in the world to go, and it was rare that a flight would even be going from our place to his. Going out on a limb, I asked the boss if I could go. Being the man he was, he said yes.

Getting to see Buck was an emotional turning point for me in a lot of ways. The crippling fear eased a bit when I saw him. I was reminded that he was in fact still real and still alive and that we had a whole life waiting for us at home. I'm not doing justice to that memory, to the feeling that came over me, with these words. Maybe it's something other wives feel when their husband comes home for R&R or when their war is finally over. I don't know. I haven't felt it since so strongly, but I was whole again when we were together. I told myself to never forget that moment and that feeling, and still I can close my eyes and conjure up exactly how it was. I would get to see Buck a few more times after that—once for an amazing R&R trip to Australia and a couple of times when real business brought me to Baghdad. But no time was ever as powerful as that first time. After that first time, I felt I was finally able to settle in to my job, to the task at hand. If we were able to see each other once, we would be able to see each other again. It was time to get to work.

The rest of my deployment was an emotional whirlwind. The overpowering fear for Buck's safety subsided into a nagging doubt that would occasionally lash out at me. I buried myself in my work to try not to think about it. I didn't really know how to handle those feelings, but I knew how to be an officer. I was comfortable playing that role and was filled with an enthusiasm that had been my companion since my early days at West Point. I loved the jobs I was doing, especially when I became a platoon leader. While some days were desperately mundane and routine, others were filled with the excitement of tearing around the country in helicopters, signing for new equipment, and being taught about the amazing new intelligent system capabilities that seemed straight out of the movies. There were times when I watched my soldiers accomplish tasks and felt a pride in them that rivals what I feel today watching my own children learn new things. And there were days when I was so angry and frustrated with what was happening around me I'm lucky I worked with senior officers that were mature enough to not punch me in the face as I felt it necessary to share my feelings. I was constantly covered in dirt rushing from place to place to check on my soldiers and the different aspects of our operations. I had equipment and collection sites scattered about the country, and I felt critical to the mission as I spent my days visiting them, solving their maintenance and personnel problems, and updating the commanders on our status. I feverously threw myself into my work, and, at the risk of sounding too prideful, I was damn good at it. I loved being an officer and working through complex problems. I spent so many years at West Point getting ready for these jobs, and I was proud of myself for doing them well.

The day I found out Gary Avery died was one my worst days in the Army. I shared many Military Science classes with Gary at West Point, and I always viewed him as one of the best our class had to offer. I found out from an email from one of our class officers that he had been killed. It was like the world came crashing down around me. However, when I looked around, everybody in the office was still going on about their business. I was amazed they had no idea about the great and crushing loss just suffered by the whole of the world from the departure of a man such as Gary.

I couldn't sit there. I left and went out for a run to try to gather my thoughts. But my thoughts were bad thoughts. I looked at that flat and disgusting Iraqi wasteland, and I hated it for being the last piece of earth upon which Gary trod. I hated the people that lived beneath the puke-colored Iraqi sky for what they did to Gary. I hated all of them. And I know an educated and decent person is not supposed to hate entire groups of people, but at that moment I found it hard not to hate them. I had been tossing around the idea for a while, since Dennis Zilinski, a fellow West Point classmate and Rakkasan, was killed earlier in our deployment by a bomb dug deep by cowards into that miserable dirt. Maybe I could hate the Iraqis because I only knew them through the sterilized lens of intelligence reports, saw them standing outside their hovels on the roadside as we passed, and watched kids much too young to be unsupervised in the civilized world dart in front of our very large trucks as we left our base. Maybe if I met some that really were trying to make that despicable country better for their own sake I would have been able to approach this dynamic with thoughtfulness like the scholar West Point trained me to be. But given the current circumstances, I couldn't see past my hate.

And then there was the day it was over. That day lived in the back of my mind for a long time, and one day it became real. We packed up our things, went through all the hassle of transferring equipment to the new unit, and explained all we had done over the year. And then we left. I went home. Back to my house. It was a stranger feeling than I expected. It was just as we had left it, although Buck would not be home for a couple of weeks. Sure, I had spent so much time thinking about it, but there it was again. The rest of the world continued to move forward, to exist, while we were gone, but this place sat just as it was. It seemed more foreign to me than the truly foreign place I had spent the last year. It was awkward feeling that this was a new routine that had previously been so familiar just a year ago. That feeling lingered for a few weeks. In fact, it felt weird to not be at work. The few hours a day at "reintegration" that first week were the only hours of the day that felt normal to me.

And then the day arrived that Buck came home. I got to fully play the role of wife and take part in the crazy process that is the homecoming ceremony from the opposite side of the field. I sat with Buck's NCO's wife and her son. It was strange to be there with her, to sit next to her as if we shared this experience and had something in common over the whole thing. She no doubt spent her time worrying and fretting for her husband, but her reality of what that place was like came solely from what he told her. She couldn't close her eyes and conjure up the smell of that place, the look of it, the feel of the dirt. But we were united in our excitement at the announcement that the plane was coming. We all moved outside, waited again, until we saw it slowly appear in the distance. It grew bigger, landed, and the line of ragged men began to exit the aircraft. There he was. Home again.

Those first few weeks home were not the honeymoon I thought it would be. We had grown apart some over the year, changed. I guess that was to be expected in some way after throwing all our time and effort in separate directions. After the initial fear subsided, I didn't really focus on the role of wife as much as I did the role of warfighter. I had had a grand adventure and felt like the conquering hero returning from battle. It pains me to admit it now that I've matured enough to recognize my mistake, but I just didn't think about what it meant to be the wife of a man coming home from war. I didn't know how to be there for him after a year where he faced the very real possibility of his own death on a daily basis. We didn't talk about any of the things that happened to him. I was too selfish and naïve, worrying only about what I needed from him and the awkwardness of my own readjustment. In hindsight, we should have talked about it. I should have known enough to ask what he needed from me. I think those things still exist for him, separate him from me in some small way to this day. It's there, in the shadows, how I let him down when he needed me because I just didn't know how to do better. He grew up that year in ways I couldn't understand and ways I regret I didn't try to. But we came through it. His graciousness allowed us to get through it. He knew much more than I did what it meant to be a team. He still does.

I didn't know it then, but that would be my last deployment. Before heading off to our respective Captain's Career Courses, we got pregnant with our first child. We didn't really discuss what that would mean or how we would balance a family. Even after the difficulties during the deployment of just learning to be a wife, the thought never even crossed my mind of how it would be to wrestle with the role of mother while still so passionate about another, and almost equally time consuming, profession. But we were fortunate. A senior officer at my Career Course at Fort Huachuca strongly urged us to stay and be stationed there. They needed instructors with our experience, and it would ensure some stability as we grew our family. Teaching and serving at Fort Huachuca was rewarding and a great experience, but it lacked the thrill and adventure of a "real" unit. I knew it was the right thing to do to be in that place and be there for Buck and our daughter, but I was still so desperate for the personal satisfaction and pride from my days in the war. When we added our second child a mere fourteen months later, it became apparent that both of us being both a soldier and parent wasn't going to work. It was a low point for us. We were burdened with anger and resentment, each feeling that we were pulling more weight than the other when it came to work and kids. Although I can't pinpoint when, somewhere in that time it became obvious to me that I would have to get out. West Point never told me that; nobody ever let me know that as the perfectionist and overachiever they tried to teach me to be I would never be capable of playing both roles to a standard with which I could be satisfied. I did learn to make a decision though, and in September of 2010 I hung up my boots. It would take me a couple more years to actually be comfortable with that decision and to stop mourning over all I felt I had lost by giving up that other part of me. It was hard to realize that all I had done was not invalidated by the fact that I wasn't doing it anymore and that the traits I liked about myself as an officer still existed in me as a person. However, through it all Buck was there for me, supportive and sympathetic to how hard the transition was.

Though my own war has ended, ours as a family hasn't. Buck is still in but fortunately with a unit that doesn't do long deployments. He travels so often sometimes it takes a few days for the kids to even notice he's gone. But it's still there, and the kids don't always understand. They miss him; they need him in their own ways just like I do. They get frustrated and angry when mommy's clay tower doesn't look like the one daddy makes or mommy doesn't sing the "sleep song" quite the same. There are still the goodbyes, but now they are quick and constant on the front porch or at the local airport. They are still hard though, and there is still that moment when I want to hang on to him, to kiss him again because it might be the very last time. However, I'm quickly reminded that it will do no good. So I play strong and watch him go and hold the kids while they cry for a minute before trying to bribe them out of their sadness with promises of ice cream.

Being home is the worst. There is no adventure in that like when you are the one in the fight. There are endless days with needy kids when you are at home. There is worry and fear, sometimes made better and sometimes made worse by knowing the reality of it all. There is living the life your family lives without a critical member of the team. And there are statements from a teary-eyed little girl like "Mommy, I'm scared Daddy is going to die in the war," wondering where she even gets this idea at her age, and scrambling for a good response like "No, baby, it's going to be OK," because you know that "Oh dear God, I'm scared of that too," is definitely not the right answer. And then there is her sweet little brother who puts his hand on her shoulder and says, "No Sissy, it's going to be fine. Daddy is the bravest man I know." She smiles and they run off to play while you can't help but be overcome with emotion at their strength and wonder how much they know that you don't.

Fortunately for us, we have always had the giddy excitement of the day that Daddy comes home. Making signs, planning his favorite dinner, and literally mopping the kids out of the house into the car so the floors can be spotless for just one second when he first sees them to help him forget about that horrible, horrible dirt. I know that smell, I know how haunting it is, and I am finally the person who knows how much he needs to forget it. There is the first kiss in a long time and the look my son gives his daddy as if he is witnessing something miraculous when he bends down to hug him. Sometimes I think all the worry is almost worth that moment, the same moment from my war when simply being in his arms again makes everything right with the world. It is such a moment of clarity when I am almost slapped in the face with a reminder of what is truly important in this life. It was a long, hard road for me to learn that, but I'm proud to say I finally have.

CHOOSING

Jay Ireland

"You now have ninety seconds to say your good-byes," the uniformed drone announced to the anxious crowd. The cyborg looked down at his watch as if to signal his seriousness, and I could almost hear him count the seconds in his head. After a moment to process the order, Michie Stadium burst into a fit of tears, hand shaking, and screams of horror.

My membership in the Long Gray Line began that day on June 29, 2000. Before I could walk down those stadium steps with my head held high, I had to face the parental units. Mom was crying, and she hugged me so hard that she bruised my ribs. Dad had those "No, I'm not crying" tears in his eyes when I gave him a hug. Challis, my sister, was there too, and she wished me luck for my new adventure. The running joke between Challis and I was always that I was never really going anywhere dangerous or scary. I was merely going to an extended summer camp. A chance to put on my swim trunks and do backflips off the rope swing. Unfortunately, it wasn't the last time that tearful farewells would happen in stadium bleachers for me and my family. They would soon become commonplace.

Why did they give us so much time? Three glacial hours? I regretted bringing my wife, Courtney, to this stupid send-off ceremony thing. We'd been married for nine months when I was to face my first real deployment.

Combat was just through the doors at the back of the gym, and it felt so real. Instead of making it quick, the Army in all of its infinite wisdom engineered a process akin to someone pulling duct tape off my genitals. We sat there, with nothing to say, and just held each other. I felt Courtney's tears running onto my shoulders, and she felt mine. For the cherry on top, the First Cavalry Division band blasted army marches as loud as their tubas would go in that tiny gym with wooden floors in an awful attempt to help us forget where we all were going. Lord.

Courtney didn't cry before the deployment. Ever. My wife was the strongest and most amazing person that I know. That made it even more difficult when she slammed on the brakes of our Jeep on our way to the gym and sobbed on my shoulder. We sat there in the pitch black, holding each other tight until the shaking stopped. Life was never the same after that kind of moment. Stupid shit didn't matter. It never did.

It was early in the morning on the day I deployed the second time. Before the sun came up, Courtney and I stood at the door of Panera Bread. The darkness of the morning concealed the Rocky Mountains and Fort Carson, Colorado. Courtney insisted that I get all the guys and their families from my troop some bagels, so they wouldn't have an empty stomach on a day that was going to suck something awful. Courtney knew about the painful pending good-bye, and she thought about the women that were going to be in that gym, terrified of the unknown. As per usual, Courtney was thinking of other people.

We arrived at my troop headquarters, drew our assigned weapons, and took accountability. The crisp, Colorado morning air felt good as we all sat around the hoods of our cars. As the troop commander, I was with my first sergeant and a few of the other more experienced guys. We all laughed and told stories about some of the epic benders we had just survived in preparation for this deployment. Even the wives added anecdotes and corrected exaggerations. I saw the LTs and their wives and knew their fear. Courtney and I looked at them with compassion and understanding. We left them alone because we both knew nothing could ease the feeling that you might never see the love of your life again.

This time around, there were not any drawn-out ceremonies, and our final moment consisted only of our good-byes. No band. No ridiculously inappropriate photos. Just friends who sat around the hood of a HMMWV, shooting bull and enjoying some quiet time before our lives got really loud. Families were not allowed in the gym. That was good. When it was time, I kissed Courtney and told her that I would come home. I would find a way. Courtney nodded, and I was off. Just like that.

The gym was nicer this time around without families. Good-byes were already said, hugs dished out, and it was time to go to work. The squadron lined up all the bags in formation for the military working dogs to look for soldiers trying to smuggle drugs into the country. Maybe it was a bad sign when the dog shit on one of the guys' bags but we just laughed about it then. Maybe we would have known that our lives would never be the same from the things we saw during that year in Afghanistan. Maybe it wouldn't have mattered if we knew.

We knew that our future destination was one of the roughest around in terms of sheer volume of enemy attacks. It sat in the base of a bowl of land near the Afghan-Pakistan border. During the months when the enemy was the most active, the Combat Outpost (COP) averaged over three encounters a day, ranging from unaimed pop shots all the way to complex, multi-directional attacks. Encounters. When said that way, you would think the Taliban wanted to kiss us on the forehead and invite us over for tea. The truth was a bit spicier.

It didn't help that right before we left, ABC released a report that included live action video of the unit we were going to replace in terrible firefights and declared our position to be "the most dangerous place on Earth." To make matters worse, the COP was renamed COP Misery by soldiers on the ground. Expecting a breakdown, I came home the night I found out the video made its way through the FRG and I was surprised to see that Courtney was completely calm.

"You're strong, Jay. Your men are strong. You will get through this. Don't ask me how I know but I just do. I don't know if I could do this if anyone else was in charge but you," Courtney said, hands on my face. Courtney's belief in me was unwavering and unchanging. She was my rock, and I was hers.

West Point was terrifying, and many of those times the fear was by design. Teaching humility to a bunch of kids who have sailed through life was priority number one. Every time I woke up, I was reintroduced to my shortcomings. It was West Point's unplanned detours that showed me who I really was. These challenges helped me sort through the extraneous priorities of my youth and glean the nature of my actual character.

For all of the times that sucked at West Point, I have ten other stories that were the funniest and most amazing experiences of my life. The time that my buddy Dave and I, after a *long* night at the Firstie Club, ran away from the Officer in Charge only to scamper into the middle of the Plain and make snow angels. My partnership with the at-risk youths across the river at the New York Military Academy and finding out years later that many of those kids graduated from high school. Bringing my girlfriend, Courtney, to military balls and being told by one of my best friends, Pete, that if I didn't marry her, he would (Pete always knew how to motivate me).

West Point broke down just as much as it built up. Don't get it? Look up the "Definition of Leather."

"The Definition of Leather"[1]—that was West Point for me. I was dipped in a solution of tannic acid and a chemical combination ensued. Just ask Courtney. We were friends all through high school but didn't even come close to dating. You could say I had some . . . uh, growing up to do. I staggered into West Point a punk ass kid and came out a man of character. That growth was invaluable when it was my turn to go to war.

Laid up on a cot in an empty tent, freezing cold, with nothing but my thoughts was unnerving. As an executive officer (XO), I was sent on the advance party to Kuwait on my first deployment to get a head start on the unsexy job of property accountability. I knew that I had little to worry about as an XO, but I had no idea what I was getting into. I knew about the IEDs, the rockets, and the insurgents, but other than what I saw on television, I didn't know anything.

XOs of a mechanized infantry company, sliced a platoon of tanks, didn't spend much time outside the wire. My day consisted of motorpool meetings, maintenance meetings, supply meetings, S4 sync meetings, XO meetings . . . pretty simple. I worked with some really great guys who made the time go by, and some of it was even bearable. My supply sergeant, Specialist Yuan, was a Chinese citizen in the process of acquiring his American citizen-

ship. In the absence of Courtney, the closest thing to a wife that I had was Yuan. We yelled, we fought, and we laughed. Things were good.

Over the fifteen months in Iraq, I also discovered just how hard war was on the entire family. When you deploy, it's foolish to think you go to combat without your family. Your parents struggle to deal with the looks from strangers when they find out their son is deployed, like you're already dead. Your sister struggles without the slightest clue about what goes on in the Army, and every death in the country of Iraq scares her. Every coffee commercial showing a soldier returning home makes her cry. Your brother, former military and combat veteran himself, knows *exactly* what you are going through and that scares him all the same. No, I didn't deploy without my family.

Courtney fought her own wars back home and had her own highs and lows. When things were good, Courtney enjoyed a Broncos game at Buffalo Wild Wings with her friend (who happened to be a Chiefs fan, but we won't hold that against her for now). Happy hours on Friday night with the same friend. Two Christmases in Disneyland with both of our families because home just didn't seem right to spend it by herself. Life wasn't all that bad, we both discovered. But then again, sometimes it was.

On the way home to an episode of *The Bachelor*, after another fulfilling day of work that helped take her mind off my unflinching absence, Courtney saw the one thing every military spouse dreads. As Courtney turned into the drive, she spotted a white minivan with government plates. The soldiers in the van, in their dress uniforms, averted her glance when Courtney pulled into the garage. Sitting in the car with the garage door closed, Courtney knew what that van meant, what those soldiers were waiting to do, and she began to cry.

Courtney was about to get a knock on the door from an Army chaplain holding a folded American flag, and her husband, who went to Iraq her hero, was coming back in a box. After ten minutes or so at the kitchen table, Courtney decided that she couldn't do it anymore and went to the window to see what was taking so long. The neighbor's husband had been killed and the van was meant for someone else. Not only did Courtney feel like crap because she had just pictured me dead, now she felt even worse because she rejoiced that it was someone else. Someone had just lost their husband, their father, and their son. Someone we knew and saw every day. Yeah, Courtney didn't stay behind when I deployed, and she didn't stay behind on my second deployment either.

The Chinook helicopter shook violently as we approached our new home, high in the mountains of Afghanistan. The thirty of us in the helicopter looked to each other, and I gave everyone the thumbs up. We've got this. For anyone who hasn't operated around a Chinook at night, in full blackout, with the enemy completely surrounding you, I can vouch for the fact that it is the most adrenaline-juiced experience of your life . . . every single time you do it. The heat from the engine exhaust, the noise from the blades, and the rocks shot around by the hurricane-force rotor wash was staggering. Men from the outgoing unit who I could only see as white smiles because of the pitch black night literally high-fived me on the way out. Thirty of my guys in; thirty of theirs out.

CPT Frank Hooker and his men, members of Apache Troop, manned the previous year. They were excited to GTFO (Get the Fuck Out). The First Sergeant for the outgoing troop whose name escapes me said something prophetic the following morning, "Every now and then, the bad guys decide to come into the bowl. That's when we make soup." In the light of day, I took in the awesome situation that was to be our lives. Our COP, in all of its military precision and brilliance, sat in the bottom of a valley, surrounded on all sides by *massive* mountains. What I always tell people who are familiar with Colorado is to picture the Rocky Mountains. Got it? Now picture another set of Rocky Mountains directly behind you. Oh yeah, one more thing. Those mountains? The ones surrounding you on all sides? Yeah, they're filled with people that want nothing more than to kill you. Welcome home!

Over the next four months, we were attacked over seventy times with every single piece of equipment in the enemy's arsenal. My lieutenants and I would joke about the absolute waste of time that key leader engagement training and cultural awareness stuff was up there. It didn't matter how much we knew about their culture, the people in the area were so sparse and so deeply embedded in the insurgency all we could do was dig in and fight. And fight we did. CPT Hooker and the units before him had done a great job preparing our new home, but the first rule of a defense is that a position is never finished. As long as there were soldiers present, the defense *must* constantly be improved, checked, war-gamed, and rehearsed over and over again.

So we went about our business, dug deeper holes, and built taller walls. That was our routine. When the sun went down, our camp came to life. Every few days, we would go out and set ambushes on routes that we knew the enemy would come through. We never had success on those missions, and as a commander, I heard the rumblings. The whispers turned into groans when I curtailed the amount of mail being delivered to make room for other mission essentials on the helicopters we received only twice a month. The boxes from families were large, and the room on the birds was limited. Fortunately, I had the best group of NCOs and junior officers in the brigade that understood what it took to win a war, so a lack of focus was not an option.

Everyone had their off days, those days where you looked to the sky and cursed your lot in life, screaming, "WHAT AM I DOING HERE?!?!" Even me. But our work brought us back to center. Each other. That was what we were deployed to that COP to do. Keep each other alive. It was hard for me, as a commander, to see my soldiers so damn worn out all the time. The constant guard requirement, coupled with aggressive patrolling of my own design, ensured my guys were always tired. I could see it in the bags under their eyes. I walked around the different battle positions during our mandatory, all-hands-on-deck stand-to in the mornings, and I tried to reassure myself that it was all worth it. That I was doing the right thing. That was command, though. Trusting your training, your men, and your gut. Most of all, command was lonely, and I looked forward to seeing my beautiful wife again.

The same stadium where we said good-bye to our parents at the beginning was our final port of debarkation on a strange journey that was the Army. West Point loves symmetry. With our brass gleaming, shoes polished to a high shine, and a crisp, full-dress uniform (except for the chevron that Pete had ripped off a few drunken nights ago, now affixed with scotch tape), we all sat patiently for the moment that we dreamed of for so long. Graduation day.

My entire family, including Courtney, was in the stands that day to watch my momentous and improbable feat. I did it! After my bars were pinned, I received my first salute from a crusty former marine who was my baseball coach throughout high school. I swear, that guy said the "F" word paired with my name more often than I care to admit. Nothing was going to keep me down. After a brief lunch with my family, more congratulations from an extremely proud grouping of individuals, I took off with Courtney to hang out in New York City. Time for my next adventure.

Much to the chagrin of my best friend of almost fifteen years, whom I promised the stag trip of our lives, I decided that Courtney would be my travel buddy on a monumental car trip from West Point to my home in Arizona. Following graduation, we had sixty days of leave, and we were going to use every ounce of it, dammit! What followed was the most wonderful, aimless, and unforgettable experience imaginable.

My Chrysler Sebring convertible meandered across the United States stopping in New Jersey, Virginia, Mississippi, Louisiana, Texas, Colorado, and Arizona. We lived off cheap beer and even cheaper motels. At one point, in New Orleans, I don't think we slept under the covers the place was so gross. Courtney swore you could catch the clap from just looking at the shower, let alone get into it.

As all good things, the trip had to come to an end. My uncle wearing a flag-adorned top hat beckoned! But before the bliss came to an end, I made an important declaration to the same friend that I jilted a month earlier at one of our stops along the way. We all drank light beer and jumped from tall rocks into crystal-clear water. As I stood on the top of that rock, looking down at Courtney, I told Austin that I was going to marry that girl down there. And almost one year later, I did.

The excitement in the bus was palpable as I finished my first deployment. Our plane from Bangor, Maine, had landed in Fort Hood, Texas, approximately an hour ago, and we were ready to see our families after fifteen excruciatingly long months in Iraq. Soldiers smacked each other on the head and wondered aloud just how much booze a man could consume before their faces melted. Others discussed how they were going to make considerable donations to aspiring junior college young ladies of the night at the first opportunity.

Fort Hood may do a lot of things differently than other places, but there is one thing that they have down to a science: pageantry! Everyone on the bus was going crazy when we pulled up to the parade field, families bursting at the seams. The buses unloaded, hiding us from the crowd on the other side, and someone encouraged the families to shout, "MOVE, THAT, BUS!" With that, the buses pulled away and every hair on my body stood on end. It was probably one of the most exciting days of my life, and I was so glad my family got to share it with me. They deserved this day, too.

After a few quick words from the general, "You guys are awesome, Iraq's rivers flow of chocolate because of your efforts . . . blah, blah, blah," we were released to our families. I did the mandatory bro hug to a couple of guys in the formation and began doing laps in search of my family. Where was Courtney? Where were my parents? After I completed a tour of the parade field, which was immense, I decided that Courtney and I were simply circling the field in the same direction. I sped off the other way and was shocked to find she wasn't there. My wife forgot that I was coming home today!

I would have to beg someone to use their cell phone, you know, to remind my loving family their hero had arrived home from *war*! I stared off into the bleachers, which were empty save for a few. From the very top, I heard clear as day, "Hey, there he is." It was my wife's brother, Kyle. I knew that spiky hair and skull and crossbones belt buckle anywhere. Moving with the speed of a Velociraptor, and attacking me with the same ferocity, a blur of a blue dress pounced. Courtney and I embraced for hours. We both had tears in our eyes. Not really caring to explain her uncharacteristic lapse of attention to detail, Courtney grabbed my arm, with the rest of me attached, and we were in the Jeep in no time. Fifteen months of waiting was long enough.

Falling asleep on my XO's shoulder, I was jerked awake when the general finally arrived at the hangar to give his speech at my second redeployment. Unlike my Welcome Home Ceremony at Fort Hood, the ceremony at Fort Carson placed a much higher importance on ensuring the paperwork was in perfect order than getting the soldiers to their families. Our plane landed over an hour and a half ago, and we were still sitting in the hangar, our families watching a live feed of us from their places on the bleachers.

What Fort Cason lacked in pageantry and show it made up for in loud, Toby Keith country music and smoke. As we burst through the gym doors like the Harlem Globetrotters, I saw Courtney front row, center. My friend in charge of the formation kicked us loose, and with that, I was back in the arms of the love of my life, the horrors of the deployment a distant memory.

The three journeys provided by Mother Army have shown me more than I would have ever cared to know about myself and about my fellow man. West Point taught me that I was nothing special and my future success depended upon my humility. Yeah, yeah, so you were your high school golf team captain for three years and you had a love affair with Gap, now what?

The deployments painted another side of the human experience. One filled with destruction, blood, and true evil. If I concentrated hard enough, I could almost taste the death I experienced on a daily basis throughout my first deployment. The Iraqis were in the middle of an ethnic cleansing that rivaled anything that happened in Bosnia, and we were right smack dab in the middle of it. Dead bodies were everywhere we drove, and I was ordering hundreds of body bags a month to keep up with them. After a while it wasn't just the civilian bodies that were turning up. Soon it was our own. Rockets never asked what your job was or what rank you were. You accepted that and just kept on going.

Afghanistan was the scariest place in the world. Unlike Iraq, where you never saw the bad guys, you just drove outside and someone blew you up, the Taliban wanted you to see them when they shot an RPG at you. To this day any sudden, unexpected noises make me jump. Those used to be rockets. If I thought hard enough on it, I could still feel bullets flying over my head and hear that snap.

That's just it, though, isn't it? I don't want to think about it hard enough. My story doesn't revolve around the bodies, killed in action, or the explosions, because I won't let it. My story revolves around the love of my life because without her, there is nothing to say that I want to hear.

Combat changed me. It made me more cynical. How can I ever believe there is good in the world when I've seen what people are truly capable of? Seeing what I saw robbed me of my innocence that those who have not seen the terrors of war can still possess, but that doesn't mean I'm allowed to stop living my life. It's about finding a way to keep going and deal with what I've seen. We all process emotions differently. We go through life the best we can, and in the end, you lie there on your deathbed and hope you don't have any regrets. War showed me that life was indeed short. You have to go out there and live it.

Even though my positive experiences outweigh the negative, it would be entirely too easy to crawl underneath the blanket of darkness and gravitate toward the pain. Feel sorry for myself. Resent those that hadn't seen what I had. Climb into a bottle. Allow myself only to focus on the more horrible images that can sneak up from time to time, but life is too short for that. Instead, I choose to picture my beautiful wife and push the rest aside. For me, it's about reframing my life experiences in a way that I want to remember them. I refuse to be defined by the worst because I believe I'm so much more.

I choose to center my story around my soul mate because she is the light. I *choose*. Darkness behind me; light in front. I have to move forward. Keep on walking away from the things that hurt, that pull me away from being a better human being. The Army sent me to war twice, and all they did was add two chapters to mine and Courtney's love story that continues every day. Throughout my story, I always reference to feeling happier than I ever have in my entire life. I do this because, first of all, as Courtney would point out, I exaggerate pretty much everything, but second, and much more important, each day that I get to spend with my wife is better than the one before.

Three roads converged in a yellow wood and standing there, only a few minutes late, was the woman I will travel down that road with forever. And *that* has made all the difference.

DISMAY

Dismay and remorse are two sides of the same coin. Both are derivatives from an experience in which the outcome was not of our choosing. Unlike dismay, remorse expresses connotations of guilt resulting from a conscious decision, while dismay captures the reaction to a situation that transpired outside of the locus of our control. The die is cast. The score is settled. Debts are paid. Dismay is how we futilely attempt to grasp the past before the future contaminated a once pristine ideal in direct opposition to our will and best efforts.

ALL THE PIECES MATTER

TJ Root

Summer in Baghdad reminds me of high school wrestling practice when our coach decided to help us all lose weight by sealing all the doors to the gym and turning the radiators up. I didn't need to lose weight. I was trying to wrestle up a weight class and was too small already. In the end, all the heat did for me was make a bad time worse. That's the best metaphor I know of for Iraq.

The city in July is putrid. Breathing feels like sucking air through a damp gym sock. Thick, viscous air. Briny. Smoky. Dusty. Acrid. Shit-filled. The effect is that much worse when the air is where you earn your living, which is an unfortunate job requirement of being a helicopter pilot.

Even with a full aviation task force, we don't have enough aircraft to give the battlespace around-the-clock scout helicopter coverage. As a result, the late afternoon shift amounts to a single team—two helicopters—instead of the three teams that overlap the rest of the day and night. It's a solitary shift—a five-hour vignette of rivers and canals and buildings and decay and palm trees and people and violence and everyday life in the big city, punctuated by two lonely green specks in the grubby sky.

Last week, one of our aircraft was swatted out of the sky by a heavy machine gun. The IEDs were so thick on the road that no ground unit could get to the pilots. It's on our minds constantly—the thought of burning in and being cut off from help.[1] We don't control nearly as much of this place as we'd all like to believe, and that fact is not peculiar to our particular corner of the war.

Only two hours to go until the next team is on station. *Christ. Two more hours.* We might have to make one more cycle through the rearm/refuel point for more fuel and ammunition.[2] Hopefully not. If we're lucky, we won't have to shoot at anyone, and we'll be able to stretch our fuel to the end of the mission. That's largely out of our hands, though, as a lot can happen in two hours. Until then, we're the only two helicopters in a battlespace that stretches across the ancient heart of Mesopotamia—from Baghdad south to Karbala, and east from the Euphrates all the way to Iran.

The blast happens in an instant. There's no boom. We're too far away and the aircraft is too loud. From here, the explosion looks like a gray boil of dust and smoke, rising up from the green elephant grass. I feel like I'm watching the silent film of old hydrogen bomb tests. It's the biggest blast I've ever seen. Actually, that isn't true. The biggest I've ever seen was four five-hundred-pound bombs that accidentally landed on a road directly in our flightpath about a month ago. I don't know if friendly explosions count, though, even if they do almost kill you.

The engine is overtaxed in the heat, shrieking over the sound of the radios as we make best speed toward the blast site. I flip-flop FM radio frequencies to bring up the battlespace owner's radio net as we cross the Tigris and check in with our callsign, Lighthorse 32.[3] The headquarters element, Battle Oscar,[4] responds and clears us into the airspace with a request that we contact their B Company element, callsign "Barbarian."

"Roger, Lighthorse 32 flight will come up Barbarian's push."[5]

I drop the FM frequency off the battalion net down to the Barbarian Ops & Intel[6] net. The ear cups of my helmet explode with the sound of Barbarian White 6 coming unglued. He's screaming at a squad leader to "find the fucking truck." *Did they lose a truck? He's out of breath. It sounds like he's running. Where is he running?*

I'm white-knuckling the doorframe, straining against my seatbelt harness to lean out of the aircraft for a better look at the ground. I can't tell where White 6 is through the settling remnant of the dust cloud. I can barely see anyone, let alone single out the man in charge whose voice is blasting across the radio. The whole scene is a big clusterfuck. I definitely don't see anyone running, though. What I can see is the hollowed-out carcass of a building. It looks like a barn. Scratch that—half of a barn. The eastern end of the structure is gone. It's disappeared. There's nothing but a crater.

White 6 is really out of breath now, barely able to form words. He finally unkeys the hand mic and lets the net fall silent. I seize the opportunity.

"White 6, this is Lighthorse 32 on O&I."

"Light . . . *pant* . . . horse . . . *pant* . . . 32 . . . White 6." *He's not running. He's hyperventilating.*

"White 1, this is Lighthorse 32. Sister ship is Lighthorse 30—we are two Kiowa Warriors on station at your location with fourteen rockets, three hundred rounds of .50 cal, one HELLFIRE missile. 1+30 of playtime. Request SITREP and frontline trace, over."[7]

Silence.

"White 6, Lighthorse 32, how do you hear me?"

"LIGHTHOR—*pant*—HORSE 32 . . . THIS IS WHITE 6 . . . *pant* . . . cough . . . MULTIPLE CASUALTIES. We can't . . . *pant* . . . find two guys. I think they got kidnapped."

His voice trails off. He's yelling orders to someone. My hackles are up at the word *kidnapped*. My first thought is of Connell. He was Coach Connell to me, since I played semipro football under him for a civilian team back at Fort Drum. To most everyone else, he was Sergeant First Class Connell, an infantry platoon sergeant. A month ago, he was killed in an ambush and two of his soldiers were kidnapped. They're still missing. They're probably being tortured.

The flight is in a tight left-hand orbit over the farm. The dust is slowly creeping off them. I can see soldiers on both sides of the road. Everything looks calm. Everything looks slow. It's quiet, but it always looks quiet from above. We can't hear the screams and the shouts and the crying children and the growling HMMWV motors and the snap of bullets and the *Allahu akhbars!* The smell, though—that we get. Misery has a smell. It smells like blood, exhaust, and shit. It churns through the rotors and into our faces. In the highlight reel of this war, that smell is the soundtrack.

"White 6, Lighthorse 32 . . . standby." I hop nets to Baghdad Radio, the catchall aircraft control frequency for the battlespace. We need a MEDEVAC bird in a hurry. Like most Army procedures, the standard 9-line MEDEVAC request format is a pain in the ass, so we bypass it. There's usually a MEDEVAC flight up somewhere, and Baghdad Radio is where to find them. It's tied up with another half-hearted advisory call from the bored female controller in her air-conditioned office. Her voice drones on and on with a string of airspace closures and meaningless administrative noise. *No fucking sense of urgency.*

"BREAK BREAK BREAK . . . Any MEDEVAC aircraft, this is Light-horse 32 on Baghdad Radio . . . Roadside MEDEVAC." Seconds pass. Nothing. I call again. Still nothing. I start to worry. *What if no one's up? How am I going to get these guys help? Getting a second-up MEDEVAC flight will take longer than these guys have. Maybe I should make another call for any lift aircraft.*

"Lighthorse 32, this is Medicine Man 44." *Fuckin' A, Medicine Man. We're in business.* He's not wasting time, either. He knows what a net call on Radio means. I pass him our location. He's five minutes out.

White 6 isn't talking to his higher headquarters, so I have to let Battle Oscar know that Barbarian White Platoon is in deep shit. I bounce back to the battalion and rattle off the eight-digit grid for the MEDEVAC LZ.

White 6 busts in. "NEGATIVE, NEGATIVE. Incorrect grid!" he sputters, and then wheezes out the grid he wants for the MEDEVAC LZ. It's ten meters off of mine. *He's not thinking. And he's still out of breath. Oh fuck . . . He's in shock. He probably got hit by the blast.*

He's all over the battalion net now, trying to cancel the MEDEVAC and send up new grids. I have to do something.

"White 6, this is Lighthorse 32. You need to calm down, son. I've got your MEDEVAC. You need to establish security and police up your casualties. I'll have birds on the ground in 5 mikes for your wounded. Do not send further grids. Prep for EVAC. How copy?"

I've officially lost my fucking mind. I just called an infantry platoon leader, who may well be older than I am, "son" on his battalion net, where God and everybody can hear it. My right-seater looks over at me. I look at him. He nods. For all that lieutenant knows, I'm a forty-five-year-old mustachioed warrant officer. He doesn't need to know that I'm a twenty-five-year-old who is as scared and clueless as he is. Honesty isn't always the best policy, it turns out.

For a moment, everything seems as calm as it looks. The calm is an illusion, of course—the result of our overhead viewpoint aided by our adrenaline-altered sense of time, which makes the seconds drag on like slow yawns. We've been working this TIC[8] for an eternity already. *Where the fuck is the MEDE-VAC? They should fucking be here by now.* I look at the clock. We've been on station for . . . two minutes. *Two minutes?* I'm sweating through my body armor. *Why is this place so goddamn hot? What kind of fucking people think this is a good place to live?* A quick glance at the dash reveals that what had been a precious chunk of ice rattling in my water bottle is now a blobby little puddle.

White 7, the platoon sergeant, is on the net with our lead aircraft. His voice is frantic. They're still discussing a blue bongo[9] truck. They're saying a blue bongo truck left the house right after the barn exploded. He's telling my lead ship that they think the two missing guys are in the bed of the truck. *Fuck.* "Kidnapped" leaps from the clatter of radio traffic. *How did we not notice that before? They already said it once. That's what he meant. Shit, how much time have we wasted?!*

Lead bends the flight over into a hard right turn. We head westbound, into the dying sunlight. Sunset has now become the enemy, too. The right-seaters are wringing all the speed they can out of the aircraft. We have to find this blue truck before it's dark. All White 7 can tell us is that it's a blue bongo truck with a tarp, and two missing soldiers are under the tarp. *Under the tarp?* White 6 chimes in and confirms the report of the blue bongo. He's still a mess, and I don't know if he's totally with us. Even if they're right, it's almost nothing to go on. You can't swing a dead cat in this country without hitting three bongos, and two of those will be blue.

My stomach feels like a lump. My mouth is dry.

FUCK. We're never going to find this truck. We wasted too much time at the TIC. These guys are fucking gone. They're going to be tortured and killed and we're going to find their bodies in the river like all the other bodies we find in the river with no hands and no heads and all bloated and rotten like monsters and their mothers will always wonder why we let this happen and it happened because we let the truck get away and if Connell wasn't dead he'd be so disappointed in me because we let it all happen again which really means I let it happen because I'm the air mission commander and I should've looked for the truck sooner but I didn't and now we'll never find it and—

"Trail, this is Lead. Blue bongo, 2 o'clock low, tarp on the bed. Looks like it just turned off the road from the TIC onto Route Chevy." *Oh thank you, Jesus. I'm sorry for all the bad shit I've done. Thank you thank you thank you.*

We have the truck in sight, too. It's definitely a blue bongo. It was definitely on the only road from the blast site. It's hauling ass. *We found it. We fucking found these kidnapping assholes.* The tarp in the bed looks lumpy, like there's something under it. Two bodies could definitely fit in the bed, side by side.

Lead sets a left-hand orbit around the truck as it bombs down the road, launching a rooster tail of dust behind it. I can't see anything in the thermal sight. The tarp is doing a good job of hiding the bodies in the bed. Not far ahead, the road dumps onto a main causeway by a market that's always teeming with vehicles. Once the truck hits that snarl of late afternoon traffic, we might lose it.

"Lighthorse 32, Medicine Man 44 is 1 mike to the northeast, inbound for roadside MEDEVAC." He's one minute out from the LZ.[10] We should be providing security, but we can't lose this truck. We should've reconned a landing zone for him. We've left him hanging. We aren't supposed to do that. He'll have to choose his own LZ now.

Lead rolls over hard and noses into a low pass over the truck. His blades chatter and pop as he breaks left over the bed to give his left-seater a good angle. No joy. The driver speeds up. He's making a run for the mass of traffic ahead. *We can't shoot him with the soldiers in the bed.* Even so, I bring up the HELLFIRE missile control page on the cockpit screen. I crane to look over the right-seater's lap at the missile hanging on the rack. The laser seekerhead is wobbling around inside the glass nosecone. Once the gyroscopes spool up, the seekerhead will be ready to fly the missile right into that truck. *How do we stop a truck with a missile? Put it through the cab? Try to land the missile in front of the truck? Those two guys in the bed will be fucked up forever, if they survive at all. I'll kill them. I know it.*

Medicine Man 44 is on the deck. The casualties are being loaded. Four in all. He's off the deck almost immediately. Two of them will die before the aircraft lands again.

Lead makes another pass on the bongo truck. Still no joy.[11] The truck is about to reach the market. If we're going to shoot him, we need to do it now. Lead doesn't want to take the shot. The decision falls to me as the air mission commander. *I don't want to kill two Americans. I don't want to, I promise. But I don't want them chained to a wall in a torture house having a power drill taken to their thighs. Or bobbing down the Euphrates without their heads and hands.*

The seconds aren't dragging anymore. They're flying by like the truck barreling toward his escape. We have to shoot him or he's gone.

We don't shoot. The truck bounces off the dirt road and lurches into the swarm of Iraqi drivers. It only takes a few moments of his weaving back and forth among dozens of identical bongo trucks for us to lose him. There are too many trucks. Too many have tarps. *Was the tarp brownish-tan or tannish-brown? Did the truck have mirrors? Was there a dent in the cab? Is that it? No, it's the one that just went under the awning. No, he's still moving. Where did he go? Fuck. Fuckfuckfuck.*

I lost the truck. Lead lost sight of it, too. My right-seater can't help much from his side, and he's trying to avoid colliding with Lead as we corkscrew in tandem over the teeming mass of cars and people as they honk and scrape their way through the narrow suburban market.

We blew it. We got a second chance and we blew it. The truck is gone and so are they. I have to tell Battle Oscar that we lost the truck with two of their guys—both probably wounded and scared to death—stashed in the back. I can barely get the words out. We're their security—their turbine-powered woobie[12] in the sky. We're the advantage the ground unit always has—that this enemy can never have . . . and we didn't do shit. We might as well have just gone home.

I'm barely finished choking out the report of our failure when White 7 jumps in on the battalion net and asks that we drop back to his frequency. He requests us back overhead ASAP.

Lead continues our turn around to the southeast, back toward the shattered barn. We're back on station in a matter of minutes. The situation looks a bit calmer now and, judging by the radio traffic, it is. *I really need some water. My mouth tastes like dust.* The remains of the platoon are still hunkered down inside the farm compound's walls, save for one squad at Medicine Man's LZ, where the dust from his rotors is settling lazily in the breeze.

"Lighthorse 32, this is White 6." He's calm now, too. I'm sort of surprised he didn't get EVAC'd. I know he's hurt. He's a good PL. I feel even worse about calling him "son."

"32 . . . disregard that truck." A wave of relief crashes over me. It feels as though the temperature drops 20 degrees. "I still have two personnel unaccounted for." The temperature soars again. *What the fuck?*

White 7 is on the net with him now. He thinks the missing guys were kidnapped and stashed nearby, maybe in a canal, or in one of the houses down the road. Thrown from the truck, possibly. The truck may not have been the one we followed. It doesn't make much sense, but even so, it's the only theory going. White 6 and White 7 are on opposite sides of the road. Two of the squads are still inside the walls. No one is moving much. White 6 is worried that there are more booby traps rigged. He's ordered everyone to stay put.

"Trail, this is Lead. Recommend we recon the canals west-to-east." From the sound of his voice, he doesn't buy the stashed-in-a-canal idea either.

"Roger, we'll cover you."

Lead drops down to about twenty off the deck and slows to a hover. He's creeping along the south side of the road. I can see the left-seater craning his head out of the aircraft, grasping the doorframe for leverage. There's no way we can cover him from up here. We couldn't get a shot off in time, and the angle would be terrible. We have to get low, too.

As we spiral down toward the ground, I get my first good look at the barn. It's an unreal sight. The crater looks like the fiery hand of an angry god scooped out the earth and scorched what he didn't take. The soldiers are all lying prone, rifles at the ready, pulling security. Filthy faces. Bloodstained pants. A vision of bedraggled misery to accompany the persistent smell.

"You look out your door; I'm watching the windows." My right-seater acknowledges as I pull my M4 off the dash. I prop one leg on the doorframe and train the sights on the windows of the grimy little mud houses just beyond the canal. Faces pop up in the shadowy holes and quickly vanish as we chatter past. Kids, mostly. A few women. I can see that Lead's left-seater has his rifle out, too. *I hope he's a better shot than I am. He probably is. I'm a crummy shot. I'm even worse from a helicopter.*

Our path takes us down the north side of the road, followed by a right turn northbound up the road the truck took to flee the blast. *This is fucking nuts. We're violating every rule. Two aircraft, hovering along a road, within fifty feet of every building in the village. Any halfway lucky asshole with an AK-47 could destroy $8 million worth of helicopter and two pilots without breaking a sweat.*

The canals are putrid. They're vats of sewage, essentially, with reeds. Tall reeds. It's like a cornfield but twice as thick. Our rotorwash sets them

frantically dancing and flopping, giving us glimpses of the oily muck beneath. *If our missing guys are in there, they're in deep shit. Literally.* So far,
though, I don't buy it. But we owe it to them to search every last corner.
Drowning in sewage would be the worst way to go. I make myself think of
something else. *Fire would be worse.*

"Trail, Lead." His voice sounds shaky. I fumble with the radio selector
switch blindly, so my eyes can keep frantically checking empty windows.
Lead is off the canal, now, beating down elephant grass in the field south of
the farm.

"Lead, this is trail, send it."

"We've got a leg here."

Leg? *Did he just say a leg?*

"Say again, over."

"We have a leg here. It's wearing a boot." The left-seater is pointing at
the ground as his aircraft slowly pirouettes around it. *A leg? A leg. A human
leg. The leg of a human. It's wearing a boot. Iraqis wear sandals.* The right-
seaters are deconflicting movements as our aircraft hops over the road and
settles into a hover where Lead had been. He's sliding east, toward the farm.

It's a leg. Half of a leg, actually—severed just below the knee. The ACU
pants are dusty, but barely frayed where they were sheared off. The flesh
and bone are tattered, but there's no horror movie gore. *It looks like meat.*
It's just laying there, as though someone packed up a picnic and left it behind as an oversight; laying there as though it was never part of a person at
all. I drop my rifle to my lap.

"White 6, Lighthorse 32. We have ID'd one leg, fifty meters to your
Southwest. More to follow."

"Roger." His answer is punctuated with a sigh. White 6 is exhausted.
The adrenaline effect is wearing off and shock is setting in.

"Which leg was it?" My right-seater's voice surprises me.

"Huh? What do you mean? It's a fucking leg, man."

"Left or right?"

"Right." *What a weird question.*

"Ok, Roger."

Lead resumes the methodical search through the grass, with our ship
mirroring him in an offset, searching as he searches. We circle counter-
clockwise around the farm, back over the road separating the troops on

the ground. Minutes pass. I spot a helmet. It's cracked and slightly out-of-round. *No blood. Maybe that guy's OK.* I let Lead know. He passes it to White 7. White 6 isn't answering anymore.

"Trail, we have another leg."

"Right or left?" I ask. *I see what my right-seater was driving at now.*

"Left . . . no, right. Yeah, Roger, it's a right leg."

Two right legs. That's both guys. They weren't kidnapped. They weren't taken. They aren't gone. They're . . . gone.

"They must've been standing right on top of it," my right-seater sighs. There's a quiver in his voice I hadn't heard before. It's unnerving. He's on his second tour and nothing is supposed to rattle him.

We repeat our earlier waltz, hovering over Lead's mark to see the leg. It's almost complete, sliced off just below the hip. The cargo pocket is still velcroed shut. It's not bloody either. Just a bit of sinew and some ratty flesh. *I thought there'd be more blood.*

The sunlight is waning. We have to find whatever else we can find. Once EOD gets here to clear the farm of booby traps, the platoon can go police up their dead, but we need to find all that we can before dark. The feral dogs will cart pieces of the bodies off if they aren't recovered quickly.

We find the torso next. My right-seater sees it and swings the tail around to give me a look. The body armor is still in place, looking almost untouched. The nametape and rank are still velcroed in place. *That's some badass armor.* Everything not covered by the armor is gone. Arms. Pelvis. Head. Pruned off by the blast.

Lead just found another leg. A left leg, obviously. He calls it up to White 6, who's back on the net again. They know what happened now. They know exactly where their guys are—in pieces, all around them. And they're stuck, helpless.

It's almost time to go. Our fuel level is critical. I can hear bits of radio chatter as the next team spins up at the airfield and checks the radios. We can stretch our gas a bit longer, though. I'm so relieved. *We didn't lose a truck with two guys hogtied in the back. We didn't blow it. I'm happy about that.* There's nothing to be done now but pick up the pieces.

There. What's that? Grass flops in the way of my view. *Is that . . . a tail? Fur?*

"White 6, this is Lighthorse 32 . . . say again number of accounted personnel?"

"32, two soldiers."

"White 6 . . . are you missing a dog?"

Silence. The mic is still keyed. I hear some background chatter.

"32, White 6 . . . Roger. One of the missing guys was a dog handler."

I'm looking at half of a dog. The back half. It's like a magician's trick gone wrong—the dog really was sawed in half. *It's a German shepherd.* The tail is fluffy and curved upward, and flops a bit in the rotorwash. The fur is still clean and has the beautiful two-tone of a shepherd. It looks soft and warm. The dirt underneath it is black and sticky with blood.

My tongue tastes briny and metallic, the way a penny tastes. The sensation reminds me of being a kid, when that taste meant I was about to be sick. I stare, unblinking, watching the wisps of fur dance around until we've hovered past and I can't see anymore. I pass the location to White 7. He thanks me. My stomach is sour. The sweat on my hands smudges my pencil.

I want to go home.

We're almost out of fuel. I check out with White 6 and promise to push the next Kiowa team to his location. He's weary but seems to be doing all right, all things considered. He and White 7 are working up a plan to recover the remains as we conduct our battle handover with the incoming team. They'll pull security until EOD and the relief force can get there. I've lost track of how many parts we found. Not all of them, that much I know. As we head for the airfield, everyone from White 6 up to Battle 6 personally thanks us on the net for all we did. *We didn't do anything.*

The rotor slowly spins down to a stop on the parking ramp. Our usual postmission jokes don't feel funny today. No one even tries. I walk across the flight line toward the other crew. Nik is smiling, mostly because that's what he always does. Josh hugs me like I'm his own kid.

"Good work, boss."

Justin lights two cigarettes and hands me one. We sit down against the t-walls beside the aircraft and smoke in silence.

Thirteen months to go.

This vignette is based—as accurately as memory will allow—on a real event. It pays homage to the soldiers we served as aircrews—the men and women on the ground who fought the good fight from the first day to the last. It is a tribute to our warrant officers—the fathers, brothers, husbands, and sons who sustained me, and one another, through fifteen months and a thousand hours of flying. It is written with the utmost respect for those two young men we tried to piece together so they could come home, too.

THE MEN I WENT
TO WAR WITH

Chris Baldwin

This chapter is dedicated to all members of the Armed Forces of the United States and her allied nations. May God continue to watch over them and protect them. I also cannot say "thank you" enough to my wife, Bridget. She is my rock and my heart.

My platoon sergeant, SFC M—, and I ran into Ben Britt and Gary Avery outside the mess tent in Kuwait one evening in September of 2005 after our unit had been deployed for a couple of weeks. Ben and Gary were going to Iraq later that night . . . to Iraq, to the war, to combat, to fight. Part of me was jealous and wondered when my battalion would follow. They were heading to do the one thing that we both trained and studied for during the past five years. *They were going to lead their platoons against our Nation's enemies.*

There are those who would say that statement is too reductive and embraces a naive sense of patriotism as opposed to an ambiguous taxonomy defined by contemporary geopolitical events. It is easy for some people to believe that soldiers take a simplistic view of war. The truth is, the opposite is the case. Only soldiers truly know the complexity of war. Only soldiers see the tragedy of civilians caught in the middle of the guns, how moments of great compassion are born in the middle of battle, how one's own life is inconsequential when it comes to protecting a fellow soldier. But soldiers also recognize the binary between good and evil, between friends and enemies. And while many soldiers might not have the academic pedigree of the talking heads on the news, they have a perception derived through training and combat experience.

The four of us sat at the cheap table in the tent in Kuwait. Since it was September, we talked about college football. Ben, who played college football before West Point, had plenty of theories and analyses that were better than that of ESPN's Sports Center. SFC M— was also a huge football fan and offered great counterpoints. Not surprisingly, the talk turned to Iraq. Rumors of IED attacks, snipers in windows, and where Zarqawi (the leader of al-Qaeda in Iraq) was hiding kept our conversations lively. We were tired of going to ranges in the Kuwaiti desert, attending classes on IEDs, receiving lectures on heat mitigation, and reading old paperbacks. We were ready to go do the real thing. My platoon sergeant, who had already fought in Iraq and Afghanistan, periodically interjected his opinions gleaned from experience into our conversation. This, of course, is one of the best things an NCO can do for young officers—keeping them focused and contained without extinguishing the flames of enthusiasm. Dinner broke up, and we walked out into the twilight. It was still hot but cooling off and the sky was pink. For some reason, I remember that fact. Our parting words were brief—telling each other to take care, promises to keep in touch, and a few handshakes. The truth is that we really didn't know what to say, and SFC M, who probably *did know* what to say, knew that this was a lesson we would have to learn on our own. I now know what I would have said to them.

If I had known it would be the last time I would see them, I would have said something else. I would have told them how much I respected them. Neither men were strangers, and thus they warranted a better farewell than what was rendered; further, if I had known that this farewell was going to be a final one, I certainly would have thought of something much more profound to say. I wish I would have talked to Ben longer at that mess tent in Kuwait. That I told him I thought he was one of the brightest men I'd ever been around. I could listen to him debate and opine for hours. I would thank him for all the advice he gave me about working out. That I was impressed beyond words about how seriously he took our profession and his pragmatic approach to leadership. I would have set definite plans with him to get another apartment when we got back. I would have told him it was an honor to serve with him. I just wish I would have known.

But I didn't know. How could I have? To me, Ben was my roommate back at Fort Campbell. We decorated our apartment with TA 50 (Aarmy combat/field equipment), old *Sports Illustrated* magazines, crushed beer cans, and a TV that sat upon a cardboard box. He was not going to be one of the first classmates to die in combat. And Gary? He was going to be watching football while adding to our crushed beer can collection. He wasn't going to die either. Perhaps my ignorance was a blessing. Maybe that farewell on that warm Kuwait evening was everything that it should have been.

A few days later, SFC M— and I were awoken at midnight and told to get the platoon ready to move north to Iraq. We finally got what we wanted.

My unit was responsible for an area south of Baghdad that consisted of miles of irrigation canals forming a spider web across hundreds of farms that had stood in that area for thousands of years. We were just outside of the towns of Mahmudiyah and Yusufiyah. The terrain did not fight my preconceived notion of the Iraqi landscape. It hated us. The summer heat transformed the lush palm groves into suffocating jungles. In the winter, mud slowed our dismounted patrols to a glacial pace and caked itself on every piece of equipment and body part. When we did use our vehicles, a few of them would always get stuck in endless fields of malevolent, vindictive Iraqi mud.

The enemy in our area was just as evil as the mud. In our Battalion's AO, al-Qaeda built car bombs that would eventually flatten entire city blocks in Baghdad. The enemy also used the area to smuggle in foreign fighters and their weapons. He did not want us here and fortified the roads with IEDs to keep us out. The IEDs were huge and were capable of destroying an entire vehicle and its crew with a single blast. They were buried in the roads, hidden in trees, or built into houses. The IEDs consisted of everything ranging from artillery rounds to propane tanks packed full of ball bearings and homemade explosives.

To take this land from the enemy, we relied on both traditional Army doctrine and what counterinsurgency (COIN) knowledge we had. From my limited perspective we did a lot right during that deployment: on patrols, we used movement techniques just like we were taught at Fort Benning. NCOs established a base of fire and maneuvered on the enemy when we were engaged. We reacted to mortar fire and rocket fire, and our forward observers called in our mortars to fight the enemy. We conducted raids that would have made any Infantry School or Ranger School instructor proud—security, violence of action, and a planned withdrawal were always part of the plan. To this day, I can hear SFC M— tell me how long we had been on the objective; remaining on an objective longer than necessary in combat is an unforgivable sin. We paid attention to what was out of place, what didn't seem right. We studied maps and planned and debated tactics and operations over endless cups of bad coffee. I quickly realized that whoever said, "The textbook goes out the window in combat," had either never seen combat or had received poor training. In the States, we trained for war, and when war came, we put our training to use. We weren't mindless drones; we just adjusted to the situation and implemented our doctrine where necessary, and if it didn't fit, we didn't use it.

As in every counterinsurgency fight, our focus was the people. However, we could do nothing until we established a relationship with them. To earn their trust, we sat for hours and talked to local leaders, farmers, sheikhs, merchants, and housewives to gain intelligence on our enemy. We ate meals in their homes and drank chai with them. You couldn't make an ally in just one meeting. My squad leaders and I learned that business in the Middle East is not as quick and to the point as it is in the West. You couldn't just walk into a home and ask someone, "Where are the insurgents?" though I did this early on several times. We had to sit and earn their trust. It was often hot and laborious work. We could feel the weight of our equipment on our shoulders as we sat cross-legged on the floor. More chai, more cigarettes, and more talk of farming, children, and how to best get crops into Baghdad, but then a name would be mentioned. A name we would recognize. A name of an insurgent—the farmer had heard it secondhand but it was a name that we had stored in a notebook or computer somewhere. Another piece of our puzzle was put into place. We continued our hunt, and as always, the enemy continued theirs. I am quite certain that my experience is not singular. Small units everywhere learned that if they wanted to take something from the enemy, they were going to need the people to do so.

My company had just come back from an air assault and was getting ready for another one when I learned that Ben was killed in action. It stunned me, made me angry, and was incomprehensible. Ben was one of the best there was. When I got the word it was nighttime, on the twenty-third or twenty-fourth of December. It was cold, and I was standing outside of my tent at FOB Striker wearing a "poly-pro top" and skullcap. I don't know what I said and I don't think I said anything; I just nodded. My commander and NCOs offered a few words of comfort. They said, "We'll get even," and that "We will settle the score." But in the back of my mind, more important than settling the score for Ben was doing my duty for him, for my soldiers, for my country. A cynic will say that is oversimplified and not realistic; that it is a form of pedestrian patriotism. But those cynics haven't served with men who love their country and have beheld the evil inflicted by its enemies. They haven't worked with professionals who would gladly, and often do, give their lives for their men and their mission. So I honored Ben by going back to my NCOs, diving into the maps and satellite imagery of our objective, and refocusing on the mission. Where should security go? Where will we be attacked from? When will the enemy hit us? We woke up at three in the morning to go out to the helicopters and go back to the war. I was with the best men I ever knew—I was with men like Ben.

Not long after Ben's death, my Company was sent to the bridge. It had no name as far as we knew and was simply known as "the bridge." We sometimes called it "Our Bridge," which was probably what the enemy called it. Al-Qaeda used the bridge across a canal to move car bombs into Baghdad, and we wanted to take Our Bridge back from them. To that end, my Company was given the mission to block the bridge with concertina wire and concrete barriers. Our 1st Platoon moved to the bridge to begin to emplace the barriers. The enemy covered the route to Our Bridge with IEDs. During the movement, 1st Platoon was attacked, and during the fight they lost a great squad leader, SSG D—. To say this NCO was something special is almost belittling. He was an amazing leader, father, and friend. The actions surrounding his death posthumously earned him a well-deserved Silver Star. His death hit our company hard. My platoon replaced 1st Platoon on the bridge mission, and a few days later we finally completed emplacing the necessary obstacles. At some point on a mission that week (I don't remember and didn't record when) or the next, I got word via a radio transmission that 1st Battalion had soldiers KIA. My RTO gave me the message, and I simply said "Roger." I couldn't dwell on it. Our platoon had a mission to accomplish. It was just another radio transmission. It went to a part of my mind, and I filed it away. It was another piece of information. When I got back to the FOB a few days later and checked my email, I found two emails expressing sorrow for the fact that we had lost another West Point classmate. This time it was Gary. He was the one of the three in the vague radio transmission my RTO had relayed to me.

I was both physically and mentally exhausted after the past week. I went to my tent and fell into a deep sleep thinking about the loss of a great friend and officer and how I could have said "morning" during that evening in Kuwait. I would have told Gary how his positive attitude was infectious, how envious I was that he took everything in stride. I would tell him that he was one of the best soldiers that I had ever been around. He had an amazing sense of duty and love of country that was matched by his field craft and physical fitness. I would tell him that he made officers to his left and right step up their game. I would have told him it was an honor to serve with him.

Change is the only constant in the Army, and after a year of leading a rifle platoon, I became the platoon leader of a weapons platoon in our battalion. The fact that it was in the middle of a war didn't matter. There were four months left in the deployment, and the weapons platoon needed a platoon leader. I shook my old platoon members' hands, thanked them, probably tried to say something clever, promised them that we would all get together back in the States, and I moved a few tents down to another company. I spent a long while saying goodbye to SFC M—, a true friend, mentor, and fine NCO. A few tents are just a few yards away in all actuality, but in the tribal world of an Infantry unit, it is miles away.

Two weeks into becoming a member of a new tribe, I was leading a patrol from the FOB when a call came over the radio. I was to return to the FOB and meet with the company commander. I was to go directly to him and to not anyone else. This could only mean one thing. Our intelligence must have identified a High Value Individual. A terrorist cell leader or senior foreign fighter at least. I was going to take my platoon and capture him. Bring him to justice, hurt their cause, and help ours. My company commander was just outside of our company TOC with a serious look on his face.

"SFC M— was just killed in action," he said.

"No. No. No. No." I said through hot tears of grief and anger.

"Maybe there is a mistake . . . maybe he's just wounded," I said/pleaded.

He grabbed me and held me, and I wept and my knees went weak.

No, there was no mistake. He was killed by an IED, and one of my old team leaders was wounded. He then told me the best thing he could.

"You have a platoon and a mission to get to. Take a few minutes, then move out."

I had lost my first platoon sergeant. The one that lieutenants are always taught about at OCS, West Point, or ROTC. He, like all other great platoon sergeants, was that improbable mix of subordinate, mentor, friend, advisor, confidant, and sage. That mix is what makes the platoon sergeant such a great asset in our Army. I would have failed without him. Together, we trained our platoon, fought the enemy, kept our soldiers safe, and even had fun. He knew war, and he knew leadership. He taught me and never let me fail. He was the only father figure some of our soldiers had ever had. I should have told him that it was an honor and privilege to serve with him, that he had taught me so much that I would never forget—him reading Psalm 91 before every patrol, that I appreciated his sense of humor, that he was everything a young lieutenant could want. Like Ben and Gary, I should have told him so much more before our final handshake.

My new commander was right; I still had a platoon and a mission. I walked around the corner, and there was my platoon. I was happy that they hadn't seen me cry like that. The platoon was hanging around our Humvees, smoking stale Arab cigarettes, checking weapons and ammo one last time. The gunners on the Humvees leaned against their turrets, the dull black of their gun barrels shimmering in the heat. It was June and the heat was oppressive. I remember my tears mixing with the hot dust, my sweat, and gun oil. Maps were brought back out, and the plan was reviewed one last time. We went forward to a place that lets you forget about inadequate farewells. We went back out to the war.

It was an honor and privilege so serve alongside these men and all the men in our unit in Iraq. A year after my first deployment, I went back to Iraq with the 502nd Infantry for another year with many of the same soldiers and a few new ones. I again stood in awe of these men and now know that I was blessed to serve with some of the best that our country had to offer. I now realize that war is terrible, but it is inevitable. To paraphrase Homer, there are no truces between men and lions. I am happy to say that I knew and served with some men and women who fought and gave the last full measure of devotion to defend the things that we hold dear. Again, cynics will say that this is overly simplistic, but they haven't seen the joy in someone's eyes when they vote in their countries' first election, they haven't seen a family devastated because a loved one was kidnapped by terrorists for a ransom that will be used to finance a terror attack, they haven't seen soldiers from vastly different backgrounds in our great country work together to take the fight to our enemies. They haven't had dinner with Ben, Gary, and SFC M— in a mess tent in Kuwait.

IT'S A SMALL WORLD

Southern Baghdad 2005

Jon Elliott and Wes Knight

A ll new cadets enter the Academy with no true understanding of the course upon which their lives will embark. September 11, 2001, transpired during our sophomore year, altering everyone's vision of Army service in the future. Our experiences do not hold greater significance over those endured by others; we wish merely to share our part of the West Point Class of 2004's story and the uniqueness of our combined experiences. We all took the oath to serve knowing full well that some of those with whom we had bonded so closely we would never see again. We were going to war.

Wes and Jon's story begins in the fall of 2001 when both scrambled[1] to the same company (C2 Circus) and, along with several other classmates, became great friends. Time at the Academy was similar to most experiences at colleges, including late nights studying, playing intramural sports together, and frequenting local establishments or visits to Jon's house in Rhode Island on weekends. During junior year branching considerations, both decided to branch Armor and seek assignment to the 3rd Armored Cavalry Regiment (ACR) at Fort Carson, Colorado. While both landed the Armor branch, post night was a different story. Unfortunately, Wes had a couple of less-than-stellar grades, causing his name to drop in selection order. He missed the last slot to Fort Carson by one pick. Therefore, while Jon headed to the

3rd ACR at Fort Carson, Wes was headed to warmer climates with the 3rd Infantry Division at Fort Stewart, Georgia.

Wes immediately deployed to Iraq in January 2005 and quickly moved north into Iraq, settling within the International Zone (or "Green Zone") in Baghdad. Jon followed closely behind in February, and while most of the 3rd ACR was in northern Iraq, Jon's squadron was task organized[2] to Wes's brigade in Baghdad. Although assigned to two different units, separated by 1,600 miles in the United States, they found themselves virtually co-located. While both Wes and Jon had been in the Army for less than a year, they could see how paradoxically small an army spread across the world really was.

Jon's unit focused on controlling a volatile region south of Baghdad, west of the Tigris River and North of Mahmudiyah and securing critical routes connecting to the Iraqi capital. Iraq's main highway ran directly through this area, which most coalition units referred to as Main Supply Route (MSR) Tampa. Running north/south and directly into the city was Route Irish or Jackson. This road served as the main access to Forward Operating Base (FOB) Falcon, where Jon stayed. These highways were used all the time by coalition forces, especially Wes's unit, who moved in and around the city regularly. On his patrols, Wes had opportunities to come across many classmates and occasionally visit Jon on FOB Falcon.

Upon assuming responsibility for their respective areas, Jon and Wes began to apply all the lessons learned at West Point and AOBC. Unlike most lieutenants, neither was afforded much luxury of honing his craft in the training environment. This was Iraq. This was real. The learning curve was steep, as mistakes were not met with after-action reviews or an ass chewing from the commander. Simple decisions here meant someone's life.

Initial contact elicits a specific chain of moments in every soldier's life where the deployment becomes terrifyingly real. The first moment begins with the sound, whether an explosion, a bullet ringing off an armored vehicle or ground, or the unmistakable "thunk" of a mortar being fired in the distance. The smells of Baghdad—seemingly made of burning plastic, raw sewage, and gunpowder—blends with the sounds of screaming over the radio and one's heartbeat exploding. The terrifying reality quickly dissipates the preconceived notions derived from books and movies. The final moment is the flood of adrenaline and excitement combining with the understanding that the only way you are going to get out of this is to rely on your training and your men.

FOB Falcon acquired its fair share of rocket attacks. During one, Jon was just outside of the building where he slept when a rocket came screaming in and scored a direct hit on his billet. Running inside, he could see that nobody was hurt and realized how fortunate he was. The rocket, a dud, had hit the ground outside, skidded across all the shower stalls, and tore off his bedroom door and part of the wall before spinning to rest inside the hallway. While every decision matters, this event reinforced the absence of control one had over certain aspects of combat. Some days you're outside your billet when a rocket tears through your room, and other days you're not.

Jon's typical day consisted of daily and nightly patrolling, observing a specific piece of terrain, or engaging with the local populace. Soon, the days began to blend with each other in a monotonous patrol cycle punctuated with the occasionally kinetic contact with the enemy. One such encounter did not simply punctuate their boredom; it would forever alter the narrative of the platoon's tour. In October, his platoon observed several rising clouds of black smoke less than two kilometers to the northeast of their position on MSR Tampa. Jon radioed to higher headquarters, which provided Apache attack helicopter support. The Apaches identified a convoy of twenty Iraqi police gun trucks that had become trapped along a canal road and were being decimated by the heavy fire of a well-coordinated enemy ambush. The identifiable plumes of smoke billowed forth from several police trucks fully engulfed in flames, some of which had rolled into the canal.

Jon and his platoon quickly moved toward the smoke and gunfire. Because of their familiarity with the area, they were able to maneuver quickly around the choke point to the rear of the enemy. As the platoon neared, the first few RPG rounds and smoke trails whooshed directly over the two HMMWVs[3] led by SFC James Bell, the platoon sergeant. This half of Jon's platoon set up in position to suppress the enemy with their M240B machine guns while the other half, which Jon was leading, maneuvered to attack the enemy. The now desperate enemy intensified their gunfire as they tried to break away from what was quickly turning into an ambush focused on them.

In training, every member of the platoon experienced the nonstop radio traffic from higher headquarters demanding updates. But in combat, this traffic coupled with internal communication shouted over a different channel shouted over machine gun fire. On top of all this cacophony, Jon could barely hear his own driver or gunner yelling at him. After what seemed like hours but was only an adrenaline-filled thirty minutes, Jon and his platoon killed and detained a few of them. Without the personnel to continue to maneuver on them, they grudgingly observed the rest disappear into the surrounding villages.

Victim to an effective ambush, most Iraqis abandoned their casualties and vehicles in the kill zone to band together behind cover. Jon's platoon established a secure landing zone (LZ) to evacuate the wounded Iraqis. Quick reaction forces (QRF) in the area arrived soon after to provide further security. What came next was unexpected and the most difficult memory of the day to shake. Jon's platoon was charged with securing several Iraqi police KIA and escorting the bodies to an Iraqi police checkpoint. Escorting the numerous dead and observing their comrades' reactions was tough. The adrenaline faded and the true reality of what just happened settled.

Upon returning to FOB Falcon, reality hit home as Jon took the time to contemplate what he had just experienced. The fear and excitement all welded together. The platoon had done their job, and he felt pride and respect for his soldier's courage. For performing admirably under enemy fire, SFC James Bell, SGT William Ora-a, and SPC Daniel Burke of 4th Platoon received the Army Commendation award with "V" Device for valor.

Another landmark event occurred later when Jon and his platoon conducted a security mission for an Engineering unit assigned to remove highway debris and fill craters to prevent future IED emplacements. The plan included closing off a one-thousand-meter-wide section of the highway by diverting traffic across the median to the opposite lanes, affording the engineers a safe space to work. After hundreds of vehicles passed without incident, a nondescript, white cargo van unassumingly moved past Jon's security perimeter. When the van suddenly cut back across the destroyed guardrails into the grass median and toward the engineers, a soldier recognized the threat and began firing at the van, causing the driver to panic and detonate the explosives inside prior to reaching the target.

The explosion Jon heard, compared to dozens of others, was unlike anything else throughout the deployment thus far. The unforgettable roar and subsequent thunder was ferocious and felt throughout his entire body. Only a debris field of parts and broken vehicles remained across a huge radius centering on one large crater in the road. While the blast destroyed several vehicles, several soldiers suffered only minor injuries. Destroyed vehicles and equipment are just metal and can always be replaced. You can't replace a father, husband, or brother.

While Jon and his platoon were conducting their patrols in southern Baghdad, Wes and his unit were conducting a different and unique type of mission. Wes's unit was not assigned specific geographic boundaries but instead escorted and protected State Department, Department of Defense, Department of Justice, and Department of Treasury personnel in around the central portion of Iraq. The U.S. government officials would meet with their Iraqi government counterparts to help improve the Iraqi government, economy, infrastructure, and security. One specific Treasury Department mission, aptly nicknamed the "money run," involved delivering vast sums of U.S. dollars, earmarked for rebuilding Iraqi infrastructure, to the Iraqi Central Bank. Wes and his platoon were able to conduct this mission several times, but one stood out more than the others due to the enormous amount of money: $1 billion.

As the platoon drove up to the scorching hot runway at Baghdad International Airport to help the Treasury Department personnel with loading, the sight of that huge sum of money was staggering. The cash came off the plane in one thousand bricks of $1,000,000. A single brick, the size of a bag of groceries, was more money than anyone in the platoon had ever seen. Of course, the jokes of making their own "money run" out of the country began. Discussion ranged from asking if anyone could fly a plane, one said he could take off but the landing was another issue, to how far their trucks could make it, and finally to the possibility of walking out with one brick. All the while, a less-than-pleased Treasury Department official looked on as the platoon refined their humorous plans. It was all talk; Wes and his platoon always did their job and escorted the money safely to the bank.

Wes's first contact with the enemy came in the form of a particular type of IED referred to as an Explosively Formed Penetrator (EFP).[4] Immediately after hearing the boom, he grabbed the radio, calling for situation reports from his other three HMMWVs. At first he heard nothing; he only saw the smoke billowing out from the vehicle directly behind him. While worried that the vehicle behind him was destroyed and the people he was escorting were hurt or killed, he could not see past it to know that his other vehicles and his own soldiers were all right. Wes's first reaction was to immediately start yelling into the radio to check the status of his platoon and wait what seemed like an eternity for their response.

That excruciating five to ten seconds was the longest of his life until his more seasoned driver, and thankfully more aware, SGT Thomas Parrish yelled for him to let go of the "hand mike"[5] button. With the button released, Wes was then able to hear every one of his trucks checking in over the radio. Immediately after getting a status, Wes and the platoon began pulling security to recover the destroyed vehicle and report to higher. The adrenaline-filled moment had Wes rushing from vehicle to vehicle checking on his soldiers and the civilians he was escorting. Thankfully, no one was severely injured.

The platoon reacted as trained, pulled security, established a perimeter around the destroyed vehicle, and gathered the passengers and equipment into remaining vehicles. The incident was a funny lesson to Wes when foolishly holding the mike, although the emotions felt at the time were genuine and far from humorous. Later that night after they completed the mission, Wes felt the "post-action crash" and began to mentally process the experience. Wes began to contemplate the fear when thinking about the small "what if" decisions such as the convoy order, crew assignments, and if they were few seconds faster or slower. Like the rocket that tore through Jon's room, sometimes you just happen to be in the right spot.

For most of us, trying to reason with our everyday anxieties, fears, and joys was, and still can be, difficult on many levels. The bonds created at West Point as classmates provided a necessary outlet as the understanding created and developed during a combat tour furthered our commonality. This often translated as simple emails or running into classmates across other FOB's who were in various stages of constant rotations. Through one of these emails with Jon, both came to realize that during one IED attack on Wes's convoy he had been calling a radio retransmittal site operated by Jon and his platoon. Conversations shared the hardships and successes that were likely to be excluded in the exchanges with family. The existence of a means to vent gave an opportunity to grieve for those wounded or killed in combat, too often a friend or classmate in a venue away from one's soldiers.

After nine months in Iraq, Wes's tour came to an abrupt end. The platoon was attacked with another EFP while escorting Department of Justice civilians and, this time, they were not as lucky. Traveling down a city road, a huge explosion rocked Wes's vehicle. Wes was initially knocked unconscious but came around to his gunner, SPC Luke Jensen, kicking his seat and yelling for him to wake up. Seeing very little except for the smoke and hearing even less with his ears ringing, Wes slowly became aware of a strong throbbing in his right hand. At first he refused to accept it, but once the pain intensified he had to look down at his severely mangled hand. Wes quickly looked over at his driver, SPC Timothy Taylor, and found him looking at his own injured hands and yelling in agony.

Everything immediately accelerated into overdrive. Reaching for his radio to call for help, Wes found it was completely destroyed by the blast. About that time, some of his other soldiers pulled him out and began applying first aid. The medic went to work on the more grievously wounded SPC Taylor. As his soldiers sat Wes down on the curb, Wes realized his mouth was filled with blood. Panicking a bit at the thought that this taste of blood might mean a far worse injury than just his hand, he pointed to his face, believing his soldiers hadn't noticed. One of his NCO's, SGT Jason Lopez, laughingly told him to stop being vain, that his cheek was sliced open but nothing more. "Chicks dig scars," he thought in a dark attempt at using humor intertwined with the surreal horror to serve as a security blanket of normalcy.

In the movies, the hero always continues to fight and bark orders all while ignoring the pain and the blood, but that simply didn't happen. Wes took off his helmet and set it down, beginning to realize it was over. The use of the word *it* to describe what was over is an intentional ambiguity. Wes knew his injury was significant but not life threatening. He is still not sure if it was shock, the weight of the situation, fear, or the fact there was no order to give since his platoon was doing everything right. Regardless of the reason, Wes sat silently on the curb, waiting for the inevitable casualty evacuation. Well trained and prepared, the platoon conducted a ground evacuation of the two wounded soldiers through the streets of Baghdad to the always hectic combat support hospital.

Upon arrival at the Baghdad Combat Hospital, Wes and SPC Taylor underwent the first of what would be countless surgeries. Hoping to return to his platoon, his injury was too serious for the Baghdad hospital. SPC Taylor's wounds were even more severe. Accordingly, both were evacuated to Walter Reed Army Medical Center (WRAMC) in Washington, D.C. Of the many things that happened during that time and after, the worst suffering Wes experienced was the sight of SPC Taylor's face fixed in agony while dealing with excruciating pain throughout the journey to D.C. The weight of Wes's decisions in route planning that day, the order of the vehicles in the convoy, the specific crew assignments, and every other minor decision replayed in his head. He could do nothing but watch SPC Taylor lie in his bed in pain.

Once again, Wes realized that war was a series of circumstances strung together by an apathetic fatalistic thread that did not care about one's actions prior to a decisive instant. The outcome of a given event was independent of the training and planning prior to its occurrence. That said, the results would have been much worse if Wes's vehicle was traveling a millisecond faster. Instead of tearing through their hands, the EFP could have very well torn Wes and SPC Taylor to pieces. Such was the case for Wes's roommate in Baghdad, First Lieutenant Kevin Smith, who died in an EFP attack. Soon after, with only a few weeks remaining in the tour, his own platoon suffered extreme losses when they were struck by another IED in January 2006 that took the lives of two of his soldiers, SGT Jason Lopez and SPC Ryan Walker.

Watching the news in the hope of updates, Wes realized that Iraq was barely a back-page story at this point. Frustrated by not being with his platoon, the constant emails and phone calls from Jon and other classmates such as Jimm Spannegal, Andrew Chegwidden, and Chris Dishong reassuring him, offering advice, and telling jokes served as an outlet for him to express his own disappointment and anxiety. The road to recovery mentally, physically, and emotionally would be difficult, he thought, but the support of classmates proved vital.

Jon learned of Wes's injury via an email from our 2004 Class President John Zdeb, informing him that Wes and his driver were evacuated to WRAMC. Questions formed with no immediate outlet available for answers. Jon understood that medical evacuation stateside meant Wes's injuries were too severe to remain in the theater. Focusing while waiting for news about the welfare of a friend was very challenging. However, Jon had no choice but to remain focused on the mission if he was to bring both his soldiers and himself back alive.

In an assignment a few years later, Jon served as a Rear Detachment Commander. With the principal role focusing on families, especially those of wounded or killed soldiers while serving as a Primary Notification Officer/ Casualty Assistance Officer (CAO), it would be the most humbling position ever held in his career. The most important task meant meeting with the families on a regular basis and providing them as much comfort, support, information, and assistance that the Army could offer. While such a small show of support could never replace a loved one, the simple act showed that the families were never and would never be alone in their grief.

In addition to those killed in action, providing support to the wounded soldiers recently returned gave Jon a small level of understanding for how Wes must have felt when he had to leave his platoon behind in Iraq. Jon frequently visited wounded troops at WRAMC in D.C., or in Brooke Army Medical Center (BAMC) in San Antonio, who had suffered serious combat injuries. While Jon was visiting wounded soldiers, Wes was also doing his part to comfort the wounded. Still in the D.C. area, Wes often visited soldiers and Chris Fierro, both on his own and with Jon to provide a personal level of support as they shared common themes of frustration and grief. "I'm fine, how are the others?" and "I just want to go back and be with my platoon" were phrases heard over and over, the same ones that Jon previously heard Wes say repeatedly.

However, there is no right thing to say when sitting with a wife and her children when their husband and father had been killed or while their loved one is fighting for life in the Intensive Care Unit after being shot multiple times. Incredible NCOs such as SFC Thomas Proffitt, SSG Brian Watson, and SSG Brian King, who served with Jon, escorted the remains of fallen heroes home. Jon and this team of NCOs ensured that every fallen soldier of Jon's squadron received the heroic homecoming to which they were entitled. Jon attended every funeral for each soldier from his unit. The funerals were in locations spread throughout the country and were attended by entire communities wanting to show their love and support for each fallen soldier. While Jon could not think of a more demanding job, he can never fathom one that would be as rewarding.

While we reflect upon our own experiences, we understand that ours mirror those of the 202 classes that came before us, as well as the countless others that will follow in our footsteps. While each fallen classmate is simply a name to those who did not know them, we view them as people with whom we share an unbreakable bond. Just as Union soldiers would cross enemy lines at night to visit their classmates fighting for the Confederacy, each member of the Class of 2004 managed to connect with each other in some fashion despite the arduous circumstances in either Iraq or Afghanistan. Being able to stay in contact with each other while in Iraq is a gift that we will treasure for the rest of our lives. As stated multiple times in this narrative, sometimes the outcomes of war are favorable, and sometimes they are tragic. Our close proximity to each other's units was definitely one of the former.

Even for those with whom we did not have a personal relationship but only a mere recognition as being one of our classmates, their death still leaves a profound impact in our hearts. We are all members of the Long Gray Line, something that can never be taken from us. To the families of these heroes, we can only offer heartfelt condolences for your loss and sincere gratitude for their dedication. Walking the far section of the West Point Cemetery is both humbling and inspiring. During every occasion to visit the Academy, it is the first place that we visit and the last before we leave. While it will never be enough, we stop to say thank you. It is because of such men and women and their enduring spirit that we live inspired.

THE DAY THE ELEPHANT CAME TO TOWN

Cory Wallace with Contributions
from Edwin "Les" Minges

A command post (CP) in Iraq is a strange place at 0300. The muffled radios punctuate a dark, suffocating stench of burning plastic, sweat, and cigarettes. The early morning of February 19, 2007, was no different. Doc Byington huddled in a black sleeping bag while I toiled on what every leader in Iraq does following a successful mission: a daunting PowerPoint storyboard requirement. Occasionally, a tired soldier in a rooftop guard post would check in on the radio. Other than the brief five-second conversation, the CP was completely silent except for the quiet tapping of my computer keyboard.

At Patrol Base North in Tarmiyah, Iraq, White and Blue Platoons from D/2-8 CAV occupied a former Iraqi police station. We enjoyed the company of our local partners until AQI,[1] or Mooj,[2] suggested it would be beneficial to the policemen's health if they stayed home as opposed to show up and work for us. Often, members of AQI would kidnap a policeman on his way home from work and film a coerced confession and the subsequent execution via a gunshot to the back of the head. Accordingly, we had the place to ourselves in the early morning hours of February 19, 2007.

Prior to OIF I, Tarmiyah was a retirement community for high-ranking Ba'athists[3] along the Tigris River. Following the capitulation of Saddam's regime, it became a truck stop for foreign fighters en route to the fight in Ba'Quaba.[4] To make things worse, "The Surge" pressed a large number of bad guys fighting in Baghdad, located approximately forty-five miles to the south, into our neck of the woods. Route (RTE) Coyotes, the main road in and out of Tarmiyah, bisected the town in half. To the east, RTE Coyotes terminated into another road called RTE Cobras; to the west, RTE Coyotes connected to the well-known Main Supply Route Tampa at a small village named Mushaada occupied by the Battalion's Bravo Company.

On February 17, 2007, a sniper killed SPC Paton during White Platoon's dismounted patrol. While half of the platoon was veterans of the Sadr City[5] uprising of 2003, the other half was just like me—a bunch of American kids who had never watched a man die a violent death. The next day, we tried to piece ourselves together and come to grips with the reality that one of our buddies wasn't going to be eating MREs with us in the morning.

Around 1500, a report came in on the Battalion tip line.[6] We were lucky enough to receive an extremely precise location to the sniper cell responsible for the death of SPC Paton. After an intensive planning session, we hatched "Operation Nice Guy" in less than three hours and executed the mission at 0100 on the morning of February 19. The mission was a huge success. We detained the sniper cell, captured their weapons, and discovered the car they used to shoot SPC Paton.

As the sun slowly began to rise, a staccato choir of small arms fire erupted. Doc and I looked at each other. This volume of contact typically didn't happen until the afternoon. While the volume of small arms fire increased, RPGs missed our rooftop fighting positions and detonated against the wall. For a brief second, we shared a grim understanding that today was going to be unlike anything we ever previously experienced. Before anyone could say anything over the ICOM,[7] it hit.

A massive explosion. Bigger than anything I could ever fathom. The explosion destroyed the barracks housing the platoons and turned the CP into a whirling tempest of razor-sharp glass shards. While SFC Housey and I missed the blender of glass and whatever else came through the CP's windows because we were standing in the hallway, Doc Byington and our communication specialist, PFC Vang, were not so lucky. Vang lost a giant chunk of his neck, while numerous facial lacerations rendered Doc Byington severely dazed.

Until this event, I never thought the scene in *Saving Private Ryan* was accurate during which Tom Hanks's character stumbles through the obstacles on the beach with an absent expression on his face. Because of my years of training, I always thought that I would know exactly what to do when the worst scenario became a reality. In my mind, I assumed that I would shout, "Follow me!" and all my soldiers would bravely charge alongside me in such a fashion that we would inspire a painting such as those that hang on the walls of every academic building at West Point. Man, I was really full of shit.

After that massive blast, we all just sat and stared at each other in a state of suspended animation. Time had stopped. No one spoke. I kept hearing the impact of small arms fire on the building that sounded as innocuous as rain falling on the roof of my childhood home. Something inside my head was screaming at me to do something, but it was to no avail as my limbs would not move. However, reality quickly extracted me from the halcyon isolation of my own inaction. I returned to the present when Vang walked out of the room next to the CP while using his fingers to plug his neck to prevent the blood from spurting out. Doc Byington came out of the CP, looked at me, and asked me what just happened. Instead of answering his question, I just stared at him with a chalked expression while trying to decide if we were dead or among an unknown number of survivors of what could only have been a nuclear explosion.

What I did not know at the time was that a bongo truck[8] packed full of military-grade explosives crashed through both of our gates and sped toward the barracks' front door. Hearing the sentry's alert as the vehicle approached, 1LT Jokinen engaged the truck with his M4 and shot the VBIED driver. This caused the driver to stray from his target—the barracks—and steer into our fuel pod and detonate his payload. The explosion sprayed five hundred gallons of burning diesel fuel all over the patrol base's perimeter, destroyed the front façade of our barracks, crippled all of our vehicles, and devastated our power sources, thus rendering us without any communication besides our hand-held ICOM radios. To make matters worse, the blast killed SSG Colon instantly and wounded everybody except for me and SFC Housey. While some of the wounded were lucky and suffered mere scratches, others were fighting for their next breath.

SFC Housey and I ran outside the command post and beheld an unbridled scene of destruction. Silhouetted against the burning fuel pod, a dazed mass of American soldiers wearing nothing but their brown T-shirts, underwear, and body armor stumbled around covered in dust, bleeding from their ears, and perforated with giant chunks of glass and concrete. We assisted the soldiers still healthy enough to walk carry those who were unable to do so back to the CP, while little kids tossed grenades over our patrol base wall.

SFC Housey fished out a Harris Radio[9] from the wreckage of his M1151. After stealing a pack of my Newports, he headed up to the barracks' roof in hope of making contact with somebody. On the roof, SSG Copeland (the acting platoon sergeant for White Platoon) and SSG Fisher identified the soldiers still physically capable of fighting and put them to work defending the barracks roof. Soon, we all heard a beautiful sound pierce the cacophony: a M240B returning fire. If I learned anything that day, it was that there is no sweeter sound than an M240B returning fire once you become decisively engaged. That sound told me that we might make it out of this alive.

As previously stated, the blast nuked all of our commo with the exception of Housey's radio. I looked at Vang, who was still plugging the hole in his neck with his hand. He and I both knew that we needed to establish communication quickly if we wanted to maintain our position and evacuate the seriously wounded. Accordingly, we headed out to the generator. While he attempted to bring the 5Kw generator back to life, an enemy RPK[10] opened up on his silhouette. I yelled at him to get down. Of course, he pretended not to hear me and continued to toil while the rounds snapped through the air above his head. Vang continued to work on the generator for another ten minutes before looking at me and morosely shaking his head. Suddenly, he jolted as if he just remembered something very important. He sprinted to a pile of rubble and began to dig through the rocks. By the grace of God, he managed to find two extra batteries for our CP radios, thus giving us a shot to restore proper communications.

The enemy became more aggressive after they learned that the SVBIED was not as effective as they hoped. ICOM traffic from the roof informed me that enemy dismounts were moving among the alleyways south of the patrol base in an attempt to exploit the breach created by the explosion on the northern side of the perimeter. We were now in danger of being overrun by the enemy.

At this precise point in time, SFC Housey managed to make contact with an AWT[11] that was miraculously within his Harris's range. While I thought we were fighting for hours prior to their arrival, I later learned the Apaches arrived fifty minutes following the blast. Every soldier who wasn't too wounded to stand couldn't help but cheer when the two Apaches vengefully screamed overhead and began to pour Hellfire missiles and 30 mm automatic cannon fire into buildings packed full of Mooj. Unfortunately, our respite was short-lived after Mooj deployed a DShK[12] and began to engage the aircraft. A 12.7 mm tracer round passed through one of the pilot's legs and his aircraft's instrument panel. The round was a tracer and lighted his flight suit on fire. He had to drop his missile pods and return to Taji all while trying to prevent his entire flight suit from catching fire.

In the subsequent gap in attack air support, the enemy forces surged against our beleaguered numbers. The fellas continued to engage visible enemy in nearby buildings that towered over our patrol base and repulsed the enemy dismounts trying to maneuver through the alleyways toward our patrol base. SSG Copeland and SSG Fisher ran between our fighting positions on the roof and provided direction to the soldiers, some of whom wore nothing more than brown T-shirts, flip flops, and body armor.[13] Soon, they began to run out of ammunition. Two soldiers volunteered to venture down a staircase exposed by the blast to our additional ammo cache. Having nothing but two black sleeping bags to aid them, they both managed to return unscathed despite Mooj continually engaging them with precise small arms fire all the while carrying two cumbersome sleeping bags full of ammunition.

While the fellas on the roof continued to delay the enemy's advance, our medics feverishly worked to keep five severely injured soldiers alive. As other soldiers have done in other wars, several of our "litter-urgent" cases didn't want to hear medical instructions confining them to the safety of the CP. SSG Stallings, missing half the skin on his head, grabbed an M9[14] and attempted to run up to the roof. Doc Byington had to place SSG Stallings in a chokehold to prevent him from joining the fight. Slowly, the loss of blood finally forced SSG Stallings to remain in the CP. That being said, I will never forget the fearless resolve in his eyes. It was almost as if he was mad at us for stopping him from killing the assholes that started this mess.

Soon after the first AWT had to leave, another miracle happened—Vang established communication with Battalion. After sending a situation report, I turned the handmike over to 1LT Jokinen in hopes of going up to the roof to conduct a better assessment only to realize one important fact:

he was bleeding out of both of his ears. The guy had not heard a single word I said in the past hour as a result of the blast rupturing both of his eardrums. Regardless, he continued to assist the medics and found other ways of being useful.

Meanwhile, 2LT Les Minges's platoon, one of the organic elements that we detached to our sister infantry company in exchange for 1LT Jokinen's Bradley Platoon, prepared to occupy their route security positions outside of his company's patrol base at Mushada. While they heard the explosion from the SVBIED, they didn't think much of the blast, for IED explosions were a common occurrence on the road between his patrol base and Tarmiyah. Believing the blast was a result of such an event, his platoon continued their daily operations.

As they prepared for their mission, the Battalion battle captain,[15] CPT Smith, contacted Les and told him to get to Tarmiyah with a "goddamn fire under his ass." Les's platoon scrambled to coalesce all soldiers not occupied with defending their patrol base, but he was only able to muster the personnel required to man two M1A2 Abrams tanks.[16] Les remembered the chaotic scene as his element prepared to depart and link up with another platoon from his company that was currently conducting a patrol:

> The patrol platoon, led by LT Burch, had two Bradleys already near our location on Route Tampa and his four M1114/M1151s were only minutes away. We decided to bring my vehicle in addition to his platoon to Tarmiyah. My tank, the only one with two operational radios had a massive electrical short and would not start, so I took my PSG's tank. Those precious seconds of going through the steps of waiting while the turbine was spooling up on the tank stretched into toe curling agony and cold sweat on my hands. My anxiety was making my throat dry. Getting into anyone else's vehicle is always weird—it seems like everything is just a little wrong and nothing functions quite the same.

After linking up with 2LT Burch, Les learned that his commander wanted the patrol platoon (led by 2LT Burch) to remain at the patrol base. Extremely frustrated, LT Burch detached his PSG's Bradley, commanded by SFC Williams, to Les's element while the rest of his platoon returned to the patrol base in Mushada. Les's element then turned toward Tarmiyah.

While Les's section sped toward our position from the west, CPT Smith informed me that a Stryker platoon was moving from the east and that the MEDEVAC birds were ready to go as soon as we could confirm that we had a secure landing zone. I quickly scanned the CP filled with seriously wounded soldiers and noticed that CPL McArn had passed away. If we had any chance of giving the other wounded soldiers a decent chance of surviving, we had to immediately establish an LZ and MEDEVAC them as soon as possible. At that point in the battle, I started to believe that these soldiers were going to die because of my own inability to coordinate a quicker evacuation to the landing zone. The feeling of confidence that resulted from having establishing favorable momentum against a relentless enemy assault dissipated again into yet another irrepressible sense of absolute panic and terror.

West of Tarmiyah, Les's section screamed toward the ever-increasing giant plume of black smoke billowing forth from our position on the horizon. He slowed his tank only enough to keep SFC William's slower Bradley in the formation. Our roof positions reported they had visual contact with his element moving into the western portion of town. I contacted Les on the radio and instructed him to secure the proposed HLZ[17] with his section and wait for the Strykers moving from the east to transport our wounded. He describes what he saw:

> Every pane of glass for a several block radius was blown out and tons of everything, from cases of coke bottles to barrels, twisted steel bars, cars and thousands of bricks were strewn for several hundred meters. Demon 5 told us that he needed someone to secure the LZ for the first MEDEVAC lift [and provided my section with] directions to the HLZ. It was a soccer field in the middle of town only about 400 meters away; however, the only avenue of approach consisted of several narrow streets that were surrounded by 3 or 4 story buildings on every side. Oops, did the tank just sideswipe a car? Fuck it. Did we just pull down a bunch of electrical wires with our antennas? Fuck it!!! Driver keep fucking going! Once we got there, SFC Williams and I took up opposite sides oriented east and west, leaving the route to the LZ area clear. It was very soft and muddy from the recent rains and our tracks dug in deep. As soon as we stopped PFC Detroit began servicing enemy dismounts in the third and fourth story windows that the

Soldiers at [Patrol Base North] were shooting at. He also transitioned to rooftop areas that the Apaches were focused on as well.

As soon as Les reported securing the HLZ, the Stryker Platoon arrived at our front gate. While I was still on the net with CPT Smith attempting to coordinate the arrival of additional reinforcements led by our Battalion Commander (LTC Efflandt), their platoon sergeant walked into our CP and yelled, "Sir, get all your wounded to my track right fucking now!" Doc Byington and Doc Patterson supervised the aid and litter teams while they loaded the wounded into the back of the Strykers. As soon as their back ramps closed, they sped toward the HLZ. From Les's position, he observed the following:

About five minutes later we could hear the Strykers making their way to the LZ. They began [driving] across the muddy soccer field. Their tires were spinning and flinging mud everywhere as they barely inched to their positions on the south side of the soccer field. "Please God, let them get out of the way so the helicopters could land," I thought. Only a few minutes later, we heard the MEDEVAC aircraft inbound. SFC Williams threw his red smoke to mark the location. The aircraft flared and landed about 50 meters from the back of my tank and their wheels sunk into the mud immediately. The flight medics jumped out to pick up the Soldiers now getting carried out of the Strykers. I wanted to get out and help as I watched the Stryker Soldiers struggling across the mud with Demon Company's Soldiers on litters and others who could barely walk or had tons of bandages, but as soon as the flight medics were 10 feet or so from the aircraft several of the enemy starting shooting AK47s at them. PFC Detroit continued to service targets with the coax[18] on the building about 50 meters in front of us. During this time, I scanned for new targets with the Commander's Independent Thermal Viewer[19] and slewed PFC Detroit onto two new locations. After what seemed like a thousand heart-beats later I got up on my CAL .50 and began firing APIT[20] to mark target areas and increase the volume of fire to the buildings to our east. The enemy's focus on the LZ immediately dissipated and refocused on the patrol base itself.

With our seriously wounded evacuated, we were afforded the luxury of solely focusing on the fight. I directed Les's section and the Stryker platoon to form a perimeter around our position. Meanwhile, CPT Smith informed me that LTC Efflandt was moving toward our position with a substantial number of reinforcements. I jokingly replied that they could take their time because I just found two packs of Marlboros and the roof still had plenty of ammo.

Les then dismounted his tank to bring us extra machine gun ammunition. He recounts his experience once he walked through the patrol gate's front gate.

Once inside, the first people we came across were SSG Ayala and SGT Alcaraz, who came to get the ammunition from us. Everything was destroyed and covered in gray, white dust, but the blood dripping off of them was bright red as it soaked down their ballistic vests. I went into the CP and found Demon 5 and PFC Dillard linked up with Doc Pat and continued to treat soldiers. SSG Colon and CPL McArn were placed in an unused room. I wanted to stay and spend a few moments with them, but I left Dillard there and ran back out to my tank. I felt ridiculous as I ran out with just my vest and pistol. The hundred meters or so stretched on for a mile. How many steps does it take to get back to the tank? After monkeying up the side and sliding back into my position. PFC Detroit asked if anyone he knew was hurt. "Yes, two soldiers died," is all I said. I did not want to tell him that one of the soldiers who died was his former team leader (SSG Colon). While we were talking, he identified someone in the girls' school who was now hiding behind one of the brick facades.

I jumped over to the loader's station and hit the ammo door switch and unlocked and loaded an MPAT-OR[21] round. "God I love the smell of propellant," I thought. The moment ended with the heavy metallic of the breech snapping closed.

"Personnel identified right here," said PFC Detroit.

"Gunner MPAT personnel. UP!" I yelled as I took the gun off manual safe. "Fire and adjust!"

"On the way!" Wooom! The shockwave was so contained in the small area of the town it seemed louder than normal. The round penetrated the building and blew up inside and left a collapsed hole about 3 feet wide and a huge cloud of dust. "Gunner, reengage, select Canister!"[22]

"Identified, canister selected!"

The breech didn't eject the aft cap of the first round. "FUCK, FUCK, aft cap stuck!" I yelled and then stuck the breech-operating handle in and yanked up and down furiously to unstick the aft cap. It fell out with an unhurried clank.

After I shoved the canister, the round in the breech went up.

"UP!"

"On the way . . . on the way . . . on the way!' said PFC Detroit as he pressed the triggers furiously. Nothing. I looked at the breech and noticed that the breech still had about one-half and an inch to go before it was locked in the closed position. I grabbed the wrench and pushed down hard to close the breech all the way.

"On the way!"

WOOOM! followed by the metallic *thwong!* of the breech opening and throwing out the aft cap against the deflector.

The thousand tungsten balls hit all in and around the hole from the previous round. Surely if the blast from the first round didn't kill him, this one would. PFC Detroit then switched to 7.62 mm coax and conducted his Z pattern sweep.

"Cease fire and continue to scan."

About thirty seconds later the Stryker next to me fired a TOW missile at the same building. Their shot hit the window adjacent to my target. It exploded in a huge cloud of dust. Then, the strangest event happened. Everything stopped. All the shooting ceased, and the whole town got completely quiet.

Within minutes, we finally pushed the enemy, who had been within kissing range at one point, to a much more comfortable three hundred meters away. Finally, our fellas could relax. At this point, we all knew we were going to make it out alive. I don't know how else to explain our mood, but it suddenly turned jovial. Soldiers began to crack jokes on the ICOM as the small arms fire faded to infrequent pot shots that were answered with a roaring volley of retribution from our positions. If my memory serves me correctly, I remember one soldier stating that he was disappointed that we were going to miss lunch in the chow hall back at Camp Taji.

At that point, LTC Efflandt, my Company Commander (CPT Barbour), and 1SG (1SG Tramel) arrived at what remained of Patrol Base North. LTC Efflandt and CPT Barbour assumed command and sent me to the roof to continue to refine the direct fire plan. There is nothing that could prepare me for what I saw on that roof. Few troopers were wearing what one could be considered a complete uniform. All of them were bleeding; some of them had giant chunks of glass sticking out of their wounds. Despite this, they were all proud inwardly knowing they had survived the rage Stephen Crane referred to as "the elephant" in the *Red Badge of Courage*. SFC Housey lit a cigarette in his mouth and gave it to me as if to say, "We made it." Seeing their exhausted faces and blood-soaked bandages, I couldn't help but ponder what kept them going when death seemed all but certain. Despite the blast wounding all but two of us, they fought their asses off to hold their position until Les and the Strykers arrived. Prior to deploying, I always had this romantic notion of war portraying men laying waste to our Nation's enemies while thinking of bald eagles and singing "The Battle Hymn of the Republic." Reality was a quick antidote to the illusion of idealism. These men weren't fighting for anything but each other. It became very clear to me that nobody on that roof was going to quit as long as one person still had the volition to keep fighting.

After nearly four hours following the initial blast, the fire decreased to absolute silence. While LTC Efflandt and CPT Barbour made plans for future operations, I had another cigarette with SFC Housey. Initially, we didn't say anything. I desperately wanted somebody to say something cathartic. Instead, I only heard an eerie sense of quiet accented with the smell of sweat, gunpowder, and the persistent stench of burning shit and plastic found all over Iraq. The only accolades this unforgiving country gave us was a quiet promise that we were going to see the sun rise tomorrow.

Eventually, another Stryker company showed up to relieve us. I can only imagine what we must have looked like when they rolled up. Many of us were covered in blood, and few were lucky enough to wear a complete uniform. As our relief began to establish themselves defensively, we headed down to the courtyard to wait for our rides home.

When we arrived back in Taji, we were met by an entourage of troopers staring at us with a collective expression of both disbelief and admiration. After we got out of the trucks, most of the fellas headed off to the aid station to get the remaining chucks of glass and concrete removed from their bodies. I continued to chain smoke my Marlboro Reds on a picnic table until the sun went down. Once again, I slowly became aware of a realization that two more of our friends who stood in our formation at Fort Hood would not be standing there when we returned. But in combat, people aren't just "friends," they're family. CPL McArn and SSG Colon were both members of our family. And on February 19, 2007, they were taken from us.

Two years later, I was at Disney World with my family. After the rest of my family went to sleep one night, I walked down to the bar to watch the news and have a beer. The place was empty except for an older gentlemen enjoying a whiskey sour. We started to talk, and I learned that he was a Vietnam vet who had seen his share of the elephant as well. We both listened to each other's stories. When we were done, he looked at me and said, "You know, nothing you do will ever change what happened to you and your men. It happened and now it is yours to own for the rest of your life. Bad stuff like that isn't important in life. What is important is how you handle your burden from here on out."

We finished our drinks, shook hands, and parted ways. To this day, I regret that I never had a chance to thank him for saying that because it made me realize that I have the responsibility of living the best life possible for the fellas who didn't make it out of Tarmiyah that week in February of 2007. And while I know the elephant's ghost will walk beside me for the rest of my life, I know that it will only rage again if I allow it to do so.

THE STRONG GRAY
LINE CONTINUES

THE FIRE INSIDE OF US

Jake Pendleton

The mess hall is best described as six large chapels attached to each other. With their large windows and six-story-high ceilings, they remind me very much of old cathedrals I've seen in Europe. In the center of all six of these is two large, stone stairwells joined together by a small stage with a microphone. There is a dull roar as the cadets move in for breakfast and stand behind their chairs awaiting the order to sit down. Small talk of the upcoming weekend and plans accompanied by the clatter of plebes passing plates and cups fill the chapels. Most are still groggy from staying up the night before doing homework neglected over the weekend.

The first captain takes the microphone and says, "Brigade attention." After hearing the same mess hall adjutant announce, "Table commandants report to the poop deck to pick up floaters, take seats," day in and day out for months now, we know the difference between the sound of his voice and that of the First Captain's. Upward of four thousand cadets all standing at attention await some sort of announcement from the highest-ranking cadet in the corps. Do the Firsties need to get their POVs inspected? Or are we going to applaud the performance of some team from the previous weekend? Is there a blood drive this week?

"I regret to inform you of the death of First Lieutenant . . ."

The room had been at attention, but you could still have easily picked out all the people who were still fumbling with gloves or whispering to each other. But now, now the mood had changed entirely. Roughly four thousand spines were straight, eyes were forward, and hands were cupped and placed on the seams of our pants. Everyone was wide awake now; everyone thinking the same thing. Everyone's face blank, staring straight ahead. Everyone perfectly still, knowing full well what was coming next.

One of our own, someone just like us, only a few years older, only a few more steps ahead of us on the same path that we are on now, had been killed. To me this, this paying of respects as a corps, as a school together in unison to all of our graduates killed in action, is the one thing that separates us most from civilian colleges or even ROTC programs. This kind of legacy, this kind of bond, it can't really be imitated or put into words. This feeling of fraternity is real. Cadets have their own culture, their own jargon, and in a lot of ways we're all family. Whether the one killed was a squadmate in Beast, a table commandant, or someone we didn't know, it still hurts and hits close to home. Because even though we don't like to admit it, these stone walls are strange. We hate them for keeping us in and denying us the privileges given to students at civilian schools, but in the end even though it's a love/hate relationship, we still consider it our second home.

But there is one thing that our civilian peers do share with us that comes to mind here. This death, this tragedy to which we are paying respect is in no way ordinary or routine. Every death is a loss and a tragedy. But it certainly isn't new to us either. Before coming to the Academy many of us knew at least one veteran of either of these wars and had buried at least one friend, neighbor, relative, classmate, or teammate. For those of us seniors and juniors, many of us have already had friends graduate, deploy, and not come back.

Ours was a generation that grew up at war. It may have been a long time ago, but not one of us has forgotten that feeling. That moment of trying to comprehend what was happening on the television. It was the mark of our loss of innocence for most of us, that moment when we realized that there was a whole world out there, and it was violent. It wasn't perfect like most of the suburban neighborhoods we grew up in. We had a hard time fathoming it. A country we had never heard of, a group of people practicing a faith so unfamiliar to us had claimed the lives of so many people. But why? We couldn't understand that kind of violence, that kind of hate just yet.

I remember when I went to visit my brother when he was at the Academy. We went to the city to see all the sites. Eventually we came uponssee that gigantic pile of shattered cement slabs with pieces of bent iron girders and rebar sticking out all over the place. Construction workers were hard at work; dust and noise was everywhere. On the scaffolding behind me I remember seeing all the faces. Faces, names, and words from family members. A collage of death and loss, chaotically pasted reassuring everyone that came by that it was real. Those faces were a testament saying "this is my friend/ dad/brother/sister, and now they are gone." This was no earthquake, no hurricane; humans did this. This somber moment caused me to ponder how that much hate and evil was possible.

9/11 was the turning point for a lot of us, a call to arms. But I would argue that my brother and I always knew deep down that the am the army was what we wanted. To serve, to belong to something bigger than yourself, and hopefully one day get to fight. My heroes were never athletes or movie stars. To me, heroes were the ones who defended others, lived in the mud, and gave their lives for causes greater than themselves. I knew at a very young age that I wanted to be one of those men. But I'll never forget at the age of thirteen staring at that pile of rubble at the collage of the faces of innocent victims. That was when I was locked in. That was when I knew that there wasn't any other place that I would rather be.

CNN and FOX didn't get any prettier for us. Soon, it was IEDs and RPGs all over the news, and two countries, of which we knew nothing about, were suddenly the topic of all the conversations of our parents and other adults. Then the funerals came. It was no longer far away on the other side of the world or just in New York City, now it was uncomfortably close. That kid down the street, that boy who played football with your brother, that one in your sister's class, yeah that one . . . he stepped on a bomb, one of those IED things.

Then they came home. Brothers, sons, and cousins came home and we put our arms around them and cried. They took to drinking, and they took to getting lost. We cried when they left, and we smiled and cried when they came home. But we didn't get all of them back. Part of them stayed over there, and a new part we'd never met came back.

"*. . . killed in the Kandahar province last Tuesday while conducting . . .*"

I can't help but wonder how the people in his company feel, much less his family. I think of my own brother, when he was deployed and how my family felt. Those were the hardest Christmases. It didn't feel right. It felt empty, and hollow. I didn't want to hear about the war; I didn't want to watch the news. I remember thinking the unthinkable and not knowing what I would do if he didn't come home.

But you have to understand how we feel. You must understand the fire inside us. The fire hasn't cooled in our hearts either. We were young when this happened; this thing for most of us is how we mark our introduction to the reality of the horrors of the world. This thing that defined us defined our generation. It's "this long" until we graduate, "this long" until we get out of BOLIC, "this long" until we get out of Ranger, "this long" until we get to our unit, and . . . we might not ever get to go over there. For most of us joining was the easy part; volunteering to fight was the only viable option we saw available. How could we not want to hit back? But now, now we might not even get the chance, the chance to see this thing, this thing that haunted our televisions, our dinner conversations, our gatherings, our radios. We will have to live the rest of our lives thinking, "I never got to take a swing at the bastard who did all this." How can we not be angry at the thought of that? Maybe not daily, but we talk about it often. At the table in the mess hall, in the shower, at the smokers' pit, at practice, before class in the hall, in our study groups, and even at the bar we talk about it. "I heard, we'll still get to go man, they're not going to be totally pulled out by 2014." "My roommate's dad is a four star and he said that we're pretty close to going to Iran." Always, always with the rumors, cadets live and feed on rumors. Some are glad, some are indifferent, but most of those I know want to go. It's not about the patch on the right shoulder, and it's not about the CIB or the CAB above the U.S. Army nametape. For us it's about so much more. We trained for this, we practiced for this, we grew up waiting for this.

"*. . . survived by his mother, father, and older brother . . .*"

But it wasn't all excitement; there was fear in my heart as well. I remember when Rick didn't come back. He was the nicest kid on my football team in high school. The kind of guy you knew that you could count on. The guy that always volunteered for stuff, whether it was helping you move or giving you a ride somewhere, he was always there and happy to do it. None of us were surprised when he joined the Marines. He seemed happy then, like he finally found where he belonged in the world. I remember how surreal it was. It was impossible for me to comprehend this idea that I would never again see my friend. My mind was flooded with memories of football and school. His smile, his truck, all the jokes, seemed lost forever. The town had a huge ceremony, tons of cars, motorcycles, cops, and firemen. The sidewalks were covered with people with signs and flowers welcoming him home. Everyone was calling him by his rightful name: hero.

"... *represented the Academy on the field. ... Join me now in a moment of silence followed by the singing of the last verse of the 'Alma Mater.'*"

The moment of silence is universal for losses. Any American can understand that feeling. But the "West Point Alma Mater" is reserved for only the Long Gray Line. I remember being told when I was at prep school that "one day long after you graduate that song will bring tears to your eyes." I was so concerned with simply trying to memorize it along with all of the other basic training knowledge in order to not get yelled at at the time that I disregarded the statement. But there's an emotion that has come to coexist with that song that I truly can't describe. A paralyzing, electric feeling, of both pride and camaraderie, is the only way that I can describe this unique feeling.

The last time we had one of these announcements, I remember walking out of the mess hall after, and I bumped into a friend. "That lieutenant that got killed, my table commandant was crying just now, he said that was his table comm when he was a plebe." I thought back to my table comm when I was a plebe, and all the other Firsties I had looked up to. As a plebe I hated most upperclassmen as well as I hated greeting them and cupping my hands. I felt as if they were a nuisance most of the time. With each upperclassmen came the possibility of being asked knowledge or tasked with some annoying duty. But some of them I legitimately looked up to, even idolized.

I thought back to my table comm. Table comms are senior cadets who sit at the head of family-style tables that the entire Corps of Cadets sits at and eats almost every meal together. Their job is mainly to ask plebes knowledge and maintain order. However, mine took a very personal interest in the plebes at his table. Why? Other than the fact that he cared, I honestly don't know. He was tall and skinny, and out of uniform and off duty, you wouldn't think he was in the Army. But I remember how much he cared about us, always stopping by my room to check on me and my roommate for no other reason than he just gave a shit. Being the company XO he had plenty of other things to do, but he made time to stop by and mentor us, giving us advice about classes, summer assignments, and everything else West Point. He wasn't even in our chain of command, but if we ever needed anything he would just say, "I'll take care of it," and he always came through for us. No excuses, no BS. I remember thinking that when it was my turn I wanted to imitate him. He always let us know when we messed up, but he gave us a reason for why we were doing each task, always making clear the purpose behind the task. He had an indescribable way about him that made me want to succeed. I wanted to be perfect in his eyes, and I never minded when he tasked us with details. I remember feeling safe around him, like I knew I was doing the right thing, that he wouldn't lead us the wrong way. He seemed invincible to me. I find it hard to imagine him ever being killed.

We're not ignorant. We hear the stories, we read the books, we watch the documentaries and the YouTube videos. We soak in every piece of knowledge that we can and desperately try to understand how combat works, what it means, what we're supposed to do. Will we go to war? Will I be ready? It haunts our every step, our every word, and our every thought. On the way to class, at practice, in class, at meals, and lying in our beds staring at the ceiling, we are thinking about our futures, possibly deployed to another place.

It's one thing to imagine what the day you take over your platoon will be like. When you stand in front of those thirty men and introduce yourself. But it's an entirely different thing when you think about the fact that we are in a time of war. Screw up in garrison and you might lose respect, even get into trouble. But screwing up downrange implied a new gravity, the lives of those you lead. Even with both the conflicts scaling down, it hasn't really stopped. The people that did this aren't done yet. They are still out there. Even then it's always likely that a new enemy will appear soon in another country and we will soon be there fighting.

Deployments aren't rare among our community. Our teachers, TACs, and sponsors have been constantly leaving and coming back from Iraq and Afghanistan. You try not to ask them about it. But every once in a while they offer to share with us their experiences, their stories, and they give us some small insight into what were going to encounter. These men and women, they talk to us with faraway eyes. They tell us stories while staring into the distance. Trying to organize their thoughts while at the same time controlling their emotions and sometimes holding back tears. Every Friday my history teacher would give us ten minutes to ask questions, anything we wanted about deployments or anything army related. When we asked him about combat he told us all about Iraq. He told us everything from downrange from food to IEDs. But when we asked him about combat, about his first firefight, I was surprised by his response. He said that he was scared. I wondered how scared we would be, if I would make the right decision when the time came. We asked him how he was able to go back, back out of the FOB after he had been attacked. He said that he had to refuse, refuse to be afraid. I've been turning that over in my head ever since I heard it. Operating under stress was what West Point had instilled in us so far, but what about true fear?

What is this place? This desert? This foreign land? No matter how many movies, documentaries, and YouTube videos that we watch, we only feel further and further from the truth and the ever-haunting question that follows us from the mess hall to class to practice. What is it like?

What happens over there? We see the explosions, the tragedies, the wreckage, the amputees, the flag-covered coffins. But what happens inside? The invisible wounds? What happens internally? Will we be ready for it when we are called?

I can't help but think about what will happen to my group of friends when we graduate. When we all go our separate ways and head to different posts. I know we will run into each other from time to time, maybe even overseas. But it's hard to imagine leaving this place, and leaving the brotherhood that we've built here. I think about all that we've been through together. And then the worst thought of all—Will they have to attend my funeral? Will I have to go to one of theirs? I've had to bury friends before, but not one of these brothers. That I can't honestly fathom.

Every time I get a chance, every time I have downtime with an NCO or an officer who has been deployed, I try to get as much knowledge from them as I can. Bullshitting on the wood line at CTLT, waiting for class to start, or even waiting in the chairs at DENTAC, I try to squeeze all the advice I can out of all of them. I constantly hear about bad lieutenants, and I don't want to be one, so I try hard to learn what I can. I vary the questions, always curious about new topics. But there's one question that I always ask, "Did we miss the boat, or do you think that we'll get deployed?"

It's funny that they always give you the same look and have the same response. Whether they've been deployed once or six times, it's the same answer. "I know you're eager and that's good. I was too. But keep your head down; keep working hard. Listen to your NCOs, put your dudes first, and don't think about it too much. Your time will come."

"*Table commandants report to the Poop Deck to pick up floaters. TAKE SEATS.*"

GLOSSARY AND TERMS

AAR: After Action Review; a sort of lessons learned after an event

ABP: Afghan Border Police

Acceptance Day: Parade and ceremony at which new cadets are formally welcomed into the Corps of Cadets following their successful completion of Beast Barracks

Airborne: Soldiers who jump from the sky under parachutes

ANA: Afghan National Army

ANP: Afghan National Police

ANSF: Afghan National Security Forces

AQI: Al-Qaeda in Iraq

Battle Captain: Position often held by captains in a tactical operations center; their role is to plan, coordinate, supervise, and maintain communication flow to ensure the successful accomplishment of all assigned missions

Beast Barracks: Beast is the first summer cadets spend at West Point and is designed to literally rip the new cadets from their civilian lives; life is not good for new cadets this summer

Branch: Each officer selects a specialization, whether it be the Armor, Infantry, Aviation, Field Artillery, Engineer, Finance, Logistics, Transportation, Military Police, Military Intelligence, or Adjutant General

CA: Civil Affairs; units that assist commanders by working with civil authorities in the commander's area of operations to lessen the impact of military operations on them during peace, contingency operations, and declared war

CFT: Cadet Field Training; training conducted during a West Point cadet's second summer meant to introduce them to the close ground fight and the associated challenges of leading soldiers in a tactical environment

CHU: Containerized Housing Unit; trailers that house soldiers during a deployment

CO: Commander; the boss

COP: Combat Outpost; small coalition outpost, many times surrounded on all sides by the enemy

Cow: Second Class Cadet or Junior at West Point

Duty, Honor, Country: West Point motto based on a speech made by General Douglas MacArthur at West Point in May 1962

EFP: Explosive Formed Penetrator; extremely lethal Improvised Explosive Device that essentially funnels all of the force of a blast in one direction

Eisenhower Hall: Large auditorium at West Point; used for performances and briefings to the entire Corps of Cadets

EOD: Explosive Ordnance Disposal; the unit that determines if an object is an explosive device and then disarms that device

Firstie: First Class Cadet or Senior at West Point

Firstie Club: The bar at West Point that is only for First Class Cadets

FOB: Forward Operating Base; where soldiers are deployed to when in combat

FRG: Family Readiness Group; spouse support group for a deployment

GWOT: Global War on Terror; includes any and all combat and other operations focused on terrorist threats, to include Operation Iraqi Freedom and Operation Enduring Freedom (Afghanistan)

Haji: Slang for someone of Middle Eastern decent; refers to the religious pilgrimage known as the Haj

HMMWV: High Mobility Multiwheeled Vehicle or "Hummer"; the army's modern-day Jeep

Hours: Cadets at West Point that receive punishment are instructed to walk "Hours," which equates to walking back and forth in full uniform for up to five hours a day

IA: Iraqi Army

IED: Improvised Explosive Device; roadside bomb in many cases

IP: Iraqi Police

JCC/JSS: Joint Coordination Centers or Joint Security Stations; after the surge in Iraq of 2005, most units were directed to establish JCCs/JSSs that acted as combined headquarters with the local forces

KIA: Killed in Action

MEDEVAC: Medical Evacuation of a wounded soldier; in combat, this happens either on a helicopter or in a vehicle of some sort

Mooj: An old colloquialism from the Soviet-Afghan War that contemporary soldiers use to describe violent extremists; it is an abbreviated form of *Mujihadeen*, which translates to "Holy Warriors"

MRE: Meals Ready to Eat; a U.S. military precooked ration pack, generally consumed during field and tactical operations in lieu of a standard meal

NCO: Noncommissioned Officers; those soldiers who are not officers and obtain the rank of sergeant or higher are called NCOs

New Cadet: What new cadets are called during Beast Barracks; you must complete Beast in order to be called a cadet

OBC: Officer Basic Course; generally, the first training officers receive at West Point that is specific to their branch or specialization

OEF/OIF: Operation Enduring Freedom/Operation Iraqi Freedeom; Operation Enduring Freedom refers to all operations in Afghanistan and Operation Iraqi Freedom refers to operations in Iraq

OP: Observation Post; place where soldiers watch for enemy activity, oftentimes for hours

PFAR: Parachute Field Artillery Regiment; a specific type of airborne unit for those with branch designation Field Artillery

PID: Positive Identification; soldiers must have PID that an intended target is an enemy combatant

PL: Platoon leader; oftentimes the first job an officer receives out of officer basic training

Plebe: Plebian or Freshman at West Point

Pogue/Pog: Noncombat type; generally a negative slang for those that do not leave the wire on combat missions

Poop Deck: Information, or "poop," is communicated via loudspeaker to the Corps of Cadets at West Point from the Poop Deck

PSG: Platoon Sergeant; a platoon leader's most senior member of the platoon and often acts as a mentor to the inexperienced officer

PT: Physical Training

Purple Heart: Medal given to soldiers wounded as a result of enemy actions

QRF: Quick Reaction Force; a unit that is designated as the QRF waits, fully prepared to leave the wire, for the order to deploy in the event another unit gets into trouble

R Day: Reception Day; the first day that new cadets arrive at West Point to begin their journey; the day is long and not fun

R & R: Rest and Relaxation during a deployment, commonly referred to as leave

Ranger: Skilled and highly trained infantry soldier; Ranger School is one of the most difficult army schools to endure and focuses on small unit tactics

Ring Knocker: A person who is very proud they went to West Point and wants everyone to see their class ring

RIP/TOA: Relief in Place/Transfer of Authority; approximately ten-day period in which the outgoing unit tries to teach the incoming unit all of the lessons learned during the previous deployment (also called a Right Seat/Left Seat Ride)

RPG: Rocket Propelled Grenade; shoulder-fired rockets

S1: Officer in charge of personnel actions; heavy administrative responsibilities

S2: Officer in charge of intelligence

S3: Officer in charge of operations planning

S4: Officer in charge of supply operations

S6: Officer in charge of communications

S9: Officer in charge of civil affairs

Special Forces: Elite army soldiers who are highly trained and operate in small units

Thayer Week: Refers to the "father" of West Point and generally means any type of week when there is a perfect storm of suck; an example would be two exams, a room inspection, two intermural matches, and two papers due all in the same week

TOC: Tactical Operation Centers, which act as the command and control headquarters for units that are deployed

Toolbag: Cadet slang for someone who lives only for West Point regulations

USMA: United States Military Academy; aka West Point

VBIED: Vehicle-Borne Improvised Explosive Device

WIA: Wounded in Action

Wire: "The Wire" refers oftentimes to a physical barrier such as walls that separates the soldiers from their base and the local people; being outside the wire refers to combat situations

Yearling: Third Class Cadet or Sophomore at West Point; also referred to as Yuk

NOTES

INTRODUCTION

1. Cadets used to receive a ninety-day furlough, or vacation, between their second and third year at West Point. "Furlough songs" were written by members of a class to sing at gatherings as they looked ahead to their upcoming furlough. "The Origin of Alma Mater: Paul Reinecke's Own Story," *Assembly*, April 9, 1942, http://www.west-point.org/greimanj/west_point/songs/vol1no1 Assembly page 9.pdf, accessed December 1, 2013.

2. United States Military Academy West Point, "West Point Classes: 2004 Profile," http://www.usma.edu/classes/SitePages/2004 Profile.aspx, accessed December 27, 2014.

FIRST LIEUTENANT DENNIS W. ZILINSKI II, KIA IN BAYJI, IRAQ, ON NOVEMBER 19, 2005

1. "Bible Gateway Passage: John 15:13, New International Version," Bible Gateway, https://www.biblegateway.com/passage/?search=John 15:13, accessed December 27, 2014.

2. Camp Buckner is where Cadet Field Training occurred between plebe and yearling year. For the Class of 2004, the training was eight weeks long. It has been shortened since they graduated.

3. STAP stands for Summer Term Academic Program. This is West Point's version of summer school.

4. The academy recognizes that military service is not for everyone and gives until the beginning of junior year for cadets to leave the Academy without owing any service.

5. A bar on West Point.

6. Cadets face four kinds of punishment boards—Company, Battalion, Regimental, and Brigade. Each board brings with it a heavier set of punishments. Charlie faced many hours of walking tours, restriction to his room, and other lost privileges. Fortunately, the punishment was light.

7. West Point calls its cheerleaders Rabble Rousers. When USMA was all male, Rabble Rousers were also all male and inspired the Corps of Cadets during football games. After the Academy admitted women, the name remained.

FIRST LIEUTENANT GARRISON C. AVERY, KIA IN BAGHDAD, IRAQ, ON FEBRUARY 1, 2006

1. Posted by the author on September 12, 2007, on the west-point.org eulogy page for 1LT Garrison Avery. "1LT Garrison Avery Eulogy," http://defender .west-point.org/service/display.mhtml?u=60373&i= 39847, accessed December 27, 2014.

2. The tribal arrangement we brokered with the al Saidi tribe led, in part, to a major pan-sectarian reconciliation and security cooperation movement in the restive districts just south of Baghdad. In October 2007, the South Baghdad Reconciliation Council, hosted at Baghdad's International Zone by the United States Institute of Peace, created a document and alliance that helped to lift the Triangle of Death out of its darkest era.

FIRST LIEUTENANT ROBERT A. SEIDEL III, KIA IN ABU GHRAIB, IRAQ, ON MAY 18, 2006

1. The upperclassmen who run Cadet Basic Training split the summer into two halves, and this break occurs while the first group of upperclassmen moves out and their replacements move in to the barracks.

2. 1st Brigade, 10th Mountain Division, is one of the most deployed units in the U.S. Army, having served as the "unit of choice" for the Army's small wars

since deployments to Haiti and Somalia in the early 1990s. The unit has been in Afghanistan and Iraq since 2001, and the division, or one of its brigades, is almost constantly deployed.

3. "Land Nav" is Army slang for land navigation, basically the ability to know where you are, and know where you are going. The fact that a team of Green Berets got lost after Rob told them they would is absolutely hilarious.

4. As the name suggests, a "dcisive operation" is the most decisive piece of an operation. Most units decide to send their best platoon, company, and others to this decisive point.

5. Staff Sergeant Gardner was Rob's most senior squad leader. He was a rock-solid dude, and did a phenomenal job taking control of the scene.

6. "Fire Base Courage" was a small American base located to the northwest of Baghdad in a rural area. It consisted of one building and a bunch of Army tents, and normally was home to two Infantry companies. We both loved and hated being in this remote and austere location, depending on the day.

7. Highly Mobile Multiwheeled Vehicle—an armored Army vehicle that we used to drive in Iraq.

FIRST LIEUTENANT AMOS "CAMDEN" BOCK, KIA IN BAGHDAD, IRAQ, ON OCTOBER 23, 2006

1. Gunny is short for Gunnery Sergeant. In artillery units, this is typically a Sergeant First Class who has the responsibility of conducting reconnaissance and establishing new artillery positions. In Mike and Amos's unit he would have the same responsibilities as a platoon sergeant. Smoke is the name given to the conventional platoon sergeant of an artillery unit. Each platoon has a Smoke and a Gunny.

2. The EFP was typically a homemade shape charge that had the ability to penetrate almost any type of armor.

CAPTAIN MICHAEL A. CERRONE, KIA IN SAMARRA, IRAQ, ON NOVEMBER 12, 2006

1. Cadets receive a sizable loan at the end of their junior year to help them pay for their uniforms and class ring. They must repay this loan during their mandatory five years in the Army.

CAPTAIN DAVID M. FRASER, KIA IN BAGHDAD, IRAQ, ON NOVEMBER 26, 2006

1. This is a West Point term for homework.
2. This is the academic building of the Civil Engineering Department at West Point.

FIRST LIEUTENANT JACOB N. FRITZ, KIA IN KARBALA, IRAQ, ON JANUARY 20, 2007

1. The PJCC in Karbala was a particularly important assignment. Not only was the PJCC coordinating emergency and local government services for the entire province, but Karbala has crucial religious significance to all Muslims. It holds particular significance to the Shia. Karbala is the site of the martyrdom of Imam Hussein and home to the Imam Hussein Shrine. Imam Hussein was the grandson of the Prophet Muhammed. Hussein's death in the battle of Karbala (AD 680) lies at the heart of Islam's rift between the Sunni and the Shia and is seen by the Shia as the greatest suffering and redemptive act in history. Every year as many as two million Shia from across the Muslim world conduct a pilgrimage to Karbala for a ten-day ceremony, called Ashura.

2. Jake's younger brother Dan followed Jacob to West Point. He graduated in 2008 and was commissioned as a second lieutenant. He served in the Infantry branch, and following his graduation from Ranger School he deployed to Iraq for twelve months with the 1st Cavalry Division. He now serves with the 4th Infantry Brigade Combat Team, 1st Infantry Division at Fort Riley, Kansas. Jake's youngest brother Ethan is now in the ROTC Corps at Texas A&M University and will also be commissioned as an officer in the U.S. military. Jacob's mother, Noala, still lives and manages the family farm in Nebraska, although his father, Lyle, has since passed. Following his capture and death, Jacob was posthumously awarded the POW medal.

CAPTAIN ADAM P. SNYDER, KIA IN BAYJI, IRAQ, ON DECEMBER 5, 2007

1. "America, the Beautiful" lyrics, USA Flag Site, http://www.usa-flag-site.org/song-lyrics/america.shtml, accessed December 27, 2014.
2. "Bible Gateway Passage: Zephaniah 3:17, New International Version," https://www.biblegateway.com/passage/?search=Zephaniah 3:17, accessed December 27, 2014.

3. "Bible Gateway Passage: Isaiah 40:28–31, New International Version," https://www.biblegateway.com/passage/?search=Isa 40:28-31 &version=ESV, accessed December 27, 2014.

4. "The Origin of the Alma Mater: Paul Reinecke's Own Story," *Assembly*, April 9, 1942, http://www.west-point.org/greimanj/west_point/songs/vol1no1 Assembly page 9.pdf, accessed December 1, 2013.

5. "Bible Gateway Passage: Matthew 8:5–13, New International Version," https://www.biblegateway.com/passage/?search=Matthew 8:5-13&version=NRSV, accessed December 27, 2014.

CAPTAIN PAUL W. PEÑA, KIA IN ARGHANDAB, AFGHANISTAN, ON JANUARY 19, 2010

1. Lead singer of The Misfits.
2. NYHC, New York Hard Core: an aggressive type of punk music known for violent mosh pits and "slam dancing."
3. A popular cadet bar outside of West Point.
4. A stereotypical haircut of Infantrymen. The sides of the heads are shaved bald while the top is reduced to little more than fuzz.
5. Cadet in charge of making sure members of a Mess Hall table upheld proper decorum.
6. Elevated platform in the middle of Mess Hall that grants permission to take seats and enjoy the meal.
7. USMA Class of 2004's Graduation Day.
8. Infantry Officer's Basic Course.
9. Parachute Infantry Regiment.
10. "Ranger Buddy" is a term used to label one's battle buddy in Ranger School.
11. Zodiacs are small rubber boats designed for tactical operations and are not intended for use in the Bering Sea during winter storms.

CAPTAIN DANIEL P. WHITTEN, KIA IN ZABUL PROVINCE, AFGHANISTAN, ON FEBRUARY 2, 2010

1. Incoming students are told to arrive on a staggered schedule based on the last digit of their respective social security numbers. I was in the final wave of receptions.
2. Seniors are called "Firsties." The Cadet in the Red Sash is a Firstie who presides over a rite of passage marking a new cadet's entrance into "Beast Barracks,"

the first summer at the United States Military Academy. A new cadet must walk up to the Firstie, salute, and report in a prescribed format. Any error requires the new cadet to endure intense yelling and try again.

3. The Bugle Notes is a small, pocket-sized book often referred to as the "Plebe Bible," as it contains various pieces of knowledge cadets are required to memorize, such as the "Alma Mater" and West Point poems, the National Anthem, famous speeches and quotes, fight songs and army songs, cadet trivia, tenets of the honor code, leadership principles, and other items deemed integral to a cadet's knowledge.

4. Discrete Dynamical Systems, or simply DDS, is the first-semester mathematics course all Plebes must take as a precursor to two semesters of calculus and one semester of probability and statistics.

5. The United States Corps of Cadets is organized into four regiments, each with eight companies, for a total of thirty-two companies. The alphanumeric code for each company corresponds to its regiment (number) and company (letter). Unit identity is associated with one's company more so than one's regiment.

6. Juniors are called "Cows" at West Point. There are several conjectures as to this nickname's origin, but no single explanation is widely held to be true.

7. Cadets refer to committing to their final two years of academics at West Point in exchange for a five-year active duty service obligation as "two for seven."

8. He opted to pursue the hardest training opportunity as a cadet platoon sergeant in the second Camp Buckner detail, so that he could participate in "Infantry Week." He did not simply go to one Army school—such as Airborne or Air Assault School—but rather he attended two Army schools. In the summer after his Yearling year, he attended Air Assault School. The following summer, he attended the Sapper Leader Course, a challenging course for combat engineers that rivals Ranger School in its physical demands despite being roughly half as long in duration. He angled for a Cadet Troop Leading Training slot with an infantry unit in the storied 101st Airborne (Air Assault) Division.

9. I cannot overemphasize Dan's love of junk food enough. I referred to him as the "fattest skinny kid I know," a testament to his ability to eat massive quantities of junk food but achieve the highest ratings on all requisite physical tasks. His company command photo is that of a chubby, red-faced, smiling Dan in maroon beret in front of an American flag. The chubby cheeks were the result of a steady diet of hot dogs and beer at the Fayetteville, North Carolina, minor league baseball stadium, where he spent a lot of time before his deployment.

10. Plebes are not authorized to wear civilian clothes.

11. Cadets "walk" disciplinary tours for minor infractions such as being late to or missing class, skipping lectures, or having chronically untidy barracks rooms. A

tour consists of dressing in the seasonal dress uniform and marching to and fro in the cadet area for up to five hours at a time.

12. Known as "turnbacks," cadets are sometimes required to spend an additional semester or two at West Point as punishment for misconduct, academic remediation, or other reasons. In our case, we had completed our academic programs and were turned back for misconduct, so our second Firstie year was flexible with regard to choice of academic program. We chose to add the additional major of Arts, Philosophy, and Literature in the English Department because of a mutual appreciation for literature and the ability to complete the full program of study in two semesters.

13. Graham Farmelo, *It Must Be Beautiful: Great Equations of Modern Science* (London: Granta, 2002).

14. Ring Weekend is typically the second weekend in the fall semester where Firsties receive their class rings. The ceremony occurs on a Friday afternoon, where the entire class dresses in India White dress uniform, assembles at the Trophy Point amphitheater overlooking the Hudson River, and receives its rings as a group. Significant others and families often attend. Immediately following the ceremony, Firsties return to the cadet area to change into civilian clothes and celebrate. It is during this return to the cadet area that Plebes recite the Ring Poop. On the Saturday evening of Ring Weekend, there is a formal ball.

15. The Ring Poop is a proud Plebe tradition consisting of a mob of Plebes interdicting the Firsties desperately trying to leave the Academy to enjoy their weekend. The Plebes will crowd the Firsties and scream the following at the top of their lungs: "Oh my God, Sir! What a beautiful ring! What a crass mass of brass and glass! What a bold mold of rolled gold! What a cool jewel you got from your school! See how it sparkles and shines! It must have cost you a fortune! Can I touch it? Can I touch it, please, Sir?!"

16. Daniel's father name is Dan, although Daniel is not a junior. To avoid confusion, we referred to him as the Old Man, or Old Man Whitten. I still do to this day.

17. Plato, *The Symposium* (London, UK: Penguin, 1999), 24.

18. In Carl Jung's archetypes, the herald is the catalyst for change, which often launches the hero on his quest.

19. Threshold guardians are the agents of opposition who challenge the hero's progress during his quest.

20. *Unus Mundus* is a Jungian term that literally translates from Latin into English as "one world" and refers to the notion that a singular reality exists as the basis for all things.

21. T. S. Eliot, *The Waste Land* (New York: Norton and Company, 2001), 5.

22. Eliot, *The Waste Land*, 6.

CAPTAIN JASON E. HOLBROOK, KIA IN TSAGAY, AFGHANISTAN, ON JULY 29, 2010

1. Academic companies are how the Corps of Cadets structures itself. Each company comprises of approximately thirty to thirty-five cadets per class (120 to 135 total), with four companies per battalion, two battalions per regiment, and four regiments in the Corps. Cadet companies live, eat, and train together.

2. The first sergeant is the head noncommissioned officer in the company structure, or in other words, he or she is the chief disciplinarian. You generally do not want to make them mad. In our case, the first sergeant for Company H3 was infamous throughout the Corps as being a "big haze."

3. Cadets typically will change companies, or "scramble," after their plebe year. The policy changes year to year—some classes never scramble, some scramble after two years.

4. The career course is a professional military school that officers attend as captains (usually three to five years into service) to "prepare them for the next level of officership." In reality, they learn to build PowerPoint slides, track tasks, and play a lot of ultimate Frisbee.

HAVE YOU PASSED THROUGH THE NIGHT?

1. IED: improvised explosive device
2. CP: command post
3. PKM: Soviet machine gun
4. RPG: rocket-propelled grenade
5. JDAM: joint direct attack munition; "smart" bomb released from fixed-wing aircraft
6. Katyusha Rocket: Soviet rocket that can be rudimentarily launched from a terrain slope or ridgeline
7. Zam Zam: cola-flavored soft drink popular in the Middle East and parts of Southwest Asia
8. RTO: Radio Telephone Operator; soldier carrying the radio typically assigned to a leader
9. wadi: dry riverbed
10. Naswar: Afghan smokeless tobacco
11. EFP: explosively formed projectile; a type of IED that penetrates armor
12. PID: positive identification; targeting term used to declare a hostile threat
13. CASEVAC: casualty evacuation; a vehicle or means of transport for a casualty

"WALKING THE LAST MILE HOME"

1. Just two weeks before this scene, my father had planned my family's escape from communist-occupied Laos. My father was a military officer in the Lao Royal Army who, after secondary school, was hand selected to attend university in Lyon, France. Once graduated, he returned to his homeland to fulfill his military service obligation in 1973 and went to Pakse, the capital of the southern province of Champasak. There, he managed the local hospital and met my mother, a pretty, dark-haired nurse; they quickly married before she changed her mind. My oldest brother, Kno, was born a year later. And a few months after that, the last American Huey hovered over Saigon, which emboldened the Pathet Lao and other communist forces to take over the rest of the country. Subsequently, the communist regime arrested and placed my father, mother, and older brother in a reeducation camp or "Seminar" in the southern region of Laos. There, for over a decade, my parents labored in the rice fields, struggled to provide basic sustenance to their growing family, and fought to maintain a semblance of community support within these camps.

2. I wouldn't learn how to swim until the last day of my second attempt at passing "Plebe Drowning" or the Survival Swimming Program at the Academy. In order to graduate, not only do cadets acquire the basic skills of swimming, they learn how to swim in full battle uniform with a rifle and to execute other water-combat survival skills. In other words, it was one of the worst experiences of my life, and the smell of chlorine, I think, haunted me years after graduation.

3. In terms of driving distance, Baqubah is located less than an hour northeast of Baghdad and about two hours west of the Iranian border. It is the capital and most populous city in the province.

4. In early 2007, in an effort to stop the unprecedented violence in Iraq, the surge operations brought an additional five brigade combat teams (BCTs) to Iraq. The troop increase brought the number of BCTs to twenty, which were about 150,000 military personnel (much of them would see their one-year tours extended to fifteen months).

5. As part of the counterinsurgency strategy, the Army wanted to reestablish internal security by making the indigenous security force more credible, and to do this, they had to reconstitute and professionalize the Iraqi Security Forces (ISF). Thus, they chose to increase the number of military transition teams in Iraq.

6. A year before my team hit the ground in Iraq, one of my former classmates, Jacob Fritz, was killed by insurgent forces on January 20, 2007, in Karbala, Iraq. The exact details surrounding his death remain a mystery, but there were reports that the ISF members were complicit or directly involved in the attack of Jacob's transition team. I used the Karbala incident as a case study for my team to look over.

7. A yearlong deployment is not easy even if one is a member in a small unit. However, we did things as a team that I think helped us bond. After almost every mission, our team would have our meals together. We'd talk about a range of topics—from the loudness of someone's fart to how our families were doing stateside. On most weekend afternoons, we would play "ultimate football" and split the teams in half according to vehicle assignments. It was a great opportunity to compete and vent off some aggression. The losers would cook dinner and clean up afterward, so no one wanted to lose. These afternoons, for me, were some of the most memorable times of the deployment, because they reminded me of playing sports with my brothers when I was younger. They were reminders of home.

8. The trip from FOB Gabe to Kanan took about forty-five minutes one way. It was a long ride, but we made the trek five to six days a week for almost three months. Later in the deployment, almost on a daily basis, we would travel almost two hours to get to our Iraqi battalion.

9. The day that Torre assumed command of his cavalry troop was the same day that I left for the Military Intelligence Captain's Career Course at Fort Huachuca, Arizona. I got a chance to see him take the guidon and assume responsibility of over two hundred cavalry troopers. It was a special day.

10. Luckily, there would be no man kiss today.

11. Or Lieutenant Amar in English.

12. Unlike some other soldiers in the battalion, he never asked me for special favors or items that I could spare. Considering the austere conditions that the unit lived in and the small salary he received, one would have expected him to have a feeling of hopelessness or doubt. But he maintained a solid optimism for the future and strong dignity to be emulated by all.

13. Muqdadiyah was the other major city in Diyala Province. It is northeast of Baqubah and straight north from Kanan.

14. Mike was in my unit when I was a Squadron Intelligence Officer. Graduating from Bowling Green State University in 2005, he, like me, was a Military Intelligence Officer who was branch-detailed to the Armor branch. Mike wanted to stay a combat arms officer, and, before I left for the Career Course, he would visit my office to figure out how he could stay in the armor branch so he could lead his platoon into combat. Looking at his 6-foot-3, 200-pound-plus frame, anyone who knew Mike understood right away that not only was he built to lead men into battle, he was down-to-earth and always placed the welfare of others before himself. On the day he left this earth, he was the epitome of the latter: leading out front and sacrificing himself to save others. Mike is an American hero.

15. At the beginning of the deployment, my team and I were at the Phoenix Academy to learn about the counterinsurgency strategy. Sitting in the middle of

the crowd, I waited to hear General David Petraeus speak to us. At West Point, he was our 100th Night speaker, and I anticipated hearing the same pep talk as that night. "Attention!" I stood up at attention, and in the corner of my eyes I didn't see the general but a blonde-haired woman walk pass me. It was Haley Dennison, my classmate, who was on the general's personal staff. The last time I saw her was at West Point, months before our graduation. She was with her soon-to-be husband, Ryan Dennison, and they were visiting friends of mine in the barracks. Ryan died in 2006, a few months after I redeployed from my first deployment from Iraq. Though I didn't know him very well, having given each other the occasional "what's up?" over the course of four years, I remembered Ryan's big smile and loud laugh emanating from Shiggy's or Jeff's rooms. I've heard this said from good friends of Ryan: the sadness of his loss underscored the power of his life.

16. I'd like to thank my wife, Jen, and classmates for editing this paper for me; it needed it. Also, I'd like to thank my Military Training Team ("Team Pyro") members for allowing me to share some accounts of our deployment: Todd Baughman, Craig Broe, Mike Coston, Robert Dodd, Woody Gebhart, Chris Goodrich, James Mosley, Daniel Munley, and Ernesto Suazo; and, our Iraqi translators: Emad, Ahmed, Mohammed, Ali, Abas, and Sarkawt. Lastly, my love and eternal appreciation goes out to my parents and siblings, Kno, Nang, and Noi. Never give up.

IN GOD I TRUST

1. Medical Evacuation. A UH-60 Blackhawk outfitted for transporting wounded service members would land inside the FOB on a marked landing zone outside the aid station.

2. Quick Reaction Force, or QRF, was a group of soldiers placed on standby to support the missions of other soldiers in the company.

3. Route Fat Boy was the main two-lane, paved road that stretched from Yusufiyah to Route Jackson (a four-lane leading to Mahmudiyah).

4. The AVLB is a metal bridge designed to move armored vehicles and troops across obstacles. Our obstacle was a canal that divided the main supply route from the JSB to a checkpoint at a major intersection nearby.

5. By chance, I met the gunner of that vehicle at Walter Reed Army Medical Center five months after that explosion. I was able to show her pictures from that day and replay the events for her from my perspective.

6. At the minimum in a Humvee, there needs to be a driver, a gunner, and a truck commander, or TC.

HIER KANNST DU NUR KRIEG FUHREN (HERE YOU CAN ONLY WAGE WAR)

1. This was the title from a story in the December 2011 edition of the *Financial Times* about the East Pakita Province. Notes: The FTD went out of business and pulled their website.

"ECONOMY OF FORCE": MY VIEW OF HELL FROM DEEP WITHIN THE "TRIANGLE OF DEATH," KARGOULI VILLAGE, IRAQ, 2007

1. Kargouli Village was an area of concern to the Coalition since the start of the most recent conflict in Iraq. During the period of Saddam Hussein's regime, this idyllic patch of fertile farmland, located along the Euphrates River approximately thirty kilometers south-southwest of Baghdad, was essentially a retirement community for older or retired members of the Iraqi armed forces. The individuals who had shown intense loyalty to Saddam were rewarded with expansive plots, many directly on the river. The local populace was composed primarily of Sunnis from the al-Kargouli tribe, hence the more common name of the village. Whereas al-Kargoulis comprised roughly 80 to 90 percent of the town's populace, there were smaller enclaves of al-Janabi and other tribes, all Sunni. The town was enclosed to the north by the never-completed Yusufiyah Thermal Power Plant, to the east by a massive concrete irrigation canal, to the south by the QaQa Weapons Production Facility, and to the west by the Euphrates River. The Yusufiyah Thermal Power Plant was particularly strange, as the Russians had abandoned construction midway through the project when the Iraqis ceased payments. As a result, the facility looked like a postapocalyptic wasteland, with half-built buildings, the skeleton of the main structure, and rusting construction equipment strewn about haphazardly. During the initial U.S. invasion, Coalition forces failed to secure the vast stockpiles of munitions at the QaQa Weapons Production Facility, and the locals had helped themselves to these and cached them all over Kargouli Village in preparation for the subsequent insurgency on which the Ba'athist had pinned their hopes and which the Coalition failed to predict. In the arid, unnamed lands directly across the Euphrates River to the west lived the al-Owesi tribe, a tribe with which the al-Kargoulis had a long-standing and ambiguous blood feud. Essentially, the Euphrates River served as an impenetrable barrier between Kargouli Village and the al-Owesi tribe, as the river flowed too quickly for regular travel and the one remaining bridge in the area was barricaded and controlled by the Iraqi

army. Finally, the east boundary of the town was marked by a massive irrigation canal (identified by Coalition forces as the Route Caveman Canal), which Saddam built to support local agriculture. In the undulating and lush (almost tropical) agricultural areas, this man-made, perfectly linear structure seemed alien. From the Water Treatment Plant in the south, one could see all the way down the canal to the Yusufiyah Thermal Power Plant. At intervals, locals had constructed ramshackle bridges along the canal, some even capable of supporting their light trucks. Past the Caveman Canal lay the town of Rushdi Mullah, another "difficult" town in which our Bravo Company established Patrol Base "Shanghai" earlier in our campaign. Generally, the al-Kargoulis had very poor relations with all the other tribes with which they shared borders, a very common condition in the factional lands of Iraq.

2. Predominantly from the Kargouli tribe, the 1920 Revolutionary Brigade counted among its members most of the former Ba'athists of the Saddam era.

3. This group was comprised of mostly Islamic fundamentalists drawing from all the tribes in Kargouli Village while also bringing in some foreign fighters and considerable resources from outside.

4. Yusufiyah is a small town located along the main east-west running road from Mahmudiyah, which is itself just south of Baghdad.

5. Nathan Hoskins, "1st ACB Repeats History with Air Assault Mission," 10th Mountain News Releases and Advisories, December 4, 2006, http://www .drum.army.mil/news/Article.aspx?List=9bf48051-598a-4759-a68f-41a214 b6d75f&ID=2785, accessed November 1, 2012.

6. Improving a defensive position usually consists of construction, digging fighting positions, filling sandbags, and building bunkers.

7. A pressure plate is a device that initiates an IED when either a soldier or vehicle applies enough weight to its surface.

CHOOSING

1. The "Definition of Leather" is one of the many bits of "Plebe Knowledge": bits of information or passages that Plebes have to memorize and recite throughout their first year at West Point. According to West Point's *Bugle Notes*, leather is defined, "If the fresh skin of an animal, cleaned and divested of all hair, fat, and other extraneous matter, be immersed in a dilute solution of tannic acid, a chemical combination ensues; the gelatinous tissue of the skin is converted into a nonputrescible substance, impervious to and insoluble in water; this is leather." "Bugle Notes: Learn This!" http://www.west-point.org/academy/malo-wa/inspirations/ buglenotes.html, accessed December 23, 2014.

ALL THE PIECES MATTER

1. "Burning in" is slang for crashing one's helicopter.

2. FARP: Forward Arming & Refueling Point. In Iraq, these were generally located on larger bases. They function as gas stations for helicopters, where rapid refueling and reloading of ammo occurs.

3. Callsigns for aircraft are pronounced by individual digits; for example, "Three-Two" not "Thirty-Two."

4. Battle Oscar is the callsign for the 1-30 Infantry HQ at Patrol Base Murray, aka "The Horse Farm."

5. *Push* is shorthand for frequency.

6. Operations & Intelligence radio net, generally called O&I, where pertinent operational information is passed. Its counterpart is the A&L or Administrative & Logistics net.

7. *Play time* is a phrase that means the amount of time the helicopters can operate in a ground unit's vicinity due to fuel or other mission requirements.

8. TIC ("tick") is shorthand for Troops-in-Contact (with the enemy or with hostile action).

9. A "bongo truck" is a Korean-made pickup truck that looks more like a minivan with a bed than anything labeled a truck in America. Every Iraqi owns one, and they come in two colors: white and blue. Blue bongos in Baghdad are like yellow cabs in Manhattan.

10. Landing Zone.

11. No Joy is standard brevity code for "no visual contact."

12. *Woobie* is a slang term for the nylon poncho liner that every soldier is issued and that serves as every GI's favorite blanket.

IT'S A SMALL WORLD

1. Cadet Companies exist of a roughly equal amount of seniors, juniors, sophomores, and freshman, and they typically will stay together in the same company as a class. Often, one class year group of cadets will be scrambled around to different companies once during their four years between freshman-sophomore or through sophomore-junior years.

2. Very simply stated sans Army jargon, a task-organized unit is detached from its organic headquarters and reassigned to another for a particular mission.

3. High Mobility Multipurpose Wheeled Vehicle (HMMWV); Model M114.

4. Made to penetrate the armor of U.S. vehicles.

5. Microphone, commonly referred to as "mike," requires a push-to-talk button.

THE DAY THE ELEPHANT CAME TO TOWN

1. AQI: al-Qaeda in Iraq.

2. Short for *mujahideen*. This word translates to "people doing jihad" or "holy warriors" in Arabic.

3. The Ba'ath Socialist Party was headed by Sadaam Hussein. They ruled Iraq since 1958.

4. Capital of the Diyala Province located thirty miles to the northeast of Baghdad. Throughout Operation Iraqi Freedom, Ba'Quaba was the scene of some of the most brutal fighting in the entire country.

5. Sadaam forced a large number of Shia Muslims into the ghetto of Sadr City—a place named in honor of Muqtada al-Sadr's father.

6. Most organizations in Iraq had a tip line made available to the public for providing information about enemy activity.

7. Handheld radios similar to a walkie-talkie.

8. A reductive version of a pickup truck consisting only of a small cab and a flat bed.

9. Compact version of our normal radios. It is roughly the size of Zac Morris's cellphone.

10. A Soviet equivalent to our M240B machine gun.

11. Air Weapons Team. In this case, our AWT consisted of two AH-64D Apache helicopters.

12. A Soviet equivalent to our M2 .50 caliber machine gun. This particular weapon fires a 12.7 mm round and is very devastating.

13. Prior to the blast, all but those soldiers on guard were sleeping in "patrol base pajamas" (brown T-shirts, PT shorts, and flip flops). The blast blew all of their uniforms out of the patrol base, forcing them to fight in their sleep attire.

14. Semiautomatic Berrata 9 mm pistol.

15. The officer or NCO in charge of directing a unit's operations in the absence of the commander, operations officer (S3), or executive officer.

16. Each Abrams tank requires four people to operate the vehicle: a loader, driver, gunner, and commander. Although not optimal, some crews conduct operations without a loader when manpower becomes an issue.

17. Helicopter Landing Zone.

18. A smaller version of the M240B mounted next to the M1A2's main gun. This machine gun operates with the benefit of being slaved directly to the tank's advanced thermal optics.

19. An independent thermal optic directly slaved to the tank commander's station. From his position, the TC can take control of the main gun or direct the gunner to view the same target as identified in the CITV.

20. Armor Piercing Incendiary Tracer: A round designed to penetrate hard targets in a highly visible manner that marks the site of impact for other forces on the battlefield.

21. Obstacle Reducing round used to destroy bunkers and other fortified positions.

22. Basically, a 120 mm shotgun round loaded with 1,300 tungsten ball bearings.

BIBLIOGRAPHY

"America, the Beautiful Lyrics, by Katherine Lee Bates." USA Flag. http://www
.usa-flag-site.org/song-lyrics/america.shtml. Accessed December 27, 2014.

"Bible Gateway Passage: Isaiah 40:28–31, New International Version." Bible Gateway. https://www.biblegateway.com/passage/?search=Isa. Accessed December
27, 2014.

"Bible Gateway Passage: John 15:13, New International Version." Bible Gateway.
https://www.biblegateway.com/passage/?search=John 15:13. Accessed December 27, 2014.

"Bible Gateway Passage: Matthew 8:5–13, New International Version." Bible
Gateway. https://www.biblegateway.com/passage/?search=Matthew 8:5-13&ver
sion=NRSV. Accessed December 27, 2014.

"Bible Gateway Passage: Zephaniah 3:17, New International Version." Bible
Gateway. https://www.biblegateway.com/passage/?search=Zephaniah 3:17. Accessed December 27, 2014.

"Bugle Notes: Learn This!" WestPoint.org. http://www.west-point.org/academy/
malo-wa/inspirations/buglenotes.html. Accessed December 23, 2014.

Eliot, T. S. "The Waste Land." In *The Waste Land*. New York: Norton and Company, 2001, 5–6.

Farmelo, Graham. *It Must Be Beautiful: Great Equations of Modern Science*. London: Granta, 2002.

"Garrison Charles Avery, West Point 2004." http://defender.west-point.org/ser
vice/display.mhtml?u=60373&i= 39847. Accessed December 27, 2014.

Hoskins, Nathan. "1st ACB Repeats History with Air Assault Mission." 10th Mountain News Releases and Advisories. December 4, 2006. http://www .drum.army.mil/news/Article.aspx?List=9bf48051-598a-4759-a68f-41a214b6d 75f&ID=2785. Accessed November 1, 2012.

"The Origin of the Alma Mater: Paul Reinecke's Own Story." *Assembly*, April 9, 1942. http://www.west-point.org/greimanj/west_point/songs/vol1no1 Assembly page 9.pdf. Accessed December 1, 2013.

Plato. *The Symposium*. London: Penguin, 1999.

United States Military Academy West Point. "Class of 2004: Class Profile." http://www.usma.edu/classes/SitePages/2004 Profile.aspx. Accessed December 27, 2014.

INDEX

9/11 attacks, 2, 11, 77, 103, 105, 147, 175, 181, 255, 281; visiting Ground Zero, 281
100th Night Show, 87

Abu Garib, Iraq, 38
al-Qaeda in Iraq (AQI), 31, 32, 155, 187, 195, 249, 251, 265; ambush attacks, 50, 90, 147–48, 183–85, 257; complex attacks, 191; *see also* attack on PB Inchon and PB North (Tarmiyah); description of, 32; double agents in Iraqi Security Forces, 155; Iraqi election interference, 176–77; infiltration routes into Iraq, 17; kidnapping US soldiers, 80, 188, 193, 196, 240, 265; kidnapping Iraqi Security Force members, 265; *see also* attack on Karbala PJCC
Alburto, Frank, 134
Anbar Province, Iraq, 176

Anderson, Michael, 47–51
Anzack, Joseph, 193, 195
Arghandab River Valley, Afghanistan, 98
Army-Navy Game, 112–13
Avery, Garrison, 27–34, 133, 135, 136–37, 216–17, 247–49, 252–54

Babil Province, Iraq, 178
Baghdad, 58, 176–77; "Baghdad Radio," 237–38; combat hospital (CSH), 202, 261; smell, 256; summer heat, 235; International Airport, 39, 175; International Zone ("Green Zone"), 177, 202, 256; Kardash District, 47, 49; Southern portion of city, 29, 30, 256
Bagram Air Field, Afghanistan, 179
Balad, Iraq, 91
Baldwin, Chris, 247–54
Bandi, Matt, 135
Baqubah, Iraq, 154

Barbour, Jerome (aka Dutch), 274–75

Bayji, Iraq, 17–18

Beast Barracks (Cadet Basic Training), 9, 29, 35, 89, 121, 124, 134; Acceptance Day, 2; march back from Lake Frederick, 121, 124; Reception Day (R-day), 1–2, 101–2, 147, 221

Bell, James, 257

Bernstein, David, 10

Bigger, Lori, 134

Bock, Amos, 43–51

Buckner, Camp (Cadet Field Training), 10, 76, 102, 285

Buerhing, Camp (Kuwait), 96, 111–12, 248–49

Burch, Matthew, 270

Burke, Daniel, 258

Brice, Patrick, 89

Britt, Benjamin, 21–26, 146, 247–49, 250–51, 253–54

Brooke Army Medical Center, 208–9, 263

Brown, Kevin, 37, 39

Byington, Brody, 265–66, 269, 272

caches (weapons and explosives), 158, 176, 192

cadet companies: E-1, 55; G-1, 45; F-1, 134–38; A-2, 95; C-2, 255; H-2, 45, 102, 113; disbandment of H-2, 105–6; F-3, 45; H-3, 121

casualty notification teams, 156, 225–26; Jon Elliot serving as a Casualty Assistance Officer, 263

Cathcart, Garret, 70

celebratory fire, 48

Cerrone, Michael 52–59

Chappell, Seth, 69–73

Chegwidden, Andrew, 262

Christenson, Adam, 88

Colon, Jesus, 267, 273, 276

Connell, James, 193, 237

Copeland, James, 268–69

"The Corps," 29, 34, 73

Courneya, Daniel, 193

Cow Loan, 56

Dacosta, Jered, 134, 137

Dallas, Jay, 134

Dauby, Cassidy, 123–24

Dennison, John, 60-67, 136–37, 159

disciplinary tours, 106

Dishong, Chris, 262

Diyala Province, Iraq, 66, 137

Efflandt, Scott, 272, 274–75

Eidson, Jerry, 23, 161–71

Elliot, Jon, 255–64

Eissler, Burt, 134

explosive ordnance disposal (EOD), 165, 244–45; route clearance, 72, 89–90

Fierro, Chris, 201–9, 263

Firstie Club, 11, 46, 104, 133, 137, 224

Fish, Michael, 85–92

Fisher, Jason, 268–69

Foley, Mick (aka "Mankind"), 206

Forward Operating Base: Brassfield-Mora (Iraq), 58; Falcon (Iraq), 256–57; Gabe (Iraq), 154; Justice (Iraq), 201–2; Liberty, Camp (Iraq), 39; Loyalty (Iraq), 51; Orgun-E (Afghanistan), 184–85; Prosperity (Iraq), 178; Speicher (Iraq), 90; Striker, Camp (Iraq), 76, 251;

Summerall (Iraq), 15, 17; Taji, Camp (Iraq), 269, 274–75; Yusfiyah (Iraq), 191; Warhorse (Iraq), 159; Warrior (Iraq), 98
Fouty, Byron, 193, 196
Fraser, David, 69–73
Fritz, Jacob, 74–83

Garberson, Ron, 9–19
Gardner, Brandon, 40
Garrett, Jordan, 52–59
Gehrels, Chris, 185
Gibson, James, 78
Given, Nathaniel, 191
Glee Club, 77, 87
Graduation Day, 2, 95, 106, 109, 227; Commissioning Ceremony, 10, 71, 95, 135

Hanrahan, Brian, 133–35, 137
Hawkins, Rick, 134
Holbrook, Jason, 121–24
Hooker, Frank, 226
Hortman, Dave, 23, 125–30
Horton, Nick, 4, 139–40
Housey, Freddie, 266–68, 275
Howald, Dave, 135
Howitzer, 3, 24, 45
Hurricane Katrina, 66

improvised explosive devices (IEDs), 148, 156, 158, 180, 193, 249, 262, 282; attacks, 90, 98, 114, 124, 191, 207, 251, 253; booby-trapped buildings, 236–37; deep-buried, 40, 184; explosive formed penetrator (EFP), 49, 50, 72, 149, 259–62; pressure plates, 191; vehicle borne, 249, 258–59

Iraqi Security Forces, 155, 178, 195; ambush near Route Tampa, 257-258; desertion of Tarmiyah Iraqi Police Station, 265; Iraqi Army (IA), 177, 189; Iraqi Police (IP), 80; working with Coalition partners, 79–80, 82; 155, 157–58, 192, 305 insurgents. *See* al-Qaeda or Taliban
Ireland, Jay, 23, 221–31

Jensen, Luke, 261
Jesser, Andy, 49
Jimenez, Alex, 193, 196
Jokinen, Shaun, 267, 269–70
Jurf Kas Sukr Bridge, Iraq, 162, 189, 196

Kanan, Iraq, 155, 157
Karbala, Iraq, 75, 79–83, 178; attack on Iraqi Police station (20 January 2007), 75–76, 79–81; kidnapping of American soldiers, 79–80
Kargouli Villiage, Iraq, 187–97; capture of American soldiers, 193, 237; search of, 194
key leader engagement (KLE), 17, 32, 180, 250; training, 226
King, Adam, 121
King, Brian, 263
Kint, Brandon, 96
Kirkuk, Iraq, 89, 98; Hawijia (small town south of Kirkuk), 90
Knight, Wes, 255–64
Kraemer, BJ, 9–19

Landstuhl Regional Army Medical Center (Germany), 204
Lawrence, Grant, 51
Livermore, Doug, 187–97

Lewis, Charlie, 9–19
Lewis, Marie (Cicerelle), 15–16
Lopez, Jason, 261–62
Lujan, Justin, 182

Mahmudiyah, Iraq, 27, 30, 249, 256
Mallard, Torre, 155–56, 159
Marks, Travis, 43–51
Maysan Province, Iraq, 80
McKee, Matt, 136
Medders, Michael, 159
Mess Hall, 21; description of,
    279; Poop Deck, 95, 279; table
    commandants, 283
Messer, Christopher, 191
Minges, Edwin (Les), 270–74
Morrow, Jack, 61–67
Mujahideen See al-Qaeda
Murphy, Christopher, 193
Mushada, Iraq, 270
Myers, Joe, 4, 133–38

Nelson, Tom, 75–83
Nickel, Joey, 145–51
Norris, Charles, 191

Orlandini, Jorge, 134
Ora-a, William, 258
Orbe, John, 181

Pafford, Brent, 16–21
Pakita Province, Afghanistan, 179;
    Steyr Gayan Valley, 185; Zhangi,
    Pakita Province, 180
Parrish, Thomas, 262
Paton, Justin, 266
Patrol Base: Bataan, Patrol Base (Iraq),
    189; attack on (19 February 2007),

266–74; attack on (12 May 2007),
    193; battle positions (BP) 151 and
    152 (PB Inchon), 190, 193; Inchon,
    Patrol
Base (Iraq), 191–95; OP4 (COP
    Tilman), 182–83, 185; Patzkowski,
    Michael, 209; role during PB
    Inchon attack, 193; Tarmiyah IP
    Station (PB North), 265; Tillman,
    Combat Outpost (Afghanistan),
    179–82, 184–85
Peck, Scott, 212
Peña, Paul, 93–99, 114, 146
Phonexayphova, Lay, 153–59
Proffitt, Thomas, 263
Provisional Joint Coordination Center
    (Karbala), 79–80

Quinn, Sean, 46

Rakkasans (3rd Infantry Brigade
    Combat Team, 101st Airborne
    Division), 14–15, 211–12
Ramadi, Iraq, 112
Ranger School 14, 16, 24, 47, 62,
    71–72, 89, 95–96, 110, 250, 282
Reid, Mark, 134
Reily, Dan, 215
Reinecke, Paul, 1; "Alma Mater," 1–2,
    5, 91, 117, 124, 159, 283
Ring Weekend, 46, 116; "Ring Poop,"
    108
Root, TJ, 125–30, 235–46
routes (Iraq): Cobras, 266; Coyotes,
    266; Chevy, 239; Irish, Route, 256;
    Jackson, 256; Malibu, 188–95;
    Tampa (main supply route), 17,
    177, 256–57, 266, 270

Rowell, Johnny (Johnny T), 41
Rumsfeld, Donald, 109, 175, 177, 206

Saturday Morning Inspections (SAMI), 54
Schaffer, Chris, 183–84
Schober, Anthony, 193
Schutte, Matt, 133–34
Seidel, Rob, 35–42
Shipman, Bishop, 29; "The Corps," 29
Smith, Cameron, 270–72
Smith, Kevin, 262
Sons of Iraq ("The Awakening"), 27, 31, 195–96; merging into ISF, 195
Spannagel, Jimm, 101–19, 262
Stallings, Chad, 269
Steele, Michael, 212
Strangio, Dan, 134–35
Strickland, Nathan, 121
Strickler, Dave, 35–42, 128–29
Synder, Adam, 84–92

Tal Afar, Iraq, 156
Taliban, 180–82, 223, 230; ambush tactics, 181, 230; ambush attacks, 185; attack in the Steyr Gayan Valley, 185; infiltration of fighters and supply, 180; local support for, 180; rocket attack on COP Tillman, 181
Tarmiyah, Iraq, 265–66
Tau, Randy, 134–35, 137
Taylor, Timothy, 261–62
Tikrit, Iraq, 211
Tramel, Glen, 274

Tribes, Iraqi: al-Janabi tribe, 187; al-Owesi, 195–96; al-Saidi tribe, 31, 32, 33
Turki, Battle of, 66
Tsagay, Afghanistan, 124

Uthlaut, Haley (Dennison), 64

Vance, Bradley, 175–85
Vang, Pao, 266–69

Waid, Courtney (Carey), 15, 211–20
Waid, Joseph (Buck), 212, 215–17
Wallace, Cory, 93–99, 266–76
Walker, Brett, 21–26
Walker, Ryan, 262
Walter Reed National Military Medicine Center, 204–7, 262
Watson, Brian, 263
Whitten, Dan, 100–19, 146
Wilbourn, Sam, 135
Wilson, Jim, 121–24
Winters, Dick, 138
Wright, Erik, 63, 134–35

Yusufiyah, Iraq, 30, 161–62, 188–89, 191, 195, 249; murder and rape of Iraqi girl and her family by US soldiers, 188, 196

Zabul province, Afghanistan, 113; Qalat, Zabul province, 114
Zdeb, John, 262
Ziemba, Nick, 23
Zilinski, Dennis, 3, 10, 8–19, 217

ABOUT THE EDITOR

Cory Wallace was born and raised in Wyoming. He graduated and received his commission as an armor officer from the United States Military Academy in 2004. He has deployed to Iraq with the 1st Cavalry Division and the 3rd Infantry Division. He and his wife, Nicole, have three children and one very grumpy, but loveable, dog. The Wallace family currently resides at Fort Hood, Texas, and is looking forward to their next Army adventure.

In addition to his undergraduate degree in English, Cory also holds a masters of arts in literature from the University of Washington and a masters of business in supply chain management from Kansas University.